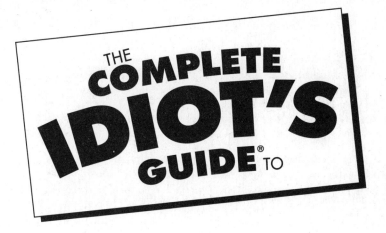

THE COMPLETE IDIOT'S GUIDE® TO

Natural Magick

D1561231

by Miria Liguana and Nina Metzner
with recipe consultant Eve Adamson

ALPHA

A member of Penguin Group (USA) Inc.

ALPHA BOOKS

Published by the Penguin Group

Penguin Group (USA) Inc., 375 Hudson St., New York, New York 10014, U.S.A.

Penguin Group (Canada), 10 Alcorn Ave., Toronto, Ontario, Canada M4V 3B2 (a division of Pearson Penguin Canada Inc.)

Penguin Books Ltd., 80 Strand, London WC2R 0RL, England

Penguin Ireland, 25 St. Stephen's Green, Dublin 2, Ireland (a division of Penguin Books Ltd.)

Penguin Group (Australia), 250 Camberwell Road, Camberwell, Victoria 3124, Australia (a division of Pearson Australia Group Pty Ltd.)

Penguin Books India Pvt Ltd., 11 Community Centre, Panchsheel Park, New Delhi—110 017, India

Penguin Group (NZ), cnr Airborne and Rosedale Roads, Albany, Auckland 1310, New Zealand (a division of Pearson New Zealand Ltd.)

Penguin Books (South Africa) (Pty) Ltd., 24 Sturdee Ave., Rosebank, Johannesburg 2196, South Africa

Penguin Books Ltd., Registered Offices: 80 Strand, London WC2R 0RL, England

International Standard Book Number: 1-59257-418-1
Library of Congress Catalog Card Number: 2005936617

07   06   05   8   7   6   5   4   3   2   1

Interpretation of the printing code: The rightmost number of the first series of numbers is the year of the book's printing; the rightmost number of the second series of numbers is the number of the book's printing. For example, a printing code of 05-1 shows that the first printing occurred in 2005.

Printed in the United States of America

Note: This publication contains the opinions and ideas of its authors. It is intended to provide helpful and informative material on the subject matter covered. It is sold with the understanding that the authors, book producer, and publisher are not engaged in rendering professional services in the book. If the reader requires personal assistance or advice, a competent professional should be consulted.

The authors, book producer, and publisher specifically disclaim any responsibility for any liability, loss, or risk, personal or otherwise, which is incurred as a consequence, directly or indirectly, of the use and application of any of the contents of this book.

Most Alpha books are available at special quantity discounts for bulk purchases for sales promotions, premiums, fund-raising, or educational use. Special books, or book excerpts, can also be created to fit specific needs.

For details, write: Special Markets, Alpha Books, 375 Hudson St., New York, NY 10014.

Publisher: *Marie Butler-Knight*
Editorial Director: *Mike Sanders*
Senior Managing Editor: *Jennifer Bowles*
Senior Acquisitions Editor: *Randy Ladenheim-Gil*
Book Producer: *Lee Ann Chearney/Amaranth Illuminare*
Development Editor: *Lynn Northrup*
Production Editor: *Megan Douglass*
Copy Editor: *Krista Hansing*
Cartoonist: *Richard King*
Book Designer: *Trina Wurst*
Cover Designer: *Kurt Owens*
Indexer: *Heather McNeil*
Layout: *Ayanna Lacey*
Proofreading: *Mary Hunt*

Contents at a Glance

Contents

Foreword

I have lived in a city, enduring incessant noise and unrelenting light and constant movement. I have climbed down into the underworld, to be transported to a worker's hell, looking in vain for a star or a moonbeam to share the night with. I have felt my soul yearn to walk free, to be caressed by the earth's breath, to trust the wind and the rain. I have longed for the feeling of soil in my hands and under my nails. And I have felt the magick growing thin, the wonder disappearing.

Before the wonder faded away, I found my way to the country. I found my way to nature. I became a goatherd, and an herbalist. I learned to live fully in nature, to walk barefoot, to be at home in the dark. Now the sounds around me are the songs of the birds, the whispers of the stars, the laughter of the plants. Tree spirits cradle me. Faeries play tricks on me. Animal totems leave me sweet presents. Green allies stand ready to help. I dance with the seasons. I dream deeply. Every breath is a give-away dance. I am surrounded by natural magick.

It wasn't as easy as it sounds. I had to work hard. And I had to do magick, without really knowing how. I had to focus my will, maintain my attention, and heed my intuition, with very little in the way of instruction. If only I had been gifted with teachers as wise, patient, clear, and comprehensive as Miria Liguana and Nina Metzner, I wouldn't have felt (and acted) like a complete idiot quite so frequently, I'm sure.

Whether you live in the country or the city, these women can show you how simple and satisfying, how effective and beneficial Natural Magick can be.

If you've ever wished that you could wave a magic wand and make a dream come true,

if you've ever wanted to stir a love charm into a soup for a special someone,

if you've ever wondered how to use the mystical light of the moon,

if you've ever fantasized about faeries, dreamed about dragons, or giggled about gnomes,

if you've ever felt the energy of earth and air, fire and water,

if you've ever sensed that a gem stone can contain secrets, or that angels are aiding you,

if you've ever listened for tree spirits, quested for an animal totem, or reached out to green ally,

then you're ready for Natural Magick. And, with the help of this exciting book, you can do it ... no matter how little you know, or how inept you feel.

Yes. It's true. Natural Magick is so simple even an idiot can do it. Without any special training, using this book, you can learn how to create a magickal space, cast a spell, summon an Elemental, and enrich your life in any way you can envision.

I love the uncomplicated instructions for nourishing wholesome seasonal celebrations. I'm delighted to find meaningful, respectful ways to cast Natural Magick spells. I breathed a sigh of relief at the common sense explanations of esoteric subjects— Feng Shui, ley lines, scrying, fire rituals, familiars. It's all so clear that any idiot will succeed, at once.

In fact, if you practice the refreshing Natural Magick presented here, you'll discover that you aren't an idiot at all: You are a God/dess, a Wise Wo/man, a Holy Fool. So take off your clothes or put on your robes, light a candle, grab your wand and your blade, your bell and this book, and get ready to unleash the magickal you.

—Susun S. Weed

High Priestess of Dianic Wicca. Susun Weed is the voice of the Wise Women Tradition; through her Wise Woman Center in Woodstock, New York, she offers workshops, apprenticeships, correspondence courses, and more. Susun is the author of four alternative health books focusing on using herbs for women's well-being for healing, childbearing, breast health, and menopause. Visit Susun online at www.susunweed.com.

Introduction

Being a Natural Magician means living a life that is mindful. It requires nothing more than paying attention to the world around you—the animate world as well as the inanimate, the world you can see as well as the invisible. One of the easiest ways to connect to the Earth's energy is to combine the tools and tasks that you use in your everyday life with some purposeful intentions to conjure up a little magick. As you'll see in this book, it doesn't require any memorized rituals and there are no rules to follow. Natural Magick is based on your own intuition and common sense.

In *The Complete Idiot's Guide to Natural Magick*, we will give you insight into how to tap into your magickal power. Following this spiritual path is simple and fulfilling. It can improve your life in ways that you have never imagined. Natural Magick will enrich your family life, strengthen your relationships, and empower you to be successful in everything you attempt to do. Don't hesitate! Let magick be your partner as you dance with the Universe.

How to Use This Book

This book is divided into a six-part exploration of how to become a Natural Magician. It's an easy process … *naturally*!

Part 1, "Practicing Natural Magick," introduces you to the role of Natural Magicians in today's world. It explains how to practice magick ethically without formal rituals or prescribed spells, but trusting your own intuition. Connecting to Nature attunes you to the living world around you. Practitioners will be surprised at how much Natural Magick they already perform unconsciously and how easy it is to include a little spellcrafting in their everyday lives.

Part 2, "Natural Magick with the Elemental Realm," looks at the connection between a Natural Magician and the four Elements—Air, Fire, Water, and Earth—plus the "fifth" Element—Spirit. It explains how to become familiar with them, how to invoke their energies, and how to honor their presence in your life. It also introduces two powerful Guardians of Elemental power—the Watchtowers and dragons—and explains how they can enrich your magick when invited into your spiritual environment.

Part 3, "Wildcrafting," takes a look at how Nature provides all the materials you need to make delicious meals, powerful potions, and intriguing crafts. Learn how to enjoy Nature at the same time you're gathering both edible and nonedible ingredients to use in spellcrafting and rituals. Whether you like camping, cross-country skiing, or just taking a walk around your city, there are ways to connect to Nature through wildcrafting. Utilizing the Winds, basking in the Sun, reveling in Full Moon glow—it's all here.

Part 4, "Natural Magick with the Faery Realm," draws upon the invisible spirit world of Elementals, faeries, and trees. Combining your magickal energy with the faery realm in its broadest definition opens you up to using the Spirits of Place to enhance your spellcrafting. Not always easy to invoke, the faeries require patience but are well worth the effort.

Part 5, "Harvest to Seed to Harvest: Nature's Cycle," offers you recipes designed to help you cook and eat seasonally and magickally. Whether you are a vegetarian or a meat eater, you can prepare meals ethically by taking into consideration what produce is in season and by remembering to thank the animals and plants that offer their Spirits to you. Just a few magickally charged ingredients can turn every meal into a magickal event.

Part 6, "Organic Craft of Natural Magick," reminds us that Natural Magick is based on connecting to Nature, eating healthfully and seasonally, and following your own magickal path. Taking care of the Earth includes charging ingredients to enhance your Will as well as uniting with other Natural Magicians to form a spiritual community. Following your own heart is the best magick you can practice. You'll also find a bonus "gem" of a chapter to help you make your magickal intent "crystal" clear!

Following these parts, you'll find four useful appendixes: a glossary of terms every Natural Magician should know, recommended books for further exploration of Natural Magick, charts of natural correspondences at a glance to help you in your spellcrafting, and a fill-in-the-blank worksheet for recording your Natural Magick workings.

Extras

Throughout each chapter of this book, we've added four types of extra information in boxes, to help you learn even more about being a Natural Magician.

Cauldron Bubble

These boxes contain practical tips and suggestions to help bring forth your best Natural Magick spells and rituals!

Liguana's Grimoire

Here Liguana shares her own personal experiences on the magickal path, including facts and advice that anyone can use to tap into Natural Magick.

Magickal Bounty _____

In these boxes, you'll discover the meanings of terms related to Natural Magick that you might not already know. And if you do already know them, perhaps you will find new magickal uses for them in your daily life.

Stir Gently ...! _____

Dabbling in magickal realms is fun, but there are a few pitfalls to avoid. Take heed with these cautions that will keep you safe and unfettered as you perfect your magickal craft.

Acknowledgments

From Liguana:

I am grateful to Lee Ann Chearney of Amaranth Illuminare for taking a lunch break conversation and turning it into a book once again. Her energy and enthusiasm never cease to inspire me. I am also indebted to the ever-dependable Nina Metzner, my good friend and co-writer. She is a beautiful, magickal lady. Then there is Eve Adamson, whose recipes are sprinkled in several chapters throughout this book. Thanks, Eve. I want to eat at your home some day! I need to tell my children how much I appreciate them for supplying countless anecdotes and for backing off when I needed time and space for writing. Derek, Devin, Shaleina, and Mason, I love you all more than I can say. Lastly, hugs to Thaddeus. Onward to the next adventure!

From Nina:

I would like to thank Liguana for her insightful writing, her determination, her funny stories, and her great good humor through it all. Thanks to Lee Ann Chearney for giving me this opportunity to work with Liguana again and for all of her positive encouragement along the way. And finally, a very special thank you to Jim Nockunas, who nursed me back to health during my broken hip weeks, fed my cats, ran my errands, and set up my laptop so I could work in bed. I love you guys.

A Special Thanks

We would especially like to thank Eve Adamson for her inspired recipes used in Chapters 17, 18, 19, 20, 22, and 23. Her easy-to-follow directions and readily available ingredients make it possible for anyone to stir up Natural Magick in the kitchen while putting a delicious meal on the table at the same time. Eve is co-author, with Marissa Cloutier, M.S., R.D., of *The Mediterranean Diet, Revised Edition* (Avon Books).

Trademarks

All terms mentioned in this book that are known to be or are suspected of being trademarks or service marks have been appropriately capitalized. Alpha Books and Penguin Group (USA) Inc. cannot attest to the accuracy of this information. Use of a term in this book should not be regarded as affecting the validity of any trademark or service mark.

Part 1

Practicing Natural Magick

You're already more into Natural Magick than you think you are. Whenever you do something nice for a friend, feed an animal, or recycle to protect the Earth, you are practicing Natural Magick. This part helps you hone those skills and focus on living more deliberately in the Universe.

Being a Natural Magician

In This Chapter

- ◆ Natural Magick defined
- ◆ Identifying yourself as a Natural Magician
- ◆ Natural Magick in a high-tech culture
- ◆ Becoming a wizard of the natural world
- ◆ Ceremony, naturally
- ◆ Attracting Natural Magick

The world is a magickal place. You can see the Earth's power in the way plants and animals re-create themselves year after year, in the movement of the water, and in the very contours of the land. When you align yourself with this natural energy flow, your magickal work becomes even more powerful.

Whether you are a bona fide practicing witch, a pagan, a Druid, or are just a person interested in living more harmoniously with Nature with a capital *N*, this book is for you. Embracing Natural Magick can be a spiritual journey that brings you closer to the Earth and all of its bountiful gifts while making you a positive force in the world.

What Is Natural Magick?

Natural Magick is, in its simplest definition, working with Nature to effect positive changes in your life. But even more than this, it means to practice your magick without imposing any negative impact on the established patterns of the Earth. Natural Magick recognizes and uses the flow of power and energy that exists all around us—the *Force*. Sometimes known as Green Magick when it involves using the Earth's green growing things, it becomes more than that when it involves connecting with the Earth's animal children, her air and water flows, her natural formations and power places. That is Natural Magick.

Magickal Bounty

In the movie *Star Wars*, Obi-Wan Kenobi advises Luke Skywalker to "use the **Force**" to tap into his natural power. This fictionalized Force actually exists in everything around us as magick. Think of **Natural Magick** as using the energy found in everyday tasks and objects to transform your life. It is much more powerful than "magic" without the "k": the sleight-of-hand tricks used by stage magicians.

Natural Magick requires an understanding of and commitment to something larger than ourselves. Whether we classify this "something" as divine, supernatural, or just plain natural, it is what allows us to change ourselves and to effect change around us. Magickal people do not need the trappings or labels of religion. We often enjoy the tools and props, but we can work Natural Magick without them.

Ritual by Rote vs. Walking the Walk

So practicing Natural Magick is much more than memorizing spells and lighting candles. It's all very well to attend rituals and practice a formalized religion, but intuitively practicing Natural Magick is, in some ways, more satisfying and more powerful. If you find yourself mouthing incantations by rote or fumbling through books for the "correct" spell to say then possibly you've lost your way.

There are many different ideas about accessing magickal energies and magickal traditions can be found in every land, even in today's modern societies. The practices of Caribbean Santeria, Hawaiian Huna, African Yoruba, and American Wicca as well as many other paths have been well documented. The forms of magickal practice may be very different, but the intent is the same—to access magickal energies and use them to cause a change.

The good news is that the magickal bounty of the Earth is in us and around us already. One need only attune to the flow of universal energy that has existed since the Earth was born. At this point, you may be wondering how to accomplish this attunement. Formal magickal study and practice is one way, but living magickally and seeking to recognize and be in harmony with the patterns of Nature is the beginning and the end of any magickal practice. Tapping in to Natural Magick is a subtle process that begins with how you choose to live in the world.

Magicians are aware of the Earth's nuances in every form they take. The hum of locusts on a hot summer night, the first song of a spring bird calling to his mate, the ghostly call of the humpback whales—all of these are part of the Earth's natural chants and hold their own power. Finding power in a thunderstorm, a blizzard, a spider's web, or a handful of grain, the Natural Magick practitioner misses nothing.

Walking and living a magickal path without the constraints of a more formalized practice is where Liguana has been heading for a long time. To be a witch, sorcerer, or magickal person without the labels, to recognize the turning of the wheel without relying on specific holiday dates, is very freeing. The world responds to Liguana when she calls out her needs and desires to it because she is a part of Nature's workings rather than being apart from them.

A person practicing Natural Magick fully uses all five senses. She or he hears the Earth's music in all its forms; sees each season's grandeur; smells the sweet fragrances as well as the loam rot; touches the soft, the hard, and the rough; and tastes every luscious taste there is—from sweet and salty to sour and bitter. The Natural Magician does all of this while keeping in mind her or his role in taking care of the Earth's highest good. If you aren't at least attempting to live in harmony with the Earth, in a nonpolluting, nondamaging way, you've missed the point and will fail to resonate with the elemental flow of Natural Magick.

Finding Our Way in a Technological World

There is a way things are designed to be on this planet, the natural pattern of Earth's energy. We are all born into this pattern, but a modern lifestyle can sometimes be contrary to a natural lifestyle. It requires not just observing the world, but blending ourselves with everything that surrounds us.

Your connection to the Earth depends, in part, on where you live. Embrace your climate and the fruit (literally and figuratively) your climate produces. Do you know which birds and animals are indigenous to your area? Are you aware of the weather anomalies in your part of the country? What herbs flourish in your garden? What fruits and vegetables should you plant? A Natural Magician makes an extra effort to tune in to her or his environment.

Shrugging Off Technology–Sometimes

It's easy to forget our deep connections to Mother Earth when we travel by the turn of a key or receive what we know about our world with the push of a button. Natural Magick is a reclaiming magick, like most nature-based religions. It is coming back to the Earth and remembering where we come from.

> **CAUTION**
>
> **Stir Gently ...!**
>
> Don't get too bogged down in someone else's rituals. Listen to your own inner voice, plan your own ceremonies, use whatever symbols of the season the Universe hands you. That's Natural Magick at its best.

So what is the easiest way to come back to Earth and tap into the power of the Universe? First of all, we should be clear that when we talk about the Earth's power, we don't mean to eliminate the stars, the Moon, and the Universe in general. A Natural Magician uses all of Nature's elements. Putting yourself back out there, into the natural world, is vital. Get up off the couch, turn off the television, put down the magazine. Here we go ….

Communing with Our Animal Friends

Witches have *familiars*, animals who aid them in their magickal practices (see Chapter 8); the rest of us have pets or animal friends. Connecting with the Earth means, first of all, realizing that we share the world with all of the other earthlings who have fur, feathers, or fins. Bringing an animal into your house is one of the best ways to connect to the magick of the animal kingdom. Adopting a pet from your local shelter or taking in a stray is not only empowering, but it also brings a new spirit energy into your environment. There is scientific proof that petting a cat lowers your blood pressure. Walking a dog lowers your cholesterol. A healthy Natural Magician is a happy magician.

If you can't adopt a pet, you can connect to the animal energy in the world by feeding the birds in your backyard, contributing to your local zoo or pet shelter, or taking bread crumbs to the squirrels and ducks in the park. Don't fall for virtual pets made up of computer bits and bytes. When it comes to animal energy, don't settle for anything less than the living, breathing originals.

Liguana's Grimoire
Recently Liguana had a lifestyle change that required her to give up her goats. She sold them to a lovely man who was also making a lifestyle change and felt that goats might be part of the answer. Liguana understands that change is part of the natural flow of the Earth. Even so, accepting change is one of the hardest things for anyone to do. Although she enjoys her new living quarters, she misses the fresh milk and cheese, as well as the gregarious, playful dispositions of her goat friends.

Eat as Close to Nature as Possible

So many of our meals come in the form of fast food, processed snacks, and frozen microwaved meals that it's sometimes hard to remember what real food tastes like. As often as possible, use the fresh fruits and vegetables available in your area of the country. Think "cooking seasonally." Strawberries in the spring, tomatoes in the summer, apples in the fall, root vegetables in the winter—you get the idea. (See Part 5 for a full discussion of Natural Magick by the seasons.) If you have an abundance from your garden, canning or freezing the surplus ensures that the food will be free of preservatives when you pull them out in the off-season.

The less food is processed, the healthier it is and the easier it will be to work Natural Magick. Eat real butter rather than margarine, brown rice instead of white, fresh vegetables rather than canned and salted, whole-wheat bread instead of white, cardboard bread. You get the picture. If calories are an issue, use portion control rather than resorting to buying sugar-free, fat-free, overprocessed, tasteless, packaged food. A natural practitioner knows that there is magick in even the simplest, purest ingredients.

Spices can add power to a spell by adding more than just flavor. Even if you're cooking dinner for just your friends or family, the right spices combined with an incantation or two can increase prosperity, incite passion, tighten the bonds of friendship, and even bring a feeling of peace into the home. Meals shared around the table in camaraderie are powerful in and of themselves. Combined with magick, the experience is positively heady. In this book, we'll show you how to stock your magickal pantry and how to combine natural ingredients to make your meals magickally purposeful as well as delicious.

Embrace the Weather You're In

How many times have you been at work or in a group of people when the conversation turns to complaints about the weather? It's too hot; it's too cold; it's been cloudy for too many days. So much energy is wasted on complaining instead of embracing and enjoying the weather as it comes. Weather patterns are a natural part of the Earth, and Natural Magicians use all aspects of a season in their spellcasting. Rain water and melted snow can be used to represent the Element of Water on an altar or used as the base of a potion. Pine needles can symbolize the Lord during a Yule celebration. Calendula flowers are sacred to the Goddess. And, of course, every Natural Magician uses the phases of the Moon to determine which spells to cast when. The point is to tune into the patterns the Earth is giving you at the time.

> **Cauldron Bubble**
>
> There is nothing quite as pleasant as walking in a warm rain under a full-size umbrella. Toss away those miniscule, fit-into-a-briefcase, collapsible umbrellas that drip rain onto your shoulders. Buy a real umbrella and walk, don't drive, to your next errand, or just take a walk for fun. Thank the Lord and Lady for replenishing the Earth's water.

Instead of constantly living in environmentally controlled buildings where air-conditioning and furnaces make sure we have a perfect 72° temperature, try turning off the technology during the summer and opening a window. (That is, of course, assuming that the heat is not just too unbearable.) Sleeping in a warm summer breeze can conjure up prophetic dreams, especially if you have fragrant flowers outside your window like lilacs, magnolias, or lavender. As your body adjusts to the change of seasons, your heightened senses will attune themselves even more to the Earth's rhythms.

In the winter, bundle up and take a snowy winter walk before coming in to a spicy cranberry cider drink. Cranberries encourage prosperity and good luck as we head into a new year. If you're lucky enough to have a fireplace, that's a great way to connect to the Lord. Or, if you're in a mild climate, build a bonfire outside.

And no matter what, stop complaining about the weather. Natural Magicians revel in the weather and use it to enhance their magickal energy and workings.

Why Natural Magick Is Important

Now let's segue into methods of magick: ceremonial vs. natural. Throughout the ages of humanity, there have always been magickal people—people who were just a little more in sync with the forces of Nature and the ebb and flow of the seasons. Whether known as shaman, medicine man, wise woman, Druid, priest/priestess, or Wiccan, these people were sought out when healing was needed for the Earth or her children.

As we've already pointed out, although ceremonial magick certainly has its place, especially in large group ceremonies, sometimes the essence of the sacred magick gets lost in the candle lighting and formalized chanting.

Pagans believe that living close to the Earth and her patterns is a way to bring harmony into their own lives. Because harmony with the physical plane brings inner peace, all pagan religions strive to be soothing to the body and spirit.

Magickal Bounty

The term **pagan** has numerous common but erroneous definitions. Many dictionaries define a pagan as anyone not of the Judeo-Islamic-Christian religions. Some people consider anyone who does not share their religion to be a pagan. Still others believe that a pagan is a person who is antireligion. To discover the real meaning of pagan, we must look back to ancient times, when the word *pagan* simply referred to a person of the country or a peasant: someone who lived on and off the land.

Can You Find Your Inner Magician?

Many Nature-based religions could be considered pagan or "of the land." But rather than relying on labels, looking at your beliefs about how the world works will tell you whether practicing Natural Magick is for you. Embracing some or most of the following philosophies might be the first steps in recognizing the Natural Magician within yourself so that you can become a wizard of the natural world:

- Believing in more than one deity and/or more than one aspect of a single deity
- Expecting the Earth to take care of your needs and not being surprised when it does
- Being mindful of the well-being of all other life forms around you
- Doing all you can to preserve the natural world while understanding that humans are also part of Nature
- Living ethically and wisely on the planet as much as possible

♦ Practicing right eating habits for your own health and the health of the planet

♦ Being a pantheist—that is, seeing the God and Goddess forces represented in everything around you

♦ Recognizing the sacred feminine as well as the sacred masculine

♦ Believing that the life force is sacred and that Nature, as a representation of that force, is divine

♦ Believing that all life forms are equal and share an equal claim to the Earth as a home

♦ Knowing that each individual is solely responsible for his or her own actions and that those actions should bring harm to no one

♦ Believing that the forces of Nature follow a pattern and can be shaped in ways commonly called "magickal"

♦ Believing that whatever actions a person takes, magickal or mundane, good or bad, come back to him or her threefold

> **Cauldron Bubble**
>
> Recycling is an easy way to help heal the Earth. Glass bottles, cans, plastic, cardboard, old newspapers—they all belong in a recycling bin, not in a landfill.

♦ Believing that there is no single path to spiritual fulfillment and that the individual determines the spiritual expression most appropriate to him or her

♦ Understanding and honoring everything about where you live

♦ Practicing the use of all your senses every waking minute

What is good for the Earth is good for its inhabitants. Recycling, planting trees, avoiding pesticides, conserving water, and refusing products from endangered species all attune you to the Earth and, therefore, to its positive energy. Practicing Natural Magick is good for all the earthlings—finned, feathered, and furred as well as two-footed.

How Is Practicing Natural Magick Different?

A truly, naturally magickal person is a positive force in the world. Not only does his or her attunement with Nature help a person create a good effect, but the Natural

Magician is a person the Earth itself cares for. Positive things happen around this person. When a magician needs money, an opportunity comes along. It might be in a promotion or a new job opportunity. If a situation requires the intervention of a friend, old friends may reappear or new friends may rise to the occasion. Most often the world seems to conform itself to meet the needs of the person practicing Natural Magick.

This isn't to say life will always be a cauldron of joy. Everyone has sorrows and difficulties at times. When you can recognize these as part of the Earth's patterns and believe things will improve, you are on your way to a sense of serenity. Making peace with what the Earth hands you is an important lesson to learn—not to be a doormat, but to accept your position in the world at that moment. It is from this place you can make magick happen. You can also recognize the magick that is happening all around you and see solutions and directions you might otherwise miss.

A Little Ceremony Is Sometimes Appropriate

Natural Magick can certainly include lighting candles, casting circles, and calling down the Elements, but it tends to take a less formal structure than Wicca, for example. This is folk magick at its best. That's not to say ritual does not have its place in the practice of Natural Magick. After all, sometimes the outward trappings remind us of the inner strength we all possess once we allow ourselves to go with the Earth's natural flow. Listening to your inner wizard will guide you in your practice of everyday magick. If lighting some incense or sprinkling some powder to create a sacred space feels right, by all means do so. On the other hand, if simply throwing an extra pinch of thyme or rosemary into a stew to encourage strength and prosperity seems sufficient, it probably is!

Use your intuition rather than preordained ceremonies and your sixth sense about empowering the Natural Magick you call forth will get stronger over time. Just like exercising a muscle to make it stronger, a magician's power gets stronger the more she or he flexes those internal hunches.

Practices to Attract ... and to Avoid

Natural Magick is an energy flow. It is like electricity, in that it is neither good nor evil. It just is. *How* magick is used makes all the difference. Many modern witches believe in the rule of three—that is, whatever you put out comes back to you three times. Have you ever known someone who always seems lucky? Good things happen to this person without her even seeming to try. Chances are, if you think about it, it's the same person who walks around with a smile on her face, who offers to help her friends when they need it, and who others trust to be honest and fair. Perhaps, without even knowing it, she's practicing a little Natural Magick. Her positive attitude is coming back to her in that powerful optimism that manifests when faith attracts beneficial outcomes. Liguana's grandfather always told her, "The old black bird comes back to roost." Make sure the black bird you send out is the one you want to get back!

> **CAUTION**
>
> **Stir Gently …!**
>
> Negative thoughts can bring about dire consequences. Before you wish someone ill, stop and think. Try to see the situation from that person's side. Have you blown the issue out of proportion? Anger hurts you more than it hurts anyone else. Take a deep breath and let it go. It's safer than having the bad feelings you send out come back to you in some way.

Most people intuitively believe in cause and effect. Another way to say this is, "What goes around, comes around." These ideas are important to those desiring balance within and attunement to the natural world. No need for us to tell you what practices to avoid. Think about it a minute. If you wouldn't want it for yourself, don't send it to someone else. If you want to manifest something good, send good out from yourself into the world.

Natural Magick Is In and Of You

Natural Magick is inside all of us; it is outside all of us. The trick is to stop whining and embrace the world and the natural energy of all of its joys and sorrows. In this book, we will offer some suggestions for understanding how your own essential nature really *is* Natural Magick. But try listening to your inner voice. It already knows the magick!

The Least You Need to Know

- Natural Magick means working with Nature to effect changes in your life.

- *Pagan* is a broad term that encompasses any nature-based religion—including Wicca, Druidism, Shamanism, Native American beliefs, and many other world religions.

- Natural Magick is less about formal ceremonies and more about listening to the Earth's patterns.

- To receive good from the world, send good out. Listen to your inner voice—it is pure Natural Magick.

2

Honoring Natural Ethics

In This Chapter

- ◆ Why acting naturally is powerful harmonious magick
- ◆ The magick of right eating
- ◆ Embracing natural ways of building and living in your home
- ◆ Practicing Natural Magick ethically

Practicing Natural Magick means showing respect to the Earth, to the Lord and Lady, and to Nature. It means valuing both the inner and outer landscapes of your life. This philosophy requires personal work to clean up both, to maintain both, and to have good visions for both.

Respecting and honoring Nature and the divine source of all things is accomplished three ways—through awareness, through gratitude, and through care. The ethical practice of Natural Magick strengthens the right use of universal energy—for you personally and for everyone and everything your magick touches. So use your natural powers wisely and well.

What It Means to "Act Naturally"

Honoring the Lord and Lady or the Source of All means respecting Nature by be-having ethically in all aspects of your life—both magickal and mundane. Cleaning up your inner life means thinking about making yourself healthy physically, spiritually, and emotionally. Cleaning up your outer life means ridding your world of clutter. You use your inner and outer energy in both magickal and mundane contexts every day. When you act naturally, you bring the harmony of Nature into your being and accept its power. The ethical concept here is one of "right use." When you do Natural Magick, you are working on the right use of both your inner and outer energy. It is in finding a balance in our lives—inner and outer, magickal and mundane—that we can work our most powerful Natural Magick.

Living Aware

Some Natural Magick can be conjured up just by paying attention to your surround-ings. This includes not just the house or apartment you're living, in but also your neighborhood, your town or city, and the people you run into every day. How many times do we seem to sleepwalk through the day, barely noticing the weather or the faces we pass? We give the cat a perfunctory pat on the head, push our children onto the bus, and say a quick hi to our co-workers, but we never really focus on any of them. Showing tolerance in our relationships is an outward manifes-tation of ethical living. Overlooking shortcomings, enjoying friends' successes and joys, lending a help-ing hand—all of these send good out into the world, which is inevitably going to come back to the Natural Magician.

> **Cauldron Bubble**
>
> A Natural Magician notices everything, and by noticing sharpens the connection be-tween herself and the natural world. Make it a point to really look for one beautiful thing each day. It might be a friend's laugh-ter, an unusual stone, or ginger-bread cooling on a kitchen counter.

Look around your living space and your ritual space as though you were seeing each for the first time. Is your house full of unnecessary clutter? No, we don't mean those special photos or talismans that conjure up happy magickal energy, but all that other stuff: In your living space, this could be the old newspapers, the outdated pills in the medicine cabinet, the 10 mismatched coffee mugs, and the drawer full of worn-out rubber bands and dead batteries and seven-year-old bank statements. In your ritual space, it could be unused magickal tools, oil that's gone rancid, herbs that aren't fresh, and the robe that's frayed and desperately needs mending.

Sometimes clutter sort of sneaks up on us when we aren't paying attention—when we aren't living aware. We need to see the Natural Magick in every moment. There's a well-known creed among folks who practice magick naturally, and we've hinted at it already: To change the outside, change the inside, and visa versa. If you're feeling a little spiritually blocked, perhaps tidying up your outside space (mundane and/or ritual) is the first step in allowing the magick to flow more freely. One of the first principles of practicing *Feng Shui* is to unclutter each room of the house to restore natural harmony, which, in turn, can help bring about prosperity, family camaraderie, good health, and good luck, among other things. Using Feng Shui can enhance your magickal workings and free up the energy in your mundane and ritual spaces. By bringing your environment into harmony with Nature through Feng Shui, your magick reveals a concerted ethical intent toward right use of energy.

> **Magickal Bounty**
>
> The practice of **Feng Shui** (pronounced *fung shway*) combines ancient Chinese wisdom with traditions of the Chinese culture and provides guidelines to be used for different situations or aspirations. When studying Feng Shui, one learns the importance of positioning objects in the home or business to create a harmonious atmosphere and maximize the flow of energy.

Using Feng Shui Harmony in Your Magickal Workings

If you've been feeling a little blocked magickally, it might mean you have to clear your ritual space of negative energy and invite chi into your space. One way to do this, using Feng Shui principles, is to add a running fountain to your altar or sacred space. Place the fountain in the center of your altar to boost the free flow of energy to all areas of the bagua, or choose one area that needs special attention. A bagua is a "map" of the locations in your house that correspond to various situations in your life. You can buy a fountain, but building your own made of rocks or seashells you've gathered yourself keeps you closer to your own Natural Magick by inviting your outside world inside. In addition, if your altar is a portable one, you may want to consider using the Feng Shui bagua to guide you toward the place where your altar will most help free your magick and connect you with potent free-flowing energy toward your magickal purpose.

Building your own fountain connects you more closely to the natural world around you. Use this map of the Feng Shui bagua to place the fountain on your altar in the area where you'd like magickal energy to flow freely.

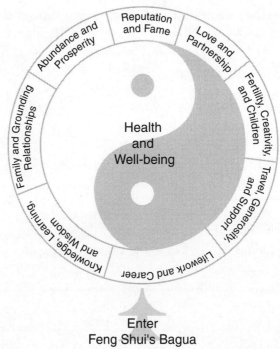

Enter
Feng Shui's Bagua

Polished river rocks make a nice filler. About four or five pounds should be plenty for a medium-size bowl. You can also use lava rocks, slate, or other clean, hard substitutes, such as marbles or beach glass. If you collect the rocks yourself, be sure they're well cleaned because any debris could clog your pump. Seashells for the top layer are a nice accent. The important thing is that the fountain be pleasing to your eye.

The fountainhead can be as simple as a few inches of rubber tubing (½-inch diameter) from the hardware store, to bamboo piping, to a larger rock with ½-inch diameter hole drilled through it. Once again, the choice is up to your own aesthetic sense, budget, and craft skills.

The first step in assembling these pieces is testing your pump in the bowl filled only with water. Learn how strong it is, and experiment with controlling the flow (most pumps have a little adjuster knob on the side). Once you have the flow you want, start filling with rocks carefully, pausing to recheck the flow periodically. Attach the fountain head and finish filling.

Once your fountain is working, invite the Water Element to cleanse your space by saying something like the following:

Soothing Water, welcome to my home,
Bring your energy and peace to my Magick,
Infuse my Life with your blessings,
And I will tend to you with love.

Be sure to clean your fountain regularly so it doesn't become covered with algae or run out of water. In addition to the soothing sound of water, which can alleviate stress, a fountain adds humidity to your home.

Expressing Gratitude

How can a person prepare for the ebb and flow of Natural Magick energy? In a word: gratitude. Liguana often does a formal thank you during her Samhain or Wiccan New Year celebration by putting animal tokens on her altar and expressing her gratitude through ritual. Giving thanks can also be as simple as offering a blessing before partaking of the meal, or when accepting cakes and wine after a ritual. Gratitude, though, does not necessarily mean you must embrace a totally vegetarian life style to live ethically. You can honor the ethics of Natural Magick and still eat meat. It does require occasionally thanking the animal spirits, as Liguana does, for their sacrifice. It also involves choosing animal-friendly products and services, such as buying personal-care products from companies that do not test on animals. A Natural Magician is profoundly aware of the need to uphold respect for and the sanctity of the animal kingdom, and the natural environment that sustains both it and us!

If you choose a vegetarian or semivegetarian diet, express your gratitude to the plants for providing their bounty. This is especially true of trees or vines that will be producing fruit year after year. Thanking the apple tree or the grape vine for its harvest ensures its continued cooperation and nurtures its innate natural magickal power.

But expressing gratitude is more than just thanking the Lord and Lady or sending out a blessing to the Universe. For the Natural Magician, remembering to express gratefulness

> **CAUTION**
> **Stir Gently ...!**
> If you feed the birds and squirrels during the winter, don't stop at the first signs of spring! Remember that there won't be seeds or nuts available until much later in the summer, and our animal friends need nutrition to build nests and raise babies.

means paying attention to the bounty you've been given and sharing that bounty with those around you—both animal and human. In sharing, the Natural Magician receives threefold what he or she has sent out.

Don't forget to save those stale crackers and that rock-hard half loaf of sourdough bread for your backyard buddies who are your allies in performing strong Natural Magick. Think before you consign something to the garbage. Who else might enjoy it? As a special treat, spread peanut butter on those slightly freezer-burned hamburger buns and provide a little extra protein for the cardinals and squirrels. Nuts, being the very seeds of life, bring health and wisdom to those who share them. Some Natural Magicians believe the sight of a red cardinal against the snow brings good luck, and watching the joy of a squirrel munching a treat increases your own joy. These simple acts connect you to the Earth, which increases your own magickal energy flow.

But as Natural Magicians, showing gratitude has an easy and obvious connection to our mundane lives. Showing gratitude includes sharing our abundance with other living beings, whether they sit at our table, grow on our windowsill, or eat at feeders in our backyard. While you're remembering the animals and plants, remember to buy some staples to drop off at your local food pantry. This simple act of human generosity toward others is powerful Natural Magick with a clear and immediate benefit—for everyone! That's because, through sharing, we receive in abundance.

Check to see what staples your local charities might need. Donating grains of all kinds will increase your own prosperity. Before you donate it, bless your offering by saying, "Lady, infuse this food with your spirit, that it might be for the health of all who partake of it." Although you should never perform magick without someone's knowledge, this simple blessing is clearly meant to bring only good things to people, so it is entirely ethical to do so.

Showing You Care

In the magickal realm, the microcosm reflects the macrocosm. In other words, showing you care about the little things also demonstrates your concern about the grand scheme of things—that is, Nature. The smallest positive energy flow increases as it spreads out and influences other living beings.

We've talked about awareness, gratitude, and sharing with our friends, both human and animal, but showing care and respect for the Earth itself is imperative! You can do this not only by recycling, but also by composting, planting, tending, and avoiding the use of pesticides and chemicals.

A Natural Magician utilizes everything to its fullest. Composting not only helps you grow those necessary herbs and flowers for spellworking without chemicals, but it also reuses waste products so they have a second life. A good Natural Magick proverb goes like this:

> *Use it up, wear it out, make it do, or do without.*

This is true of everything in your life—slivers of soap, recyclable containers, used clothing. It is the ethical way to savor the Earth's offerings to you. Pass them on!

If you have a backyard, composting is relatively easy—you can just use a little corner of your yard for the compost pile. If you live in the city, it's a little more challenging but still possible.

Start with three large (at least five-gallon) flower pots. Put your veggie-based kitchen scraps mixed with a little dirt in the bottom pot. When it's almost full, nest the next pot inside the first one and keep filling and stacking. By the time the top pot is full, the bottom pot is finished compost. Place a pot tray on the bottom to water the compost and another tray on the top to keep the fruit flies and gnats away. The whole thing takes up about 1½ square feet of space. It even fits under the sink. You can use this compost to grow luscious balcony flowers or vegetables. Be sure to share your compost with your apartment mates. A little compost, a pretty flower pot, and a package of seeds makes a lovely present. Giving them basil seeds will increase their wealth, rosemary can bring love into their lives, and sage can help them in their work endeavors. Think about what your friends might "need" and select your herbs accordingly.

Liguana's Grimoire

Liguana discovered that an easy way to stir her compost was to compost where her chickens could enjoy it. The compost bin was open on one side and the top, and it was a favorite hangout for the feathered set. Chickens love leftovers! Her favorite thing to feed them was spaghetti noodles. They flipped noodles around in the air, at each other, and around their neck and beaks, and generally had a merry time of it. What does this mean for your Natural Magick? Your animal friends are infusing your compost with their own essence and insight.

How will a Natural Magician show ethical compassion, though, toward pests and weeds—not always typically thought of as helpful creatures? There are magick-friendly ways to discourage pests from taking up residence. Sprinkling cinnamon or talcum powder around an area infested with ants will drive them away, and concentrated lemon juice around your garden border will keep them off your vegetables. Using these chemical-free solutions is the ethical way to discourage pests without damaging the birds and backyard friends who live off them.

And besides, sometimes "pests" and "weeds" are necessary. If you have peonies, black ants are vital so the plants will flower. Peonies are good to add to potpourri to attract affection. And dandelions, which most people spend hours digging out of their backyards, actually attract wealth when tossed in a salad or turned into wine. Even poison ivy has a purpose! It keeps humans and animals away from an area that might need protection, such as a new stand of trees. Don't be hasty in writing off something as a pest! A Natural Magician listens to the Earth and respects all of her inhabitants.

Likewise, using poisons to eliminate mice can endanger any children or pets in your home. If a cat munches on a poisoned mouse, it may also die. Stuffing steel wool and moth balls in any cubby spaces that look mouse-friendly will discourage them from entering without introducing toxic fumes into your environment. Mouse energy can fill a house with ambition and industriousness. You just don't want them munching on your crackers! Keeping them outdoors will suffice.

Although it's tempting to want to destroy the creepy crawlies, an ethical Natural Magician knows that every living thing serves a magickal purpose. Recycling, composting, avoiding chemicals—every small act of caring ties the natural wizard more deeply to his or her magick and its success.

Ethical Eating

Many spiritual practices have rules and guidelines for eating to keep the body healthy and enliven the spirit. The *ayurvedic* diet, as one example, calls for lacto vegetarianism and eating specific types of food based on what body humor or dosha may be out of balance.

Magickal Bounty

The word **ayurveda** comes from two Sanskrit words, *ayus*, or "life," and *ved*, meaning "knowledge" or "science." Ayurveda is translated as "science of life" or, more precisely, "the knowledge of life span."

Keeping your dosha in balance further connects you to Nature. When you are healthy, Earth's energy can flow freely through you into your magickal intent. And, of course, being healthy works in your mundane endeavors. Eating ethically nourishes your spirit and your body.

The definition of *health* in an ayurvedic tradition doesn't just mean "absence of disease." Health is where mind, body, spirit, emotions, and senses are all in perfect balance, the way Nature designed them to be. In our high-stress, sleep-deprived, eat-on-the-go, get-it-all-done-yesterday world, having our systems go out of balance is easy. Eventually, imbalances manifest themselves as disease. Rather than popping a pill, ayurveda encourages right eating. Ayurveda maintains that balance is the key to health.

Natural Magicians who make good use of ayurveda connect to the Elements through balancing the doshas and drawing closer to uniting their physical bodies with natural energy in a harmonious way. The three doshas are vata, pitta, and kapha. They are structured from the five senses and the five Elements. Vata is the essence of Air and touch. Pitta is the essence of Fire and Water and sight and taste. Kapha is the essence of Water and Earth and taste and smell. Spirit encompasses them all.

Each dosha has qualities that control basic functions of the body, as well as qualities that can be identified in food, in the environment, and in all other material substances. Vata is movement, quick, light, dry, cold, and rough. Things with these qualities might include an icy wind, popcorn, or a fast-moving ice hockey game. Pitta is sharp, hot, acidic, light, and slightly oily. Pitta qualities are found in hot salsa, a shrill siren, and the full noontime sun in August. Kapha is heavy, slow, oily, steady, solid, and dull. Cheese and ice cream, the gait of an elephant, and the heaviness one feels after an afternoon nap all have Kapha qualities.

Doing Natural Magick ayurvedically isn't so much about specific recipes and spells as it is about a style designed to balance the doshas. In ayurvedic cooking, there are six tastes: sweet, sour, salty, bitter, pungent or spicy, and astringent. To feel completely nourished, all six tastes should be present at every meal. Eating all six tastes strengthens your immune system—as well as your magick! (For more on ayurvedic recipes, see Chapter 22.)

Here are two sample recipes based on ayurvedic principles. For a list of specific magickal correspondences for each recipe's ingredients, consult Appendix C. Try these recipes at home, or prepare them with intent for your next magickal gathering, to promote the ayurvedic lesson of ethical balance in right eating.

Vegetable Stroganoff

This dish produces a rich tomatoey sauce that aspires to a Russian heritage. Serve it over wide, flat egg noodles or fettuccini.

2 TB. olive oil

1 cup fresh parsley, chopped

1 tsp. dried basil

½ tsp. dried thyme

¼ tsp. dried rosemary

1 sweet bell pepper, finely chopped

1 carrot, grated

1 zucchini, grated

4 cups ripe tomatoes, chopped

¾ cup water (or vegetable stock)

1 bay leaf

⅔ cup sliced carrots

⅔ cup sliced zucchini

½ cup peas

⅔ cup cauliflower, broken into small pieces

1 cup cooked garbanzo beans (cook the day before according to package directions)

½ cup sour cream

Salt and pepper to taste

In a large Dutch oven, heat the olive oil. Add the parsley and dried herbs, and sauté for about 30 seconds to release their aromas. Add bell pepper, grated carrots, and grated zucchini, and sauté for about 7 minutes more. Add tomato, water, and bay leaf. Cover and simmer over very low heat for 2 to 2½ hours, stirring occasionally.

Steam carrots, zucchini, peas, and cauliflower until tender. Stir them, along with cooked garbanzo beans, into the sauce. Heat until piping hot. Add sour cream and salt and pepper to taste. Serve over pasta. Serves 4–6.

Yam-Pecan Casserole with Dried Cranberries

A nice winter treat, this is easy enough to serve during the week or to grace a holiday Yule or Candlemas/Imbolc table.

4 cups yams, cooked, peeled, and puréed

¼ cup melted butter or ghee

½ cup packed brown sugar

1 tsp. cinnamon

1 TB. lemon juice

⅛ tsp. salt

⅓ cup crystallized ginger, finely chopped

½ cup dried cranberries

½ cup whole pecan halves

Preheat the oven to 350°F. Butter a 9-inch pie plate. With an electric mixer, beat puréed yams, butter, brown sugar, cinnamon, lemon juice, and salt until smooth. Gently fold in ginger and cranberries. Spoon the mixture into the pie plate. Decorate with pecan halves and bake for 30 minutes. Serves 4–6.

Eating "Live Food"

Today the "live food" trend encourages people to consume the spark of life from food without processing it into oblivion first. Eating live food keeps you closest to the way Nature is offering you her bounty. It respects her choices and honors the way she offers her plants to our benefit. Living and Raw Foodists believe in eating only an uncooked, unheated (not above 116°F), unprocessed, and organic plant–based diet.

There are many reasons why Natural Magicians might embrace a raw and living foods diet or incorporate it into ritual. People who eat this type of diet sometimes experience improvements in their general physical and mental health. Some people find a live food diet too extreme but certainly including more fruits and vegetables in your diet and ritual—farm-rich from field to table—is an achievable goal. Because you no longer have to cook as much, you don't use as much electricity, which helps save the environment. Because you eat only organic agriculture, it helps to save the planet from the overuse of chemicals. Most live foodists become more in tune with their bodies, and many report definite spiritual improvements. Finally, because no animal products are used, the animals appreciate it.

Embracing a totally live food diet requires some commitment and perseverance. If you'd like to try easing into it gradually or practice only it occasionally, start with these two simple recipes.

"Raw" Apple Pie

Apples are significant in many symbolic ways. In the Wiccan tradition, for example, they symbolize the Mother. If you cut them in half, the core appears as a natural pentagram, another powerful talisman. They represent a fruitful autumn harvest, and as a mundane ingredient, they are just plain healthful!

For the crust:

> 1½ cups sunflower seeds
>
> ¾ cup raisins
>
> 1 TB. carob powder

For the filling:

> 5 or 6 medium-size Granny Smith apples, peeled and cored
>
> 1 TB. cinnamon
>
> Juice from half a lemon
>
> ¾ cup raw, unfiltered honey
>
> Dash of cloves
>
> Shredded fresh coconut

Make the crust by placing sunflower seeds, raisins, and carob powder in a food processor and processing until finely ground. The mixture should stick together. Spread the mixture into a 9-inch pie pan and pat firmly.

Next, put apples into the food processor and pulse into small pieces. (Be sure not to overdo it and make applesauce!)

In a bowl, mix together chopped apples, cinnamon, lemon juice, honey, and cloves.

Scoop the mixture into the pie crust. Sprinkle coconut on top of the mixture. Refrigerate for at least 1 hour before serving, to allow pie to set.

Hot and Spicy Coleslaw

This recipe has several magickal components. Mustard seeds and peanuts both tend to draw newfound wealth into your life. Dates and tomatoes increase the power of the spell, and coconut promises a visit to an exotic land (or just a well-earned break from your everyday life). Cumin seed and jalapeños can add spice to a romantic relationship. It's all good!

> 3 cups finely chopped cabbage
>
> 3 cups ripe tomato, chopped
>
> 1 minced jalapeño pepper, or to taste
>
> 1 cup fresh grated coconut
>
> ½ cup raw, ground peanuts
>
> 1 large pitted date, soaked and mashed
>
> 2 TB. lemon juice
>
> 2 TB. peanut or olive oil
>
> ½ tsp. ground mustard seed
>
> ½ tsp. ground cumin seed
>
> ¼ tsp. turmeric
>
> Salt and pepper to taste

Mix together cabbage, tomatoes, jalapeño pepper, coconut, and peanuts. Set aside.

In a blender, add the remaining ingredients and blend until smooth. Pour the dressing over the cabbage mixture and toss until well coated. Serves 4.

Vegetarian Eating the Old-Fashioned Way

Basically, vegetarians do not eat meat, fish, and poultry. Their creed is to eat nothing with a face. Vegans are vegetarians who abstain from eating or using all animal products, including milk, cheese, and eggs or wool, silk, and leather.

Among the many reasons for being a vegetarian are health, ecological and religious concerns, dislike of meat, compassion for animals, belief in nonviolence, and economics. The key to a healthful vegetarian diet, as with any other diet, is to eat a wide variety of foods, including fruits, vegetables (including plenty of leafy greens), whole-grain products, nuts, seeds, and legumes. As with any healthful diet, limiting your intake of sweets and fatty foods is a good idea.

Good protein sources for a vegetarian are lentils, tofu, low-fat dairy products, nuts, seeds, tempeh, legumes, and peas. Many common foods such as whole-grain bread, greens, potatoes, pasta, and corn quickly add to protein intake. We'll be sharing more vegetarian recipes with you throughout this book. Let's say again, though, that you *don't* have to be a vegetarian to practice ethical Natural Magick. But you may find that you'll want to use vegetarian principles and apply them to your Natural Magick rituals to enhance specific magickal workings where that is appropriate.

Why Does Right Eating Equal Natural Magick?

Remember this basic principle: Natural Magick is a flow. It very much has to do with energy moving in and out of the body, as if the body were a conduction wire. Training yourself to be a conduit for magickal energy means physical as well as spiritual conditioning. Food is the body's fuel. Eating ethically conditions the spirit so you can be receptive to magick. It also gives you a foundation for creating organic spells and rituals with increased Natural Magick potency and power because the substances you are using and the methods and respect used in their preparation are in tune with natural energy.

Ethical Building

Natural Magicians should be aware of the building they live in and where they do any indoor rituals. We understand that it is sometimes difficult to control the building structure you live in, but to the extent that you can, your Natural Magick will strengthen. Liguana presently lives in a house built using materials harvested from the land cleared for its foundation. Finding ways to build that are not wasteful or polluting is another way to show respect and care for Nature.

Using recycled materials in constructing our homes is an additional way to help our living space be a focal point for Natural Magick. Homes or barns can be made of hay bales covered with adobe plaster or a mix of plaster and perlite. Building with short sections of logs covered in plaster is another good use of resources. If trees must be removed, better they are used with respect and gratitude in the structure that is taking their place.

Living and practicing ethical Natural Magick, such as in ethical building, is actually easier than it may seem. Listen to your inner wizard or witch. If it feels wrong or destructive, it probably isn't a good idea. Face the world calmly and optimistically, and your magickal energy will come back to you. If you are not able to influence the construction, then concentrate on having only natural objects in your home, or construct your altar using only natural materials.

Practicing Ethical Magick, Naturally

Natural Magick practiced ethically hurts no one and comes from only the best intentions. A natural wizard doesn't try to bend other people to his or her will, but "goes with the flow" that the Earth automatically presents. In other words, you can't—and shouldn't try—to cast a spell to make someone love you or to stop someone else from getting "your" promotion. Instead, you can do a ritual to make yourself more open to the opportunities for love and advancement, and then listen to the universe.

An ethical wizard doesn't allow opportunities to go by unexplored. That isn't to say you'll fall in love every time you go out on a date with a new person, but you might find a new friend. Likewise, going after a job or a promotion doesn't necessarily mean you'll get it, but it might give you a chance to learn something about yourself that will make the next time easier. Don't let yourself think of "failure" as a negative thing. Sometimes it's just a way for the Earth to help you sort through your choices.

Drawing Down (an Ethical) Circle

When the time comes to perform a Natural Magick ritual, you might want to cast a circle to represent a formal, sacred place. When you look for a good place to cast a circle with ethical intent, the spirits of place should be considered and the land honored. Indoors, you may want to honor the Feng Shui energies of the bagua, which we discussed earlier in this chapter.

Stir Gently ...!

If you're casting a circle outside, be sure to look for a space that affords you some privacy. Ethical magicians don't want to make neighbors uncomfortable, either.

Natural Magicians can make a sacred circle by using flour or barley to mark out the ritual space. Sprinkling the grain in a large circle is an outward sign of your inward intentions. Circles are most often cast on flat ground, respecting the natural contours of the land. This is not only for the sake of convenience, so you're not jumping over hummocks and stumps, but also to respect the natural lay of the land and energy flows therein.

Once the circle is cast, milk, honey, or small cakes or other foods are sometimes offered to the spirits of the place. Honoring these spirits, whether they're from the fairy world, the Druid world, the plant world, or the animal world, reinforces the positive energy you are trying to invoke. After all, as you've learned, nothing is more ethical than saying thank you.

Good Magickal Karma

In Buddhist teaching, the law of karma says that for every event that occurs, there will follow another event caused by the first, and this second event will be pleasant or unpleasant, based on whether its cause was accompanied or unaccompanied by envy, resistance, or delusions. In other words, the urge to nourish pain and squash joy is living unethically and will result in only bad things coming back to you. Nurturing joy and trying to eliminate pain means living ethically. Happy days will be heading your way!

Being fully ethical is said to be impossible for those who make a distinction between themselves and others. In the Christian religion, it is known as the Golden Rule: Do unto others as you would have them do unto you. In Wicca, the Rede is, "And it harm none, do what ye will." Hindu sacred literature says, "Let no man do to another that which would be repugnant to himself." This rule exists in some form in every ethical religion practiced in the world. It's no wonder, then, that practicing Natural Magick requires the thoughtful consideration of how your actions affect those around you.

Natural Magick harnesses the spirit of karma, the Golden Rule, and the Wiccan Rede so that the magician can dwell in harmony within the natural cycle of everything that lives on Earth and in the Universe. An ethical magician honors these cycles and all spiritual quests through respect and compassion.

The Least You Need to Know

- Living ethically in the world means connecting to the positive energy flow in the universe.

- Ethical Natural Magick requires awareness, gratitude, and care.

- Ethical eating provides the healthy body necessary for Natural Magick to flow freely though you and to you.

- Caring for the Earth by composting, recycling, and building wisely is a part of practicing Natural Magick.

Chapter 3

An All-Natural Pantry: Magickal and Mundane

In This Chapter

- ♦ When is a pantry magickal?
- ♦ Putting the all-natural in your pantry
- ♦ How to organize your magickal pantry
- ♦ Using utensils and magickal tools

To eat and drink ethically and magickally you need a well-stocked wizard's Natural Magick pantry. We've already mentioned that less processed foods are more magickal and better for you than more processed foods. What then do you put in a Natural Magick pantry?

Actually, you stock the same foodstuffs you would for a mundane pantry for the most part. The difference is in the intent you stir into a ritual meal or magickal dish. No one casually looking at a wizard's magickal pantry would even guess there was spellcrafting in the works. No eye of newt in a jar or frozen bat tongues waiting to be defrosted. Just wholesome ingredients but brought together with love and perhaps an incantation or two.

Stocking Magickal Staples

A Natural Magick pantry is not necessarily a specific room in your house. Think of your pantry as your cool, dry cupboards; your spice rack; even your freezer and refrigerator. Wherever you store your staples makes up your pantry. The best part of gifting yourself and your loved ones by starting a Natural Magick pantry is that your natural pantry represents a wonderful, healthful lifestyle choice—regardless of your religious beliefs. Anyone attracted to natural, unprocessed ingredients, lovingly prepared, is ready to enjoy what every Natural Magician knows: Living in harmony with Nature is right living. But just what are staples for Natural Magick?

Cauldron Bubble

Don't think you need to buy all of your staples at once. Decide which spices and oils you will use most often and then add to your Natural Magick pantry as your purpose or working requires.

Every kitchen, whether magickal or not, needs to have a ready supply of edible oils, herbs, spices, and basic cooking supplies and utensils. A Natural Magick wizard is always prepared with ingredients to serve every purpose, magickal and mundane: for guests popping in; for the impromptu ritual that takes advantage of the natural energy flow of the season, day, or moment; or simply for the family relaxing at home. With just a few essentials always on hand, a magickal feast can be just an hour or so away from your table, your altar, or your ritual circle.

Start with Spices and Herbs

The art of seasoning foods in such a way that an ordinary dish becomes one transformed with magickal energy and intent is definitely the mark of a talented Natural Magician. Spices not only add flavor to a meal or to a ritual offering, but they can also promote health-enhancing benefits, aid in digestion, and stir up more than a little Natural Magick.

Here are some common spices and herbs you should have on hand and what they most often are used for magickally. (For more herb correspondence, see Chapter 10.)

Magickal Spices and Herbs

Spices/Herbs	Magickal Purpose
Allspice, basil, cloves, ginger, nutmeg, tarragon	Wealth and prosperity
Caraway, celery seed, mustard, rosemary, summer savory	Wisdom
Anise, asafetida, cumin, curry, dill, fennel, parsley, pepper, oregano	Protection of loved ones
Bay leaves, cinnamon, peppermint, saffron	Psychic awareness
Cardamom, chili powder, marjoram, paprika, thyme	Passion and to attract love
Vanilla beans	Enhance memory

Sometimes a recipe calls for fresh herbs. Choosing fresh herbs adds an exquisite power to the magickal significance of each season. You'll learn more about this in Part 5. But using dried herbs is perfectly acceptable and often more practical when fresh are not available. However, you can't substitute the same amount of dried herbs for fresh in a recipe because the flavor of dried is much more concentrated, although the magickal potency is the same. To substitute dried herbs for fresh, the general rule is to use a generous 1 teaspoon of dried leaves for every tablespoon of the fresh herb finely chopped. But it's usually better to add a little, taste, and add more if necessary. Spices should enhance the flavor of the food, not overwhelm it. When practicing Natural Magick, a little hot spice, such as pepper, cumin, or chili powder, goes a long way to adding passion to a relationship. Use these sparingly—or you may find fireworks that get a bit out of hand! (See Chapter 5 for more on the Fire Element.)

> **CAUTION**
>
> **Stir Gently …!**
>
> Store your spices in a cool, dry place—*not* above your stove. Their potency, for both magick and flavor, will suffer. Buy small containers that you can use within a year. Stale spices are no longer potent for magick.

Salt of the Earth

In addition to bringing out the flavor of food, different salts can produce different magickal results. If you are accustomed to using only iodized table salt, you're missing out on taste and magick. Try these specialized salts for a little wizardry:

◆ **Gray salt**—Harvested in Brittany, this salt is rich in iron, calcium, zinc, potassium, and iodine. It also attracts the Water Element, which is good for psychic endeavors and protection. Plus, it tastes good!

◆ **Hawaiian red salt**—Almost fruity with a slight peppery taste, this salt is tinted pink by iron-rich island clay. As a magickal ingredient, it calls out to the Earth Element and provides stability.

◆ **Fleur de Sel**—From France, this delicately flavored salt calls to the Earth Element and ensures prosperity.

◆ **Jurassic salt**—A pure salt from an ancient North American sea, this salt calls to the Water Element and can help you connect to and honor your ancestors.

◆ **Black salt**—A boldly flavored mineral salt, this salt calls to the Earth Element and increases psychic abilities.

◆ **Kosher salt**—A course salt with no additives, kosher salt is used for healing and blessing magick and calls to the Earth and Fire Elements. In the Jewish faith, kosher salt is used in the preparation of meats.

◆ **Sea salt**—A salt made by evaporating seawater, this salt is used for cleansing and for dispelling negativity; it calls to the Water and Fire Elements.

Whole-food stores also sell salts infused with herbs, or try a website such as www. napastyle.com. The herbs bring their own magickal properties to the dish. Sundried tomato garlic gray salt strengthens a spell, provides protection, and heightens psychic abilities. Citrus rosemary gray salt heals broken hearts, calls for prosperity, and heightens psychic ability. Experiment with exotic salts until you find one that seems to speak to you and enhances your magickal workings in just the way you desire.

You will want to use plain old table salt in your protection rituals or in casting a circle. It works well for those rituals and is much cheaper. Save the expensive salts for edible food magick.

Onion and Garlic Magick

Onions and garlic are very protective. Onions help cleanse a space of negative energy and also attract money. You can use them in soups and stews or weave them into a braid to hang in your kitchen as a talisman.

Any onion can be used in a recipe, but each type brings a slightly different magickal energy to the meal. Yellow onions draw in positive energy, whereas white onions are better for protection. If you're weaving onions into a protective talisman, don't forget to consider adding leeks and shallots. They're onions too! Each knot you make becomes a holding place for magickal energy, so the more knots you include, the better the magick.

Oils Facilitate and Extend Natural Magick

A good selection of oils is one of your most important Natural Magick pantry items and should be thoughtfully chosen. Oils can add a flavor or a texture, or they can be used as a neutral medium that enhances the flavors and magickal potency of the other ingredients you choose to mix with them. Whether you use a strongly flavored oil or a relatively bland one depends on the magickal effect you want. You'll also want to consider the *smoking point* of the oil you select for your recipe or specific magickal purpose.

Virgin olive oil is a basic oil for your Natural Magick pantry. Throughout history, olives have represented all that is beautiful, peaceful, and sacred. Sautéeing herbs or vegetables in olive oil adds subtle flavor while enhancing the flavors and magickal power of the other ingredients. Olive oils lend calmness and harmony to magickal preparations. Do not use olive oil to deep-fry food; it has a low smoking point, which is not good for deep frying. Investing in the purest oils will achieve the highest results, both culinary and magickal. Following is a list of qualities to look for in selecting your olive oil for magickal purposes, and qualities to avoid. You may be surprised!

Magickal Bounty

The **smoking point** is the temperature at which cooking oil smokes when heated. When oil reaches the temperature at which it begins to smoke, a chemical breakdown occurs that is dangerous as well as unhealthful. Oils with high smoking points, such as peanut oil and corn oil, should be used for deep-fat frying because of the high temperature the oil must reach.

Magickal Qualities of Olive Oils

Enhancing Qualities	Detracting Qualities
Astringent: Cleansing and mentally focusing	*Briny:* Too much salt
Bitter: Green olives especially, adds bite	*Overly bitter:* Overpowers other magickal ingredients
Fruity: Lends maturity, though fruitiness may wane over time, so use fruity oils promptly	*Dirty:* Has absorbed the smell and taste of processing vegetable water
Grass or hay: Adds flavor of leaves or twigs, boosting Earth Element	*Earthy/Musty:* A musty, humid odor that obscures the magick
Harmonious: Well balanced, facilitating magick	*Flat:* No flavor or aroma
Nutty: Lends Earth energy	*Metallic:* Takes on undesired influence from contact with metals during processing
Sweet: Lends mellow energy	*Moldy:* Prepared from rotten or fermented olives, spoiling the magick

Many other oils, often those pressed from nuts or seeds, can add their magickal flavor to a dish. These oils may be difficult to find, but you can order many of them online. Buy specialty oils in small quantities, and use them quickly so they don't turn rancid. To find the magickal correspondences for many of the nuts and seeds used to press oils, turn to the discussion of nuts and seeds later in this chapter.

Although we recommend deep-frying rarely, sometimes a recipe, such as tempura, or a magickal purpose, such as a ritual honoring the Lord, just calls for it. Some oils have a high smoking point and are also mostly flavorless, so they can be used in recipes in which you don't want the flavor of the oil to stand out. These include corn, peanut, vegetable, canola, and sunflower oils. Any of these oils connect you to the Fire Element and add positive energy and passion to the meal.

An ayurvedic alternative to oils to use in Natural Magick is ghee. Most health-food stores carry ghee. It is easy to digest, doesn't spoil easily, and adds a light, buttery taste. Ghee is clarified butter—the butter oil, without the lactose and other milk solids. The word *ghee* is pronounced with a hard *G*, as in *go*, and a long *e*, as in *glee*. It is traditionally prepared by gently heating butter until it becomes a clear, golden liquid with the milk solids floating on top. Skim them off and the resulting "oil" will keep much longer than butter. Ghee adds a subtle passion to a dish and, in the ayurvedic tradition, helps balance pitta (see Chapter 5).

Stir Gently ...!

Oils are volatile and can spoil easily, becoming rancid if they are stored too long or are kept at too high a temperature. Buy your oils in small quantities unless you are cooking in volume, and store in a cool, dark place out of sunlight.

Vinegars

So you have your wine that cost you $12, and you settle down on your couch with your fuzzy slippers, your blanket, and a good book. Then you sip the wine, and gack! Spew! Yuck! You just don't like it. No worries. Just leave it uncorked, with the mouth of the bottle covered with a cloth. In a few days, you will have wine vinegar.

Now, don't think that just because the wine represents celebration and gladness and the positive side of life the vinegar does too. We don't use a lot of vinegar in magick because it represents things that have soured.

This can be tempered by flavoring your vinegar with herbs, which is easily done by suspending the fresh herbs in your bottle of vinegar for 10 days or more in a dark room or pantry. Here are some common vinegar herbs and their magickal associations:

- **Basil**—Prosperity, romance
- **Dill**—Protection, wealth
- **Fennel**—Protection, purification
- **Lemon balm**—Romance, happiness
- **Raspberry**—Contentment, calm
- **Rosemary**—Love and passion, wisdom banishing negativity
- **Sage**—Wisdom, longevity

Grains and Dried Goods

Grains represent fertility, protection, and wholesomeness. Powders can be used to dust doorsills and windowsills to keep out bad luck and to seal in good. Natural Magick foodstuffs to have on hand are baking powder, baking soda, cornmeal, wheat flour, rice flour, oatmeal, quinoa, barley, rice, dahl, and any other grains you use often. Here is a list of some magickal correspondences:

- **Amaranth**—Healing, protection
- **Barley**—Love, offering
- **Corn**—Nurturing, divination
- **Dahl**—Stability, balance
- **Oats**—Wealth
- **Quinoa**—Health, psychic ability
- **Rice**—Fertility, longevity, blessings
- **Rye**—Loyalty
- **Wheat**—Fertility, abundance

More mundane than magickal (whether fresh or dried), pasta is always good to have on hand as a staple for highlighting the pure magickal energy of the ingredients used to top it. Pasta made with spinach enhances wealth; tomatoes, of course, add passion. Keep a variety on hand—spaghetti, fettuccini, farfalle, angel hair, macaroni, and lasagna. Pasta lightly tossed with fresh herbs and a good oil makes a quick and magickally potent meal.

Nuts and Seeds

A good protein source for vegetarians, seeds and nuts also help add some magick and connect us to the Earth Element. After all, nuts and seeds tie us to the way our feathered and furred friends dine outdoors and are graciously offered to us from our tree and plant companions.

It's best to buy raw, unsalted nuts. Otherwise, they have added oil and way too much salt, so their magickal energy is diluted. Because nuts are naturally oily, they can become rancid unless properly stored. They will last longest if you freeze them, but they'll keep up to two months in a cool, dry cupboard and up to three months in a refrigerator.

Toasting nuts brings out their full flavor and adds Fire to the Earth Element. Spread the nuts on a cookie sheet and place them in a 350°F oven for 15 to 20 minutes. Stir them every 5 minutes and watch them carefully; they can go from golden to burned to a crisp in seconds.

All nuts and nut oils connect you to the Earth Element and to Earth's animal spirits.

Magickal Bounty

Cousins to the sage plant, chia seeds boiled in water or fruit juice produce a type of gelatin that can be sweetened, mixed with fruit, and served as a dessert in place of the usual animal-based gelatins. They infuse wisdom and grounding to your dish, and are usually found in whole-food and health stores.

Magickal Properties of Nuts and Seeds

Nuts/Seeds	Magickal Properties
Acorns	Fertility, wisdom
Almonds*	Wisdom, prosperity, enduring love
Cashews	Money
Chia seeds	Grounding, maturity, wisdom
Grapeseed*	Banishment of negative energies or influences
Hazelnuts*	Fertility
Macadamias	Wealth and empowerment for women
Peanuts*	Male sexuality, grounding
Pecans	Wealth, work
Pine nuts	Psychic power, intuition
Pistachios	Physical health, peace
Poppy seeds	Restful sleep, psychic dreams
Pumpkin seeds	Honoring the Spirit and ancestors
Sesame seeds*	Love, strength, abundance
Sunflower seeds	Abundance, wealth, new opportunities
Walnuts*	Wisdom

*Indicates this nut or seed is commonly pressed for use in oil form.

Perishables

Once your basic Natural Magick pantry is stocked with staples, you'll want to take a look at perishables. Be sure to take advantage of the seasonal produce when planning your meals. Eating ethically means taking advantage of the fruits and vegetables as the Earth offers them to you. In addition, in-season foods are usually cheaper. If a crop is destroyed by a natural disaster—oranges or tomatoes, for example—do without until the source of All offers them up again. Not only does this put you in tune with the flow of the Earth, but it forces you to vary what you eat, which is a nutritious way to live.

Fruits and Vegetables

We know a health Natural Magician can call up powerful magick, and what could be healthier than fruits and vegetables? Besides being good for your body, particular fruits and vegetables can be selected depending on the spellcrafting you want to perform. It's best to choose produce that is fresh and in season, but frozen fruits and vegetables will work, too. Use the following table as a starting point, but substitute your own wisdom any time.

Produce and Their Magickal Correspondence

Fruits/Vegetables	Magickal Correspondences
Apples	Love, enhances magick
Artichokes	Prevents unwanted attention
Asparagus	Enhances sexuality
Avocado	Beauty spells
Bananas	Humor, sense of well-being
Beans	Reconciliation, protection, exorcism, resurrection
Beets	Love, passion
Berries	Protection from disease, passion
Cabbage	Fertility, profit, good luck
Carrots	Lust, fertility
Celery	Psychic power, mental work
Corn	Protection from negative forces

Fruits/Vegetables	Magickal Correspondences
Cucumbers	Healing, lunar magick
Endive	Love, fertility
Fennel	Victory, clear vision, purification
Grapes	Fertility, money, mental power
Lemons	Cleansing, protection
Lettuce	Contentment, divination, sleep
Melons	Intuition, creativity
Mushrooms	Peace, healing, prophetic dreams
Oranges	Prosperity, love
Peas	Fortune and profits in business
Pears	Love, enhances magick
Pineapple	Draws good luck, hinders lust
Potatoes	Wards away illness
Tomatoes	Repels evil, inspires love

Dairy and Nondairy Substitutes

Liguana loves dairy food and finds it a comfort food. Milk is nurturing and mothering. That's why cows and goats often correspond to these qualities (especially cows, because goats are pretty playful and capricious, not quite as strong a symbol for nurturing). Milk is for love. It is also a food given to the sidhe, the faeries and the spirits of place.

Dairy products can include yogurt (especially homemade), cheeses, ice cream, and cream. If you turn to nondairy products, you miss out on some of the Natural Magick of milk. However, soy-based nondairy products can add grounding.

CAUTION

Stir Gently ...!

Don't offer faeries nondairy products. Like cats, they know the difference! The luck they offer you can turn sour if you try to thank them with a substitute. Whole-milk offerings only, please!

Meat, Meat Substitutes, and Fish

For ethical Natural Magicians who want to include a little meat in their diets, making sure the meat is as fresh as possible and raised and slaughtered humanely is the key. Making meat the centerpiece of a meal isn't a good idea, for all kinds of health and environmental reasons. Stretch the meat in your diet with vegetables, rice, or pasta. A good stir-fry or vegetable-rich pasta sauce can stretch a pound of meat to serve six people.

Meat consumption tends to slow all body processes, including the magickal ones. A person may eat animal flesh to incorporate the magickal properties of that animal. Always remember to thank the spirit of the animal for enriching you with its essence. Ideally, any animal you eat should be free-ranged and not cruelly treated in its living or in its dying. Meats are associated with the following magickal qualities:

- **Chicken**—Vitality, light-heartedness

- **Beef**—Kindness, parenthood, nurturing

- **Duck**—Loyalty

- **Pork/bacon**—Intelligence, wealth

- **Turkey**—Integrity, leadership, protection

"Free range" conveys a positive image of animals living outdoors as Nature intended. Historically, the term *range* means that, in addition to living outside and getting exercise, the animals are able to sustain themselves on the land on which they are living. Chickens and turkeys raised under those conditions are much more preferable than poultry that has been mass produced and force-fed. Nothing ethical about that! Be wary of chicken labeled "free range." Government requirements don't specify the number of chickens limited to a certain space to be called free range. Chickens packed into a gravel yard full of feces may be getting some outdoor exercise, but they aren't being allowed to range—that is, feed themselves. Buy only from reputable companies.

Other meats, such as beef and pork, may be eaten as health and conscience allows. We suggest always avoiding veal, which treats calves as objects rather than as living beings. Always recognize the animals' dignity and value in the world, and give thanks for their sacrifice and generosity.

If your Natural Magick practices can't condone killing animals, you can use meat substitutes for flavoring and in recipes, although they don't add the same magickal

energy. For example, *seitan*, a popular substitute, adds the same qualities wheat adds:
fertility and abundance.

Fresh fish should be firm, with no "fishy" smell.
If it has an odor or if it feels slimy to the touch,
it's past its prime. Be sure to ask your grocer
whether the fish was previously frozen. Those
Natural Magicians lucky enough to live on a
coast where the fish can be really fresh should
take advantage of it. Those land-locked wizards
will have to settle for slightly less.

Magickal Bounty

Used as a meat substi-
tute, **seitan** is a wheat protein
with a firm, chewy texture. You
can make your own, which takes
about as long as making homemade bread, or buy it at your
local health-food store in the
frozen food section.

The trouble with fish as an entrée is that the world's oceans are being seriously over-
fished, leaving some species, such as cod and Chilean sea bass, in danger of extinction.
If you want to know which fish are "safe" to eat ethically and which to avoid, the
website of the Marine Conservation Society (MCS) at www.mcsuk.com is an excellent, up-to-date resource. Or go to www.audubon.org/campaign/lo/seafood for a
wallet-size printout of what fish to eat ethically.

If you're buying fish from a supermarket, look for the blue MSC logo that guarantees
that the fish comes from a sustainable source. After all, extinct is forever. An ethical
Natural Magician wants to replenish a species, not destroy it. A good rule of thumb
is to vary the fish you eat by eating less well-known fish, such as saithe and pollack.
Keep asking the question "Is this fish responsibly fished and from a sustainable
source?" If the answer is no, pass on it.

Any fish recipe introduces the Water Element, which enhances intuition. In general,
fish also enhance memory and increase wisdom and common sense. No wonder we
call fish "brain food."

Teas

Teas infuse whatever herbs you use to your magickal intent. Using fresh spring water
connects you to the Water Element. Black tea brings energy. Green tea brings health,
while white tea brings purity. Chamomile introduces calm. Peppermint is good for
digestion, grounding, and attracting romance.

Honey is the Mother's sweetener and attracts the Earth Element and fertility. Add
honey to your tea instead of refined sugar. Molasses also is calming and attracts psychic energy, although it has a stronger taste (you probably won't want to add it to
your tea).

Snacks

In today's world, snacks have gotten an increasingly bad name but it's largely because of the overprocessed, highly salted, oversugared junk food that passes as snacks. Instead of stocking your Natural Magick pantry with low-fat, no-taste cookies or oily crackers, keep the ingredients on hand to make your own.

Pack your cookies full of oatmeal, dried fruit, nuts, seeds, and fresh coconut. Bake them with a lot of love and share them generously. Homemade crackers are a little more challenging but well worth the effort. If you make your own, you can be assured that the ingredients are fresh and can limit the amount of salt and oil you use. Remember that your magick is stronger when your body is healthy.

> ### Liguana's Grimoire
>
> Liguana and her daughter made shortbread for a PTA bake sale one October. Although they put loving thoughts and magick into them, the shortbread didn't break into the little wedges they liked to see. They packed up their oddly crumbled cookies and set them up with a sign saying "Unattractive, but oh, so yummy!" They were the biggest-selling item at the sale. In a quiet way, Liguana and her daughter shared their magick with the community by making shortbread cookies while baking blessings into them for all who ate them.

A good magickal kitchen also keeps on hand a variety of fruits (both dried and fresh), nut butters (especially almond and cashew), natural juices, raw veggies, homemade jams and jellies, and popcorn (which can be flavored with various herbs and spices). If you crave ice cream, make it yourself or make your own yogurt. Remember that foods as close to their natural state as possible are best for you. Before you buy a pre-packaged food, look into healthful alternatives you can prepare instead.

Storing Foods Both Magickal and Mundane

Storing foods with respect to their magickal properties is one way to set up a Natural Magick pantry. For example, place foods and spices designed to draw in love and luck on the right side of your pantry or kitchen, and those designed to draw in wealth and health on the left. Order your kitchen in whatever way works best for you.

Labeling spice jars with rhunic or theban script is a good way to learn the writing and refocus daily on the notion that you are a magickal being. Or label a jar on one side with the ingredients and on the other with the magickal properties. This makes an easy reference guide as you begin to put your Natural Magick pantry into action.

In some ways, all foods have magickal properties. It's through good nutrition that our bodies most easily connect to the Earth, to the All, and that Natural Magick flows freely. It isn't necessary to store food with magickal properties and mundane food separately. Work within your own space, organizing it so that cooking is a pleasure—whether you're cooking up a family dinner or a potion for your next ritual circle. If you prepare what you cook with care and good intent, Natural Magick is sure to happen!

Ritual Tools to Cook With

Basically, whatever cooking utensils you have on hand is where you have to start building your tools. Old pans handed down from a wise woman can imbue powerful Natural Magick. Liguana prefers to use wooden spoons and cast-iron pans. Is this magickal? She doesn't know, really. It seems to connect her not only with the natural organic world, but also an earlier time when pots and pans had to withstand the cooking fire. Reclaiming old pots from yard sales and second-hand stores is a great way to recycle. Be sure to clean them thoroughly, bless them, and, in the case of cast iron, to cure them.

Cauldron Bubble

There is no such thing as a ruined cast-iron skillet. If you're lucky enough to find one at a yard sale, no matter how rusted, snatch it up. Scour it with steel wool until the rust is gone, and then coat it thoroughly with oil and put it in a 350°F oven for an hour. Turn off the oven and leave the skillet inside with the door shut until cool. This cures it. Wipe off the excess oil, and you will have a nearly nonstick surface in an indestructible pan.

You can sweep your magickal cooking space with your magickal broom. Sweeping in the direction that the Sun moves, from east to west, is empowering and invokes the power of the Lord.

Although you should never slice meat or cheese with your athame, some Wiccans use a white-handled knife to slice bread at ritual feasts. The knife would most likely be blessed and used only for magickal rituals.

A cauldron can be a traditional ritual tool like the one Macbeth's witches cackled over, or it can be a magickal wizard's old stock pot, a wok, a roaster—whatever container speaks to the cook. The shape of the container isn't important. What's important is the love that goes into the pot.

And don't forget a goblet. A goblet can be used in ritual as well as for more mundane meals, although use of a lovely wine glass instead of plastic can elevate any meal to magickal realms. Liguana has a red goblet she sometimes fills with water and leaves on her windowsill for 24 hours to charge the water with the Sun's energy. You can do the same with a blue goblet in the window to catch the Moon's glow. Solarized water is for energy and will. Lunar water strengthens peace and health.

The Least You Need to Know

- Stocking a Natural Magick pantry means keeping staples on hand and learning about the magickal properties of the ingredients you choose.

- There is no one right way to organize a Natural Magick pantry. Take stock of your own space and let common sense be your guide.

- Eating meat can be part of an ethical diet, as long as the meat comes from a source that is sustainable and raised and slaughtered humanely.

- Buying old pots and kitchen utensils not only recycles valuable items, but also can bring a touch of wise woman magick to your cooking.

Part

Natural Magick with the Elemental Realm

Even Natural Magick calls out to the basic Elements—Air, Fire, Water, Earth, and Spirit. In addition, Natural Magick taps into the strengths of the four Watchtowers or Guardians—North, South, East, and West. These are powerful resources that need to be welcomed into your life, but in a controlled way so they don't spiral out of control.

Chapter 4

Summon Air

In This Chapter

♦ The subtle realm between physical and spiritual

♦ Chi in Feng Shui, ayurveda's vata

♦ Smudging rituals with herbs

♦ Meditate in harmony with the Air Element

♦ Crystal magick to stir Air Energy

One of the four Elements, Air is thought to be the subtle material realm between the physical and spiritual planes. This is where all thought develops and where our spirit goes to be nourished. It represents new beginnings, the intellect, and creative imagination.

Air provides a way for your magick to be carried to the ears of the Goddess and God so they can hear your request. Air is generally considered masculine, yang energy and has been associated with breath—the spirit or soul of all living creatures.

Blowing in the Wind

In the Wiccan tradition, Air is the Element of the East and might be represented on an altar by incense, feathers, or an athame. It can be as soft as a whispered breath and as violent as a tornado, so it isn't an Element to be taken lightly. It should come as no surprise that particularly persistent winds have even been given names—the Scirocco winds in the Mediterranean and the Santa Ana winds on the United States West Coast, for example. When these winds blow, they can literally change people's temperaments and often fan wild fires. When mixed with another powerful Element, Water, Air can produce a fury we call hurricanes.

But Air is a necessary and benevolent Element, too. Without even thinking about it, we use our breath to blow out candles, sing songs of celebration, and whisper secrets. How often have you "stepped out for a breath of fresh air"? Used during meditation and to alleviate the pains of childbirth, the Element of Air is healing and vital.

Symbols and Associations

Air has the qualities of coolness and dryness and associations with breath, life, and communication. In astrology, Air rules the Zodiac signs Aquarius, Gemini, and Libra. People born under the Air signs think, communicate, analyze, and theorize. They love freedom, truth, and justice, and have the ability to change circumstances with amazing speed. As thinkers, they rely on rationality rather than on intuition or emotions. Their philosophical approach to any situation allows them to endure hardships. Air signs can tolerate almost any circumstance, as long as there is a rational explanation for it. They have great leadership capabilities, with a reputation of being fair. Interested in almost everything, they are lifelong students.

The Element of Air becomes a negative one when Air folks require family and friends to uphold the same standards they live by. Air people cannot understand why everyone does not think and act as they do. When they make a mistake, they tend to rationalize instead of using the situation as a learning experience. They are devoted to abstract ideas and have difficulty making decisions, making them sometimes exasperating to work with. In addition, they tend to procrastinate.

Spirits of the Air

The Elemental spirits associated with Air are called *sylphs*, and their ruler is named Peralda. The word *sylph* comes from the Greek word *sylpha*, which means "butterfly." When you see butterflies fluttering on the wind, sylphs are inevitably nearby. Sylphs may be the easiest entities to invite to a ritual because air exists as easily in a tenth-floor apartment as it does in an outdoor circle. Sylphs especially tend to gravitate to creative endeavors, so they are most easily called by artists, writers, poets, and musicians. They inspire the creative spirit, much like muses, and aid in shaping clear communication. It isn't unusual to feel a sylph touch your hand or toss your hair while you're busy creating. Don't be alarmed; they are just giving you some creative encouragement.

Sylphs stimulate mental balance, freedom, and curiosity. They assist us in coordinating our perceptions and in verbalizing them. They enhance the power of speech, music, and the written word, especially poetry. They teach us about the relationships between all things, which allow us to see and know the great web that connects all of life. This, in turn, brings about a desire for greater harmony. Sylphs stimulate creativity, intuitiveness, and inventiveness, and they awaken the intellect. They can open us to the realm of ideas and help us with mystical experiences and world views.

> **Liguana's Grimoire**
>
> In the Latin Alchemical language, Air is called Flatus, or gas. In Ritual Magick and Kabbalah, it is the Element overseen by the sword-wielding archangel Raphael. In mythology, the air image relates to Mercury or Hermes, the winged messenger of the gods. In Christianity, good news is heralded by angels. All religions and myths recognize the spirits of the Air.

Like the wind they dance on, sylphs are changeable, volatile, and occasionally flighty. If you've ever experienced writer's block, you know what it means to have the sylphs disappear and take their creative energy with them. But it's easy to call them back.

An Air Ritual for Calling the Wind

The first step to working with the Elements is remembering what it felt like in the past when you encountered that Element. Remember and focus on as many details as you can. What did the wind feel like on your skin? Was your hair tousled? What smell was in the air? Did the wind whistle or howl? As much as you can, relive the experience in your mind. This puts out to the Cosmos that you are ready for this experience. You are open.

Practice going through your day noticing what the wind and the air around you feel like. In the evening, try to recall as much of the experience as you can. This is like an ongoing meditation. The more you do this, the easier it will become to call up the wind. You are focused.

The first few times you call up the wind, do it alone. Company can distract you from your magick. Also, these things take practice, and your first few attempts might not put you in the wizards' hall of fame; it's between you and the wind.

Go to an open place outdoors. Higher ground is better. Use an athame, if you have one—or your extended arm, if you don't—and draw a magick circle around yourself to mark your sacred space. Open to the experience of the wind moving around you. Focus your mind and bring up images of more wind blowing all around you.

Liguana's Grimoire

Liguana once had a friend who ran an espresso stand. She and her friend were arguing one calm summer day about whether people could actually connect with the spirit of an Element and cause an effect. The friend became vociferous in his claim that it was all nonsense until a freak dust devil blew up out of nowhere and sent a stack of paper coffee cups flying. Liguana just smiled as her friend gathered the cups and conceded the argument.

Try to incorporate as many senses as possible when you remember wind and visualize wind. Now reach down and pick up a handful of dust or grass. Holding your arm out to your side and slightly above eye level, slowly let your hand's contents filter through your fingers. Watch the air between your hand and the earth catch the offering. You may want to quietly chant, "I call the wind. I call the air. I call the mother's breath." Concentrate hard on experiencing wind. Focus as hard as you can. Hold the feeling for several minutes, and then stop. Clear your mind of your wind images completely. Wait for the breeze to pick up and the wind to answer your call. Be confident.

Air in Feng Shui

Feng Shui, which we introduced briefly in Chapter 2, means literally "the way of wind and water," or, symbolically, "the natural forces of the Universe." These forces affect everything in our world. Europeans call the science of Feng Shui geomancy. Hawaiians and Native Americans practice their own form of Feng Shui, each seeking to live harmoniously with nature. The ancient Chinese believed in and lived their lives by these natural forces. One of the strongest and oldest natural forces is called chi.

Chi, also known as the breath of nature or as "the dragon's celestial breath," is everywhere and, many believe, represents the truest abstract energy in the Universe. (You'll learn more about dragon's breath in Chapter 9.) Chi is an invisible energy that circulates everywhere but gathers in certain places, which are said to be good in Feng Shui. Chi enhances happiness, prosperity, and longevity, and it is the life force inside all living things. Good relationships, a healthful lifestyle, and meditation can increase levels of chi energy.

In Feng Shui, winds are sometimes thought of as bad because they scatter chi rather than accumulate it. When selecting a place to build a home or to hold a ritual, avoid places that are windswept. This can be hard if you live on the prairie or beside the ocean, but in those cases, just try to schedule your rituals on days when the wind is calmer. If you have a home where it's windy, you might want to perform a weekly ritual to encourage the sylphs to leave chi where they found it.

A Spell for Protection from the Winds

Draw down a protective circle. Light some incense and focus on the smoke as it curls skyward. Pick an incense that appeals to you in some way—lavender, sandalwood, and musk are good choices, but any fragrance you like is fine. Say something like the following:

> *Children of the winds, Guardians of Air,*
> *Listen to my words. Harken to my prayer.*
> *Breathe upon me gently. Breathe upon me*
> *   warm.*
> *Guard my home and family. Keep us safe*
> *   from harm.*

Be sure to thank the sylphs for their attendance and their cooperation. You might hang a wind chime in a window, on a porch, or in your backyard so you can "hear" the sylphs as they hover near you.

CAUTION

Stir Gently ...!

Feng Shui theory warns against using glass wind chimes. The sound of breaking glass can be distressing. Stick to brass or wooden chimes, which are more soothing.

Vata in Ayurveda

Vata, which is identified with the cosmic Element of *vaayu*, or Air, and *akash*, or ether, is responsible for respiration. Vata controls the body's auto functions, such as nerve impulses, circulation, respiration, elimination, and heartbeats.

People classified as vata or "Air people" tend to be of slender build. Creative, quick to learn, and imaginative, they also generally walk and talk quickly. Usually impulsive, their skin and hair are dry and their hands and feet are often cold. Their appetite is variable and they have a tendency toward constipation. When vata is in balance, vata types are joyful and enthusiastic.

A vata-pacifying diet, to balance your wind dosha, is one that is made up of foods that are mostly heavy, warm, and slightly oily. Sweet, sour, and salty flavors are especially important. Almost all vegetables are good for vata, as long as they are cooked. Two vegetables that are especially balancing to vata are cucumbers and radishes. "What?" you're thinking. "Not eaten raw?" If you're adventurous, try adding steamed or sautéed cucumbers to your next vegetable medley or stew. Radishes minced into small pieces and sautéed in ghee or oil have a mellow flavor when added to a soup or casserole.

For a light vata lunch or ritual offering to the Air, mix together one minced radish, ½ cup shredded carrot, ¼ cup chopped onion, and 1 cup each of broccoli and cauli-flower flowerettes. (Or substitute any of your favorite vegetables.) Stir-fry them quickly in a tablespoon of ghee or peanut oil. Add dried hot pepper flakes, if desired. Serve over brown rice. Makes 1 serving.

A vata's Natural Magick pantry can include all dairy products, lots of nuts and seeds, most fruits (avoid "light fruits," such as apples and pears), and fish and poultry.

Smudging and Herbs to Honor Air

There are always experts to tell you which herbs are associated with a particular Element. Although it's true that some are more traditionally aligned than others, you should always use your own instinct as a Natural Magician to pick the herbs to use in a ceremony.

Smudging as an Air Ritual

Smudging is an easy Air ritual designed to purify, provide balance, cleanse, or sanctify a sacred space. You can smudge a room, a piece of furniture, or even yourself.

Let's say that you "inherit" a bookcase from your new boyfriend's ex-girlfriend. You need the extra room, but you want to eliminate her essence (but not do her any harm!). A smudging ritual can purify the bookcase and bring some harmony back to your living space.

There are any number of smudging herbs, but some are more traditional than others. These three are most closely related to the Element of Air:

   ◆ **Sage**—There are several different kinds of sage, and all types work for smudg-ing, but perhaps the king of sage is white broadleaf sage. It is the most aromatic and is excellent not only for smudging to cleanse and purify, but also for medita-tion.

- ◆ **Sweetgrass**—As its name suggests, sweetgrass produces a sweet, light fragrance when burned. Believed to attract only positive spirits, it is excellent for cleansing a sacred space.

- ◆ **Lavender**—Most useful for attracting peace, happiness, and restful sleep, lavender imparts a lovely aromatic, refreshing scent when burned.

Smudging can be accomplished by using a smudge stick or by burning loose herbs in a smudge pot or a firebowl. First dry the herbs by hanging them upside down in a still room, a pantry, or some other dry room where they won't be disturbed. They will need to dry for several weeks.

> **Cauldron Bubble**
>
> It is almost impossible to dry herbs in damp places such as basements or garages. Herbs are likely to mildew or mold before they dry, damaging their magickal purity and potency. Make sure you put drying herbs somewhere where the air is dry and where the herbs won't be disturbed.

If you want to use a smudge stick, cut your dried herbs into 5- or 6-inch lengths, bundle them together, and bind them tightly with red thread, which represents the Fire Element. Use a candle to light the bundle because you will want to hold it in the flame long enough to get the stick really smoking. The combination of Fire and Air purifies the space or object and disperses negative energy. Use a feather or your hand to fan the smoke into the corners of the room you're purifying. Smudging is the equivalent of spiritual spring cleaning. You might find that the house feels cleaner and brighter, even though you haven't dusted or vacuumed.

Sweetgrass is often braided into a small rope to be used in smudging. Tie off the ends with red thread. Although you can find sweetgrass growing wild in some prairie places, it's rare; you might have to grow your own.

Smudging Yourself

Smudging yourself is an especially good idea if you've been around someone who is ill, depressed, fearful, angry, or generally emotionally unbalanced. Smudging helps you achieve a calm state to prepare you to meditate or just face your day. If you are experiencing an unusual amount of stress, daily smudging can be beneficial.

Smudging yourself is easy. If you're using a smudge stick, light the stick in a candle flame. Using a feather or your hand, gently fan the smoke onto your body, starting at the top of the body and moving downward. (Although a feather isn't required for smudging, using a feather that one of your bird friends has offered up to you can also encourage the Air Element to assist you in your cleansing ritual. Or, if you have a pretty fan, that can work, too.) Get the back of your body as best you can (it is often easier to use a smudge pot and loose herbs for this). When you're finished with your outer skin, inhale a little of the smoke (just a little!) to purify your insides.

Magickal Bounty

Being **skyclad** means to be naked, or to literally "wear the sky." Some Natural Magicians prefer to perform rituals in the nude to more closely connect to Nature, but it isn't a requirement.

If you're using a smudge pot and loose herbs, light the herbs (using self-lighting charcoal) until they are smoking well. This is best done outdoors in an open space. Put the smudge pot on the ground and stand over it with your legs spread and feet on either side. Weave back and forth in the smoke until you have been thoroughly cleansed. Clothing is optional for this approach, and smudging in the nude (*skyclad*) is recommended for a more thorough cleansing. Again, when you're done, inhale a little of the smoke to purify your insides. People often feel more relaxed, lighter, and brighter after smudging.

Meditation Breathing

All meditations, including such structured ones as transcendental meditation or yoga, start with focusing on breathing. Yoga theory is based on five principles: proper exercise (asana), proper breathing (paranayama), proper relaxation (savasana), proper diet (vegetarian), and positive thinking (vedanta) with meditation (dhyana).

Breathing revitalizes the body by nourishing the central nervous system, clearing the mind, and establishing bodily and emotional harmony. Even insomniacs and joggers are taught breathing techniques to help them relax into the moment. In yoga, there are three basic types of breath: clavicle (shallow), intercostals (middle), and abdominal (deep) breath.

Most people breathe only shallowly through the mouth and nose without using their diaphragms. Breathing in this way allows only a small amount of oxygen to be taken into the lungs, which decreases vitality and lowers resistance to disease. Correct breathing involves deep and full inhalation through the nose, expanding the abdomen. As the abdomen expands, the diaphragm drops, massaging the abdominal organs. Exhaling through the mouth should contract the abdomen, pushing the diaphragm up, and massaging the heart. It is especially easy to start breathing shallowly when you are angry or afraid. By controlling your breath, you can learn to control your mind and calm your emotions.

Breathing exercises are the simplest path to inner calm. Fifteen minutes a day can significantly lower stress and blood pressure. Concentrating on your breath rather than your thoughts is a good way to begin meditating. Feel the air move in and out of your lungs, and watch the rise and fall of your chest and abdomen. If your mind drifts back to stressful thoughts, refocus on your breathing. Breathing is one of the only bodily functions controlled by both the voluntary and involuntary nervous systems. Therefore, breath, as the manifestation of the Air Element, or chi, forms a bridge between our inner and outer selves.

Crystal Magick

Another breathing meditation is to focus on a crystal closely associated with the Element of Air. Those stones traditionally aligned with Air are any clear crystals, amber, jasper, and mica. Place the crystal on your altar or table, light a candle, and call on the Guardians of the East to join you:

> *Guardians of Air and breath,*
> *Join me in this meditation,*
> *Strengthen my creativity and intuition*
> *For the good of All. So mote it be.*

Once you feel the air stir (the candle may flicker), focus on the crystal, drawing in a deep breath and releasing it slowly. Clear your mind and relax into the moment. After 10 or 15 minutes, thank the sylphs for their presence and, using your renewed breath, blow out the candle.

Adding lavender or lily of the valley to your meditation ritual is an added bonus. Both Air scents, they tend to attract the Element to your side.

Connecting to Air can boost your creativity, calm your stress level, and strengthen your immune system. An often overlooked Element, Air is a vital part of a Natural Magician's practice and brings cleansing wisdom as it allows for valuable insights.

The Least You Need to Know

- Air is an Element closely tied to intellect and imagination.
- Sylphs are the spirits most closely associated with the Element of Air.
- Eating heavy, warm, slightly oily food can help balance vata (your wind dosha), according to ayurvedic principles.

◆ Focusing on deep, controlled breathing during meditation can alleviate stress.

◆ Always use you own judgment when choosing herbs or crystals to use in a ritual.

Summon Fire

In This Chapter

- The spark that energizes spirit
- Conjuring Fire
- Using ayurveda's pitta energy to balance Fire
- Fire walking
- Staying safe in Fire's midst

Fire is the Element that embodies the very spark of life itself. Fire is passion and zeal; it is where our spirit goes to be energized. It represents emotions, activity, temper, purity, and transformation. Fire is generally considered masculine, yang, as is Air; it has been associated with blood, the liquid warmth of all living creatures.

In Natural Magick, Fire strengthens a ritual and brings an earnestness to your spellcrafting and requests to the Spirit world. Fire is the Sun's heat; warming life, it is the Element that invokes enthusiasm. It is the one Element we are forbidden to touch.

Burning Bright

In the Wiccan tradition, Fire is the Element of the South and is usually represented on an altar by a candle or a wand. Fire can light a Fourth of July sparkler in celebration or burn a city to the ground. A highly volatile and powerful Element, Fire is treated with the utmost respect by Natural Magicians. Ritual bonfires are a staple in almost all nature-based religions. Candles can light our way, send a wish to the Goddess, and focus our attention during a spell. In Nature, Fire can be related to volcanoes, comets, and, well, forest fires.

Symbols and Associations

Fire has the qualities of heat and dryness and associations with blood, deliberate movement, and passion. In astrology, Fire rules the Zodiac signs Aries, Leo, and Sagittarius. People born under the Fire signs are charming, active, fun, mischievous, and easily excitable, and they change emotional states rapidly. They love change, bright colors, and stimulating environments. Fire signs are the leaders and the cheerleaders of the Zodiac. They provide us with much needed inspiration, motivation, and creative energy. Their attention spans are short, but they generally accomplish twice as much as everyone else in half the time. They sometimes shortcut directions because they're impatient, which can cause problems for their fellow co-workers. They tend to make snap decisions based on gut-level intuition.

Liguana's Grimoire
In Greek mythology, Prometheus stole sacred fire from Zeus and the gods. As punishment, Zeus commanded that Prometheus be chained for eternity to a rock where a vulture would eat his liver. Each day the liver would be renewed so the punishment was endless, until Heracles finally killed the bird. This is just one myth that demonstrates the universal value of Fire. It "belonged" to the gods.

Fire people are extremely passionate, jealous, and forceful. They live life to the fullest and have powerful emotions. Everything about them is intense, and if nothing is happening, they will create something, even if it means trouble. They will do almost anything to avoid boredom. Their minds are always active. They are generally quick to anger and quick to forget about it. They also tend to get readily involved but lack the staying power of the other Elements. They are full of zest, are usually brilliant, and live for the moment.

Fire leaps upward and can help carry spells into the clouds and beyond. After all, the Sun and the stars are fire in the sky. The Sun is a God symbol in many pagan religions. Fire ideas can often be very distant and innovative from the ideas of this Earth. Although fire consumes, it also creates new life. Forest fires remove the old and nourish the new. Some plants even wait for the fire to release their seeds. Of all the Elements, Fire captures our attention the most. Fire lives on and above the Earth, so it connects us closely to the God force. Fire is consuming and captivating; it creates the new and removes the old.

Spirits of Fire

The spirit of Fire is the *salamander*. The word *salamander* was used in the eighteenth century to mean "a woman who lives chastely in the midst of temptations" and "a soldier who exposes himself to fire in battle." It most likely comes from the Greek work *salamandra*, meaning "fire." The salamander is characterized as a lizard or a little dragon. The myth is that a salamander is a creature whose body is so cold that it can live in fire or even extinguish it. In other words, it is a being that can stand a lot of heat! Salamanders can be "seen" in the sputtering of a candle or in the fireballs and sparks in a bonfire or fireplace.

Djin (pronounced *dee-YIN*) is ruler of the salamanders and can be invoked when you are calling upon Fire. Salamanders are easily out of control, so approaching them with some healthy caution is best. If you build an outdoor bonfire, having water or sand on hand can reduce the chances of having a potential disaster, in case the salamander's energy takes control. Candles should be in stable candle holders so they don't tip over. And fire screens in front of a fireplace keep the salamanders contained.

> **Liguana's Grimoire**
>
> In Ritual Magick and Kabbalah, Fire is the Element overseen by the archangel Michael. In mythology, the Fire image relates to Zeus, the Sun god. In Wicca and Christianity, candles on the altar represent the Light of God. All religions and myths recognize the spirit of Fire.

Because the Fire Element incites strong emotions, extra caution should be taken to make sure your intentions are pure if you call salamanders. If you have the slightest inclination toward revenge or vindictiveness, be cautious about invoking salamanders. Instead, use them to encourage passion, excitement, laughter, creative genius, and love. They represent sheer will and can be useful when you are facing a difficult task or situation because they give you protective strength.

In medieval times, people followed the practice of walking their livestock between two bonfires during a summer solstice celebration to cleanse them of negative energy.

This can be affective for humans as well. If you don't live in a place where you can have bonfires, or if you just don't want to work that hard, you can use two rows of votive candles to light a path of purification. This is especially good when starting new endeavors, such as moving into a new home or leaving home to go to college. Just walk the path and have someone else extinguish the candles when you pass by pinching the wicks (not with their breath, which adds unintended Air energy from that person).

Summoning Fire

Let's just say it right now: this is not a ritual. This is not a spell. This is conjuring, and it takes practice. Your intention is to raise energy up through your hands and create an etheric glow as if Fire were coming out of your fingertips.

Go into a darkened room. Feel the floor beneath you. Sense the Earth beneath the floor. Let your mind's eye see deep into the center of the Earth, to the magma, glowing red and yellow. In your mind, pull the Fire energy upward, through the many layers of Earth. Each time you breathe in deeply, see the flame rise up closer to you until at last an electric charge begins to fill you and make your body tingle. Move your hands in a scooping motion, as if gathering energy from your own aura. Extend your arms in front of you, palms facing you. Now visualize the energy you feel in your body flowing through your arms and up to your fingertips. Watch carefully for flickering light at your fingertips or in your palms. This is magickal Fire. It's probably not what you will use to light candles, but it is evidence of your innate Natural Magick. And remember, if at first you don't succeed ….

Another common Fire conjuring most wizards cut their baby teeth on is flame enhancing. Light a candle and sit comfortably looking into the flame. Concentrate most strongly on the experience of the fire, its color, its movements, its brightness. Connect in your mind with the flame so that you are part of it. Send your thoughts into the fire. "Flame grow larger. Flame grow wider. Flame show me your power and my own." You may see the flame waver. You may see it start to grow larger. Perhaps nothing unusual will occur this time. Keep trying. Summoning Fire is one way to inspire Natural Magick practitioners, letting them know that Elemental Magick is real and attainable.

Fire in Feng Shui

Fire as a Feng Shui remedy is powerful and potent. Used incorrectly, Fire can bring about illness and separation. Used correctly, it can bring about money and help build solid relationships. In general, it is believed to enhance chi, the Universe's positive energy flow.

The Fire Element is the most "*yang*" of the Elements.

You might assume Feng Shui would use a candle to represent Fire. Although candles or hurricane lamps are sometimes used, it isn't practical to leave a candle burning.

Therefore, the Fire Element in Feng Shui is often represented with an object that is purple, red, burgundy, maroon, mauve, or pink. If it is hot, it is even better. A red night light or table lamps with a red shade make excellent Fire remedies. If you prefer the look of candles, just make sure they have a red hue; that way, they represent Fire even when they aren't lit.

Placed in the right area of your house, Fire helps the flow of chi and brings you prosperity.

Magickal Bounty

In Chinese philosophy, **yin yang** represents everything in the universe, two opposite energies that need each other to function. Yin is female and associated with the Moon; yang is masculine and associated with the Sun.

Fire in the Vedic Sciences

Vedic sciences include vastu, ayurveda, yoga, and jyotish. All of them offer spiritual solutions to material problems. The value of vedic wisdom is the guidance it provides for progress in science, economy, politics, and the life of the modern individual. It relies upon experience as the sole basis of knowledge, not experience gained through the senses only, but experience gained when the mind, becoming completely quiet, identifies with the Universe.

The basic ingredients of any ritual are prayer, offerings, chanting, recitation, songs, oblations, libations, charms, consecration, formalized spells and visualizations, breathing, movement, colors, forms, and symbols. Sometimes the liturgy is specified to the smallest detail, as in the Veda's; sometimes it is more free. Sometimes it is just a small routine, such as saying thanks before eating; sometimes it is an extended sacrament with many routines.

Sacrificial Fires are especially powerful because they involve both external and internal preparation. Before the ritual, the bonfire needs to be built and the sacrificial objects gathered together. Next, the participants need to focus on their intent and put the intention into words. Finally, the ritual is performed, which involves active participation and mental acceptance.

Homa: The Ancient Fire Ritual

Homas are an ancient form of Fire rituals, with their roots thousands of years back in the vedic science. A homa can help you to get well, have good relationships, find a partner, and have children, and it may even remove bad karma or negative aspects in a horoscope or with *vastu*.

Magickal Bounty

Vastu in Sanskrit means Nature, a surrounding or environment. This can include a house, shelter, or apartment building. *Shastra* in Sanskrit means systems. Vastu shastra is an ancient art and science of constructing buildings that ensure a harmonious balance between man and Nature, and thereby bring all-around happiness, health, wealth, and prosperity.

Although Fire constitutes the basis of the homa, the procedures and ingredients are quite different, depending on the purpose. Enlightened dasajis or trained leaders generally perform the ceremony, which includes throwing sacrifices into the Fire. The Lord is worshipped by tossing ghee, grains, flowers, spices, and fruits into the blaze, which acts as the mouth or consuming agent that carries the offering to Vishnu. The offering is accompanied by vedic mantras that address the Lord in a specific form and carry a specific request.

One of the biggest and most dramatic Fire festivals of all is Up Helly Aa, which takes place in Lerwick, Scotland, on the last Tuesday of January. Locals dressed as Viking warriors drag a "longship" through the dark streets before ceremoniously setting it alight.

Pitta in Ayurveda

Pitta is actually made up of two Elements. Pitta contains Fire, but it also contains Water. It is the source of the flame but not the flame itself. Compare pitta to gasoline—it is not hot to the touch, but it can be the source of flames.

Pitta is responsible for all types of transformations in the body and has the qualities of being hot, sharp, liquid, and oily. Therefore, anything (food or lifestyle) that has those qualities will increase pitta because of the rule "Like increases like." So the hot summer months, tropical weather, and spicy food can be difficult for people who are physiologically pitta.

People with more pitta in their constitutions tend to be of medium proportions, with a frame that is neither petite nor heavy, warm skin that is very fair or ruddy and may be sensitive, and fine hair that tends toward premature graying or thinning. They are sharp and determined in thought, speech, and action. There is an element of purpose to their step and an intensity to their voice. Ambition is usually their second name. They are moderate sleepers and gravitate toward cooler environments. Self-confidence and an entrepreneurial spirit are hallmarks of balanced pitta.

But if the qualities become extreme, or more pronounced than usual at a given time, the pitta in you has likely become aggravated or imbalanced and needs to be brought back into balance. It is then time to follow a pitta-balancing diet and lifestyle to help restore the level of pitta to its normal proportion.

Factors that can cause pitta dosha to increase include a diet that contains too many hot or spicy foods, fasting or skipping meals, overexposure to the Sun or to hot temperatures, and emotional trauma.

Signs that you need to balance pitta include feeling unusually irritable or impatient, experiencing heartburn, feeling flushed, being unusually thirsty, and losing your temper over little things. You might find yourself obsessed at work, unable to stop even for lunch.

Following a pitta-balancing diet and lifestyle can help restore balance to pitta. Cooling foods are wonderful for balancing pitta dosha. Include a few dry foods, such as cereal, crackers, granola and cereal bars, and rice cakes, in your daily diet to balance the liquid nature of pitta.

Include some "heavy" foods that offer substance and sustained nourishment, and some foods that are cool, to balance the fiery quality of pitta. Focus on foods that are sweet, bitter, and astringent. Eat sweet, juicy fruits, especially pears, milk, sweet rice pudding, coconut, and milkshakes made with ripe mangoes and almonds or dates. All of these are examples of soothing pitta-pacifying foods.

Summer Fruit Salad

Any sweet, juicy fruit helps balance Fire energy. This light and sweet salad can be eaten as a dessert, an afternoon snack, or used as a pancake topping. Use only fresh, ripe fruits.

If you're using Fire in ritual, serve this salad afterward to help keep the Fire energy from flaming out of control. The fruit in this dish invites friendship and love into your life while the nuts provide stability and wisdom.

1 mango, peeled and diced

2 pears, peeled and diced

½ lb. strawberries, halved

¼ cup raisins

¼ cup chopped walnuts

1 or 2 TB. unsweetened coconut milk (depending on how juicy your fruit is)

Stir all ingredients together gently and let sit at room temperature for about 30 minutes to allow flavors to blend. Serves 2 to 4. Be sure to refrigerate leftovers—if you have any!

Avoid spices that are too hot or pungent. Ayurvedic spices such as small quantities of turmeric, cumin, coriander, cinnamon, cardamom, and fennel offer flavor, aroma, and healing wisdom.

Fire people should walk away from arguments and avoid exercising in the heat of the day. Air-conditioning is definitely a pitta's best friend!

Bonfire Safety

The first priority when working with Fire outdoors has to be safety for the participants and the surrounding area. A minimum of the expected height of the bonfire doubled is needed for a safe zone.

Stir Gently …!

Never use chemical accelerants for starting ritual fires. Besides adding toxic fumes to the atmosphere, they can cause a controlled bonfire to spiral out of control. Remember that Fire is a powerful Element and must be approached with great respect.

Be aware of clothing that is especially airy or highly flammable. Mow as much of the surrounding area as possible and clear the space of dried brush or weeds. Keep shovels, water, or water-soaked burlap bags handy. Embers can be carried 50 feet or more into the air, only to fall back down on participants. Everyone needs to watch out for each other, especially if there are children in attendance. Nothing is worse than a flaming pagan!

Walking on Fire

Fire walking is very old and was practiced in many cultures, including in ancient Greece, India, Fiji, and China. Many Fire walkers are still performing the ritual today. Some cultures build a log fire, whereas others use white-hot coals. A path is laid and set on fire, and hours later the Fire walkers perform the ritual. Some rituals require the participants to walk the path seven times to complete the ceremony.

Generally, the ceremony is performed to show respect and devotion to the Lord. After the ritual, the Fire God is celebrated with a feast and thanked for his protection.

Please do not try this at home! If you want to try Fire walking, we recommend using the Internet to locate a reputable instructor and following all safety precautions. Fire is not an Element to be toyed with or treated lightly. You can do Fire-walk meditations, which can be equally (and sometimes more) effective!

Liguana's Grimoire

Liguana once attended a seminar that culminated in walking barefoot on hot, fiery coals. When walking on coals, her concentration was not on the heat and fire under her feet, but rather where she would end up when her walk was finished. Liguana learned that this can apply in everyday life as well. If you have a challenging situation to go through, focusing on the difficulty intensifies it. Instead, visualize the best possible end result for yourself and put your concentration there.

Candle Magick

A much safer (and perhaps saner) way to invoke the Fire Element is to light candles. Years ago, before lights came on with the flick of a switch, candles were an invaluable commodity. Without them, people were helpless between the hours of sundown and sunrise. No wonder Fire was revered! It banished the darkness, cooked food, and provided warmth during cold seasons.

A simple candle ritual can work amazing results. You can send a blessing, call for wealth, ask for health or peace of mind, or just give thanks. Any type or size of candle can be used—tapers, votives, pedestal, or even birthday cake size, if that's what you have available. But for a Natural Magician, beeswax candles are best because they are made from Nature's bounty. Pick a place in your home or apartment that has little traffic. A bedroom is usually a good choice, but use your own intuition.

Cauldron Bubble

Practicing visualization—that is, seeing something in your mind's eye—can make it easier to do during a ritual. For example, close your eyes and picture a red apple. Look at the color of the peel. Notice its texture and the wooden stem on the top. Hold the apple in your mind for as long as you can.

You might want to anoint the candle with oil before you begin. Oil is another Fire symbol. If you are performing a ritual to draw something to you, such as money, love, or luck, dab the oil on your fingers and spread it on the candle from the top to the middle and then from the bottom to the middle. If you are trying to eliminate something from your life, such as excess weight, a broken relationship, or bad luck, spread the oil from the middle to the top and from the middle to the bottom. Don't use a back and forth motion, which scatters the energy. Use any fragrance of oil that appeals to you.

Place the candle in a sturdy holder on a flat surface where it won't tip over. Open your mind to the Universe by stating your intentions out loud, and then light the candle as you visualize the outcome you desire. For example, if you are facing a stressful presentation at work, picture in your mind's eye standing in front of your audience, relaxed and smiling. See yourself finishing the presentation and being congratulated by your boss and co-workers. You might even picture being awarded a bonus for your efforts. Focus on the candle's flame as you breathe in and out slowly. Concentrate really hard on your desires. Hold the picture of you succeeding in your mind as long as possible. Thank the Fire Element and release the spirit by blowing out the candle.

The Fire Element is a vital, powerful force in our lives, whether we invoke it deliberately in ritual or just nudge the thermostat up a notch on a cold winter's night. The next time you put a pot of water on to boil for tea, remember to thank the Gods for this Elemental spark.

The Least You Need to Know

- Fire is an Element closely tied to passion and transformation.

- Salamanders are the spirits most closely associated with the Element of Fire.

- Fire can carry spells and blessings up to the Gods and Goddesses, whether it's a bonfire or a candle.

- Eating hot, sharp, liquid, and oily food can help balance your pitta dosha according to ayurvedic principles.

- Always use extra caution when holding outdoor bonfires so that you don't lose control of Fire.

Chapter 6

Summon Water

In This Chapter

- ◆ Water, the psychic shape-shifting Element
- ◆ Feng Shui fountains to soothe your spirit
- ◆ Be the Water
- ◆ Inviting Water indoors
- ◆ A fishy dish to serve

Water may be the Element closest to us because our bodies are made up of approximately 65 percent water. Water is responsible for every living thing—plants, animals, and humans.

Whether it's a summer shower or a meandering river, water plays a significant part in our lives. Water exists in the most unlikely places—as fog, as snow, as sidewalk puddles. Even the desert protects its few water sources, and when the rain falls, the desert blooms. It is a magickal Element that brings transformation to everything it touches.

Water, Water Everywhere

Water is malleable and can take on the shape of any container it is poured into. Therefore, like Earth but unlike Fire and Air, it has form and volume. Water is generally considered feminine, yin energy. Water can rise high with the help of Air but generally doesn't move upward. When it does move upward, it inevitably falls back to the Earth as rain. Water flows freely downhill unless impeded by natural or human-made barriers. Water is extremely powerful and will always find its own level. If artificially constrained at a high level, it will eventually break free. Water can flow at a trickle or flood with the raging force of Nature. Water is impressionable and reflective. For the Natural Magician, Water relates to feelings, dreams, fantasies, intuition, and psychic powers.

> **Liguana's Grimoire**
>
> In Ritual Magick and Kabbalah, Water is the Element overseen by the archangel Gabriel. In mythology, the Water image relates to Poseidon or Neptune, the trident-wielding god who rules the oceans. In Wicca and Christianity, Water is used to purify and to welcome newcomers to the faith. All religions and myths recognize the spirit of Water.

In the Wiccan tradition, Water is the Element of the West and is represented on an alter by a chalice or a bowl of water. Water gives life, provides recreation, cooks our food, and can wipe out an entire community when raging uncontained. Without it, crops wither and die. With it, Earth's plants and animals flourish. Natural Magicians are especially protective of bodies of water because they know polluting streams and lakes means destroying an Element that is vital to every living being.

Symbols and Associations

In astrology, the Water signs of the Zodiac are Cancer, Scorpio, and Pisces. Water people are very sensitive to their own feelings and to the feelings of the people around them. They are generally good-natured, introverted, quiet, contemplative, and sometimes even melancholic. They approach life through their emotions. They are concerned with what "feels" right, with their hunches, rather than with what is practical or rational. Water can raise people to the heights of bliss but can bring them down to the depths of despair. Like the waves on the ocean, they rise and fall easily. Water people need close emotional relationships and rarely have superficial affairs. They are romantic, sentimental, and affectionate. They can be very nurturing and very possessive of their family and spouse. They have fixed opinions. They communicate in nonverbal ways, emotionally and psychically or through creativity such as art, dance, music, poetry, and photography. Their beliefs are based on feelings rather than on reason or practicality (although what they express can often be surprisingly reasonable and practical—or not!).

Water Spirits

The spirits associated with Water are called *undines*. These beings are beautiful to look at and are very graceful. They exist within the water itself, so they are often seen riding the waves of the ocean. They can also be found in rocky pools, waterfalls, rivers, lakes, streams, marshlands, and even puddles. The size of the undine is determined by the size of the body of water.

The undines work with the vital essences and liquids of plants, animals, and humans. They are present in everything containing water. The undines also work with the plants that grow under the water and with the motion of water itself. The ruler of the undines is a being called Necksa. The undines love, serve, and honor her unceasingly.

They are emotional beings, very friendly and open to being of service to humans, although they can also be capricious and whimsical.

Undines assist Natural Magicians in absorbing and assimilating life experiences so that they can use them to the fullest. They heighten psychic feelings as well as emotional ones. They help us to see and feel the fullest ecstasy of the creative acts of life, be they sexual or artistic, or working at a job or duty with the right emotions.

> **Liguana's Grimoire**
>
> Close relatives of the undines are mermaids and sirens. Sometimes accused of luring sailors to a crushing death on the rocks through their beauty and songs, real Elemental Spirits would never deliberately hurt people.

Water in Feng Shui

Feng Shui philosophy encourages the use of fountains both indoors and outdoors as an invitation to embrace change, to blend and flow with life rather than struggling. This is right up a Natural Magician's alley! By reconnecting with natural Elements such as Water, and the stones and plants that lay in and near Water, we can be revitalized by the subtle currents of the life force and beauty that flow through the landscape. In this way, we nourish our human spirit through Natural Magick.

Moving water in the garden is good Feng Shui. It refreshes chi and soothes the nerves. Putting goldfish in your garden pond encourages wealth, but make sure to keep the pond clean and never let it stagnate. Pools of water that empty into each other are very good for moving energy. The plants and flowers that accent your fountain garden are a reminder of life and growth, and lily pads attract undines.

The bubbling sound of a small indoor fountain relaxes people and introduces a natural background noise. (Remember that we gave instructions for making your own Feng Shui water fountain in Chapter 2.) The humid atmosphere created by the gentle splash and spray of water is perfect for growing ferns and moisture-loving plants close by. An underwater light, a candle flame, or a mirror near the fountain garden casts a brightness symbolizing life and happiness.

Like wind, flowing water, such as a rushing stream, can scatter chi. If you live next to rushing water, a backyard fountain can help anchor chi close to you for your benefit.

Calling Water

If you are lucky enough to live near a beach, practicing calling the waves is easy. Your objective is to feel the essence of the Water spirits and connect with their energy, not to create waves you can surf on.

Go to the shore and stand where the incoming waves just touch the tips of your toes. Concentrate on the motion of the waves. Hear the sound the water makes. Smell and taste the salt air as the waves build and break against the beach. Open yourself to the total experience. Now visualize the breakers growing larger. Feel the water splash over your feet, up to your ankles. Whisper to the waves:

> *Water ebb.*
> *Water flow.*
> *Water build.*
> *Water grow.*

Pull the waves toward you with your mind as the larger waves break against the shore.

But wait just a minute here. Won't this happen anyway with a rising tide? Yes, it will. Start out practicing this at a rising tide. When you can cause the same effect on an ebb tide, you will be ready to move on to more complex Water working.

Connecting to Still Water

What if you need to connect with the energies of still water? For this exercise, you need a small lake or pond. Wade into the lake until the water is a few inches above your ankles. Focus on the feel of the water against your skin. Listen carefully for the sounds of the water as its surface is rippled by wind or as it moves around rocks and reeds near the shore.

Now lift a foot out of the water and take a step. Do this slowly and carefully. The object is to walk through the water without causing ripples. The water itself is fluid and does not resist its own motion. The more you become like the water in mind and movement, the calmer the water will be as you walk. Experiment with different depths of water. Generally, the deeper the water, the more difficult the exercise. Remember, attuning to the Elements takes practice. Don't expect to be the perfect Water walker right away. The important thing about this is your growing affinity for the Water Elementals, not your nonrippling promenade.

> **Cauldron Bubble**
>
> The trick to working closely with Elementals in Natural Magick is to become one with them. Be that thing: Water or Fire or Earth or Air. Be part of it. That connection is where the Magick originates and the Spirit lives.

An Indoor Ritual

If you're a landlocked Natural Magician, the spirit of Water can be experienced in a bathtub instead. It just takes a little ingenuity to raise it above the level of mundane understanding.

Think of things that seem to correspond to water. Blue flower petals in your bath might be just the thing. Light a blue or green candle and turn off any electric lights. Put lapis, turquoise, or sodalite stones into the bath water. Many magickal or occult book stores sell blends of incense corresponding to Neptune or rain. Light some appropriate incense.

Next, step into the water and stand a moment, feeling the water against your skin. Sink down slowly and relax into your tub. As with all the other Elemental exercises, try to use all your senses to experience everything. Move about in the Water and be part of it, not just an outsider, somebody in a tub. If you live near a hot spring or a natural spring, this exercise is enhanced by the heat and mineral action the water provides, helping you melt into the Water essence. At home, you can approximate this by taking a warm bath (not *too* hot!) or by adding mineral salts to your bathwater. On the other hand, if it is bracing mental clarity you desire, take a cold bath; actress Katherine Hepburn is said to have taken cold baths regularly!

CAUTION

Stir Gently ...!

Although a backyard cement pool can help you connect to the Element if you have an affinity for pools, the artificiality of a built-in pool can be a deterrent. The water is contained in a space in which it doesn't belong and is filled with chlorine. Better to go to a natural source or to invite the undines to join you temporarily in a blow-up children's wading pool you can empty after you use it.

If you have only a shower, you can still invoke Water. Use the same preparations. Turn on the water and take a minute to listen to the sound it makes as it hits the shower floor. (Think waterfall or rain shower.) Step into the shower and let the water wash over you. Try to feel each stream of water as it hits your body. Again, the trick is to try to become the Water, not just someone getting clean. Stay in until your fingertips are pruney.

When you get out of the tub or shower, spread some body oil on your still-damp skin to hold in the moisture. Choose a fragrance that appeals to you. Lavender, lotus, lily, and magnolia all attract the Water Element.

Daily Connection to Water

Once you've become really familiar with Water through immersion, you can touch base with the Element through more mundane tasks. Washing your face in the morning or plunging your hands into soapy dishwater can remind you what an important role Water plays in your life. Respect the Element by not wasting it!

Pick just one day and make it a point to thank the Water Element each time you use it throughout the day:

> *Water, which gives life to all living things,*
> *Bless this task for which I turn to you,*
> *And nurture my Spirit as I drink you in.*

Watering plants, washing your child's hair, making soup, scrubbing a floor, filling a wading pool—we use and commune with Water constantly. You'll be surprised.

Note that if you live in an arid climate, it is unethical use of the Water Element to try to keep grass and plants in your yard that really do not belong there. Natural Magicians cultivate the plants indigenous to the region. Cacti can be the "trees" in a desert climate.

Water Witching

Some Natural Magicians have such an affinity to Water that it calls to them from underground. These magicians, sometimes called Water Witches, actually have nothing to do with Wicca or witchcraft. The term comes from the fact that early diviners often used witch hazel sticks as their divining rods. Dowsing or divining is usually used today to find water and determine where a well should be dug.

Today Water Witches often use freshly cut peach tree branches, cherry branches, or grape vines shaped in a capital *Y* configuration. Using fruit limbs naturally draws toward Water because fruit itself is full of natural juices, and as we've said, "Like calls to like." The diviner holds the branch so that the *Y* points away from his or her body and is parallel to the ground. The stick will point toward the ground when the diviner passes over underground water.

> **Liguana's Grimoire**
>
> The first recorded anecdote of finding water with a forked twig is in Georgius Agricola's work, *De re metallica*, written in 1556.

Dowsing is also often done with two metal rods bent in an *L* shape. The dowser holds the short ends in his or her hands, one in each, with the long ends pointing forward and the hands held close together. These divining rods react to underground water and also other electromagnetic influences. When using the rods, try to keep your hands very still and walk forward. When there is a water source, the rods will open to the side, making a wide angle. When moving away from the water source, the rods move back together. (Slipping straws over the metal rods can make it easier for them to move in your hands. The rods can rotate inside the straws while your hands hold the rods steady.)

A divining rod also can be made with a slim, straight stick. Slice the stick down the center three quarters of its length. Bend the sides back and forth at the fork several times so they are almost floppy. Pull the two sides back together and hold the stick straight out in front of you as you walk. The movement of this type of rod is harder to see. The sides will move apart and come back together, just not as dramatically as the metal rods.

Divining also can detect magickal energy fields. Try this experiment. Have a friend stand on one side of a room while you stand with your divining rods on the other. Walk toward the other person slowly. Note how close you get when the divining rods move away from each other. Back up a few paces and have your friend focus on sending out energy and force from their hands. Watch the rods react now. It might just amaze you.

Natural Water Wonders

Of course, Water exists in Nature in all kinds of ways. In the Midwest, it falls as snow and ice during the winter. In tropical climes, it cascades down mountainsides as waterfalls. And almost everywhere, it falls as rain.

The next time you have a chance, take a walk in the rain. A walk in moist weather is great for your skin. Imagine those Scottish beauties walking on the foggy moors. No wonder they look so healthy—it's Nature's moisturizer! Pick a warm spring or summer rain, if you can. Dress in old clothes and head out without an umbrella. Not only does this connect you to Water, but it also is great for moisturizing your complexion! If you can, begin the walk in a westerly direction because that is the direction associated with Water.

Really feel the Water against your skin. Let it soak into your hair and clothes. Listen to the noise it makes as it falls to Earth. Watch how the plants, birds, and animals react to it. If you do this often enough, you will begin to feel as though you're blending into the rain, becoming rain. You might almost become invisible to passersby the more you practice this exercise. (Watch out for cars!)

Snow Play

So you live near a snow-covered mountain or on wintry plains? Lucky you! Another way to connect with water is to, well, play in the snow. Undines love whimsical play and will readily join you.

Liguana's Grimoire
If you're brave enough, you can try polar bear swimming. Liguana did this recently and found it an exhilarating experience. She plunged into icy Puget Sound, thought she was going to die, and then walked out of the water with her hands held over her head like a winner! Everyone cheered!

Downhill skiing, cross country skiing, and even building snow people are ways to connect with the Water Element during the winter. Pick up a handful of snow and look at the crystals. Taste the (clean!) snow. Feel the moisture seep into your mittens or gloves. Smell the sharp, cold scent. Be sure you're living fully in the moment.

Collecting Sea Salt

If you have a chance to go to a body of saltwater, you can collect its salt for use in Natural Magick rituals. This salt is *not* edible but can be used for protection rituals and to draw in positive energy or to cast a circle.

Take a gallon jug that you have thoroughly cleaned of its previous contents. Fill it with sea water and take it home. Fill a shallow bowl or a cookie sheet with sides with 1 or 2 inches of water and place it in full sunlight. As the water evaporates, it will leave a white layer of salt. Crumble the salt into a bowl or plastic bag and repeat until you've used up the water.

Small amounts of this salt tossed into the corners of a room provide protection, increase your psychic powers, and draw in positive energy.

Foggy Inspirations

Fog is actually the combination of Water and Air. Taking a walk in the fog can heighten both imagination and intuition. Think of it as walking through a cloud. Imagine you are high above the Earth. Feel the soft rush of the moist air as it brushes against your face and hands. Watch objects loom out of the fog and see if you can intuitively predict their appearance. Breathe the fog deep into your lungs until you are immersed inside and out in the fog. Fog is a mystical, magickal way to connect to Water.

Inviting Water to Your Table: Poached Fish

Serving "Water food" encourages fascinating table conversations and adds light-hearted good fun to your meals. Dishes that are poached, boiled, or seasoned with sea salt all bring the Water Element to your table. Of course, serving sparkling water as a beverage is another way to invite Water.

Water is often associated with autumn. Presenting your guests with a delicious poached fish is a great way to usher in the season and to say good-bye to the Lady of summer as you welcome in the season of the Lord. Poaching the fish puts it back into the Element it came from, which enhances its magickal properties. This dish has a Southeast Asian flavor.

4 garlic cloves, minced

2 TB. ginger root, peeled and minced

1 cup spring water

1 cup white wine (or substitute chicken or vegetable broth)

1 cup fresh basil, minced (or 2 TB. dried basil)

4 6-oz. firm fish steaks (halibut and red snapper are both good)

In a deep skillet, combine garlic, ginger, water, wine or broth, and half the basil. Bring to a near boil; reduce to a very low simmer. Add the fish and cover. Poach for 10 minutes per inch of thickness until fish flakes with a fork.

Remove fish to a serving platter or individual plates and cover to keep warm.

Raise heat and cook poaching liquid at a steady, high simmer (do not boil) until reduced by half. Strain and serve over fish. Garnish with reserved chopped basil or a light dusting of dried basil.

Serve with lightly sautéed Chinese cabbage and onions. Keep them tender crisp. Add a side of brown rice. Serves 4.

The fish invites intuition and psychic abilities into your life. Ginger adds a touch of magickal romance. Garlic is for protection. And basil invites newfound wealth. As you present the fish to your guests, offer thanks to the Lord:

> *Guardians of the West,*
> *Bring your blessings to this table,*
> *We welcome the strength of the Lord*
> *And prepare ourselves for the coming harvest.*

The Water Element is a necessary and vital part of a Natural Magician's world. A powerful force, it brings life, sustains life, and makes life glorious!

The Least You Need to Know

- Water is an Element closely tied to intuition and feelings.
- Undines are the spirits most closely associated with the Element of Water.
- Water can be called to you like the waves of an ocean.

◆ If you don't live near water, a bath or shower can draw you closer to the Water
   Element.

◆ A ritual fish dinner can invite the Water Element and honor the Lord in an
   autumn festival.

Chapter 7

Summoning Earth

In This Chapter

- Honoring Mother Earth
- Gnomes of Earth unite
- Back to the caves
- Bringing Earth inside your home
- Root vegetables to bring Earth to your table

Earth is our home, so naturally Earth is an Element we most revere and honor. Earth is the beginning of the journey forward. Earth symbolically represents both the womb and the grave. Earth is the Element that brings forth life and then reclaims it. We are born on Earth, and our bodies will be either buried in the Mother's bosom or scattered by the Wind as ashes when this particular journey is over.

Magickally, Earth is viewed as the place where the other Elements can physically manifest their nature.

Big Blue Marble

Earth is the Element of our Universe that represents substance, renewal, and regeneration. Earth is solid. The Earth Element represents matter.

You can touch what exists; you can see it and hear it. Earth is real and objective because it is perceivable by the five senses. Of all the Elements, the Earth Element is the most easy to confine and capture. It is rigid, fixed, and stable. Most often called feminine, with yin receiving energy, anything that is attainable is "down to earth" and not "high in the sky." Archetypal Earth is real, heavy, and the basis of all achievement. It is the foundation of all that is. Like the real Earth, it is fixed, stable, organized, and predictable. It is limited and disciplined.

In the Wiccan tradition, Earth is the Element of the North and is represented on the altar with stones and rocks or a small bowl of salt. Earth people are born under the Zodiac signs Taurus, Virgo, and Capricorn. Earthy people are cautious, premeditative, conventional, and dependable. They are loyal, practical, and persevering with an inner strength, and the ones to turn to in a crisis. They live by a practical, common-sense code and seek physical well-being more than spiritual enlightenment. The expression "down to earth" sums them up. They are responsible, methodical, and concerned with detail. Children of the Earth Element are, therefore, well suited to life on this planet. They are realistic, builders, and hard workers. They are pragmatic and materialistic, and they reduce everything to what is practical, useful, and observable. They particularly value skills and abilities.

> **Liguana's Grimoire**
>
> In Ritual Magick and Kabbalah, Earth is the Element overseen by the archangel Uriel. In mythology, the Earth image relates to Demeter. In Wicca and Christianity, Earth is used to signify the corporeal body of the Deity. All religions and myths recognize the spirit of Earth.

Earth types are successful businesspeople, in the sense that they can stably maintain things. Whereas the Fire type is an innovator, the Earth type is cautious and practical, more interested in established business activities than new, innovative ones. They think about what is rather than what might be. Occasionally, they lack imagination. They can sometimes be too fixed to rules, regulations, and procedures.

Spirits of the Earth

Guarding the Earth and all Her wonders are the precocious yet ever-watchful *gnomes*. The name *gnome* was given by the medieval scholar Paracelsus, in an attempt to describe the most important of the Earth spirits. According to Paracelsus, they move as easily through the earth as humans walk upon the ground. Some sources claim they spend the hours during daylight as toads. They are related to goblins and dwarfs. The gnomes are the oldest of Mother Nature's spirits. Bent and gnarled like the ancient oaks, these dwarflike creatures protect the land and all that lies upon it. The gnomes live in the forest among the roots of giant trees and deep within the hollow hills.

The gnomes' job is to protect the physical nature of the Earth. Gnomes live under the earth, where they guard treasures. Gnomes are traditionally associated with healing because they have knowledge of all the plants and their medicinal properties. In times of failing health, the gnomes are summoned for their expert assistance. When out of control, the gnomes strike back through earthquakes, landslides, and pestilence. Their virtues are endurance, responsibility, and thoroughness. Their vices can be a tendency to be dull, lazy, melancholic, and slow.

Ghobe is the ruler of the Earth Element. He is a solemn, shadowy being, with wary eyes of sharpened crystal and delicate clothes made of ferns, sewn with glistening dewdrop webs by busy elfin hands. This Elemental king is much more shy and less forthcoming than the other kings. His power is indomitable and his strength without comparison, but he normally remains hidden in the secret meadows and groves where humans do not go.

However, if we look very carefully, and if we earn his trust, we may find that he will show himself, sometimes peering from the undergrowth, or maybe standing almost immobile with his back to a tree trunk on the edge of a woodland stream. This silent, somber being can be as gentle and protective as a shady tree, or as brooding and heavy as a forest at night. He is unusually sad these days, due to the way we are destroying the earthly treasures he has given us.

Earth in Feng Shui

Earth is an interesting Element in Feng Shui, despite the rather commonplace conception of dirt. Arranging your environment to promote a healthful flow of energy is bound to include Earth! Use Earth solutions for nurturing, receiving balance and stability, and feeling total support from the Universe and your choices. It is helpful for starting a family, making steady progress, gaining security, and inviting harmony.

Terra-cotta pots filled with potting soil make a great Earth remedy. Many times Earth is recommended for a larger environmental solution. In this case, large granite boulders or a beautiful clay statue can be used. A bowl filled with rocks and stones you've picked up can also act as an Earth remedy. Earth-tone colors can be used, but they are not nearly as effective as the actual Element.

Money Frogs

In China, frogs are the bringers of good luck. The three-legged Money Frog holds a Chinese coin in its mouth and sits on a protective bagua or a pile of coins. It is usually placed near cash registers, reception areas, managers' desks, and offices of many successful businesses in Oriental countries.

> **Liguana's Grimoire**
>
> The Money Frog is a mythical creature said to appear every Full Moon near homes in which the residents will receive good news the very next day. This good news is usually increased wealth or monetary gain. In ancient China, these mythical frogs are believed to be the bringer of fortune, which is why you often see them bringing a string of coins in their mouths.

At home, the Money Frog is placed in the corners of the living room or family rooms to enhance the wealth chi of the household. The Money Frog is also kept in the corner diagonally across from the entrance to a room. The corner of a room is known to be the focal point where chi gathers. The Money Frog is placed in these corners to activate what is traditionally believed to be the "wealth luck" of the household. In addition, placing him inside your front door facing inward symbolizes money coming into your home or business.

House Placement

Obviously, we can't always plan how our houses are situated, but if you are moving to a new house, there are some balances you need to take into consideration. Don't buy a house if the main entrance is facing south. Almost any other direction is more beneficial. Make sure the road in front of the house isn't higher than the front door. Choose a house with windows that let in the light and where rooms naturally flow one to another. Small, choppy rooms with low ceilings will need an Earth remedy to encourage the flow of chi.

Building a House, Rishi-Style

India's traditional science of architecture is called Sthapatya Veda. According to Sthapatya Veda, every inch of the Earth is in perfect harmony with cosmic order. When we disrupt a part of the Earth, we disturb this order. From this perspective, we have no right to disturb the Earth by putting a building on it. Of course, humans need shelter to live and work. How can we achieve that without disturbing the harmony of the cosmos? Sthapatya Veda shows how to incorporate the naturally occurring cosmic order into the design of a building and re-establish the inherent order that was disrupted by raising the building. It structures the home as a vessel for cosmic consciousness in which your life and being will naturally expand. This ancient system of design and construction has been used to engineer some of the most high-tech and harmonious homes.

Earthy Ayurveda

In ayurveda, *kapha* is the term used to describe an excess of the Water and Earth Elements. People who are low in Fire have a tendency toward this condition, one that is characterized by slow digestion and an excess of *ama*.

Going back thousands of years, the great sages of India taught that disease begins in the stomach with bad digestion. Although modern medicine probably wouldn't concur, similar thoughts were held by the Iroquois and many other traditional cultures.

Magickal Bounty

Ama is a word that can be broadly interpreted to mean phlegm or mucus. An excess of mucus dampens pitta and needs to be put back into balance.

A kapha-pacifying diet is based on foods that are light, dry, and warm. The primary flavors are pungent, bitter, and astringent. Kapha balance is achieved through eating low-fat dairy; small amounts of oil; light, dry fruits such as apples, pears, or apricots; all vegetables except sweet, juicy ones, such as tomatoes; and any spice except salt. The only meats consumed should be white-meat chicken and seafood, but only baked or poached, not fried.

Spelunking in Mother Earth

Crawling into a cave is not for the faint of heart, but it is the perfect way to connect with the Earth Element. You have to rise above the mundane exercise of exploring and feel yourself crawling into the Mother's womb. Find a place to sit comfortably and meditate on the Earth surrounding you. Pay close attention to the smell of the damp earth. Listen to the air as the ground breathes around you. If you're lucky enough to be in a cave inhabited by bats, enjoy the noises they make as they rustle in sleep or take wing into the night sky.

Ask the gnomes' permission to take a rock or a handful of dirt to remember the encounter. If you have an altar, place the rock to the North to honor the Earth Element and the Mother.

CAUTION

Stir Gently ...!

For safety's sake, never go caving alone. Wear sturdy shoes and take along a flashlight with fresh batteries. If you feel compelled to go alone, let others know exactly where you're going and when you'll be back.

Thank the Earth for nourishing you and enfolding you in her arms. Visit the Earth womb as often as you can. For a Natural Magician, this meditation provides stability and calm.

If you don't have access to a cave, you can achieve similar results by going deep into a forest, sitting beside an ocean or stream, or lying in a wild grass meadow. The point is to become part of the Earth by using all of your senses to be aware.

Collecting Earth

There are so many ways to honor the Earth by bringing its symbols into your home. It can be as simple as picking wildflowers for a table centerpiece or adopting a pet at a local shelter. Picking up a rock every time you visit a natural spot not only honors the Earth Element, but it also can remind you of a special time you had.

Be the Bush

One of the exercises Liguana uses to train her students is blackberry picking. The berry bush has thorns to defend itself from predation. If you are merging with the bush and being like the bush, it has no reason to defend against you. See how much you can relate to the blackberry vines as you reach for that big, fat berry way back in the branches.

If a berry drops to the ground, let it be an offering of thanks to the bush, Mother Earth, and the spirits of that place. Never pick all the berries. It is just plain rude to the bush, and you deserve the scratches you may get!

And by the way, no matter what kind of fruit you're picking, always remember to thank the plant for its gifts. It's the polite thing to do.

Panning for Gold

Striking it rich! It's a miner's dream. Unlike professional gold seekers, recreational gold panners benefit mostly from the adventure. As a Natural Magician, it is more about the benefit of connecting to the Earth than it is about becoming a millionaire. The entire family can share in the fun of prospecting and gold panning.

Recreational gold panning is a privilege. Be aware that panning can adversely affect water quality, thereby impacting vegetation, fish, wildlife, and, ultimately, people. During the process of separating soil from minerals, silt may be washed into streams, creating muddy water. Fish, fish eggs, and aquatic insects have difficulty living in heavily silted water because of its reduced oxygen supply. Avoid washing soil and vegetation into streams, and do not dig in stream banks. This increases silt in the stream and is also dangerous. Many banks are unstable and can slide without warning. To reduce silt, dig only in active stream gravels. Return rocks or boulders moved during your efforts to their original positions. Aquatic insects, an important food source for salmon, often make their homes under these rocks. A little care will help ensure a healthy water ecosystem for both miners and anglers.

Be sure to follow all national forest rules, such as camping limits, discharge of firearms, and use of trails. It's a good idea to check with a state's Department of Fish and Game before panning. Some states, such as Alaska, limit the time of year you can pan for gold, to protect the spawning season for fish.

Cauldron Bubble

Gold corresponds to Earth's abundance. It also is the solar or yang metal when worn for jewelry (as opposed to silver, which is lunar and yin). Calling to Earth's metals attracts wealth and honors the Lord and Lady.

How do you know if you've struck gold? Gold has a rich yellow color or "kindly" appearance, turning paler as its silver content increases. Gold is relatively easy to identify when you know its properties, but novices can confuse it with minerals such as pyrite and mica. Both can occur with gold. Pyrite, or "fool's gold," is brassy light yellow and brittle, so it shatters when crushed. Mica is light yellow to bronze and very lightweight. Whether you strike gold or pyrite, the pretty rocks will bring good luck into the house when placed on a northern window sill.

Collecting Flowers

Picking flowers that can be dried and pressed between the pages of a book is another way to bring Earth into your environment. Pressed flowers can be turned into bookmarks, pictures, or additions to a scrapbook. Just picking a bouquet to place on your table or alter works, too. Don't forget to add leaves, ferns, and branches to your collection.

Stone Energy

All stones are of the Earth and can be used to represent and invoke Earth energies. Many stones correspond to other Elements as well. Here is a short list of stones you may want to display in your home or put on your altar:

- **Agates**—Geodes promote psychic abilities and enhance magickal energy of all sorts. They also promote psychic visioning. Moss agates promote success in weather work and gardening.

- **Bloodstone**—Lightens the mood and promotes energy and vitality.

- **Jade**—Promotes beauty, wealth, and spiritual growth.

- **Onyx**—Very protective; repels negativity.

- **Quartz crystal**—Promotes focus and channeling of magick energy, especially healing energy.

- **Red jasper**—Helps in relating to family and community, gives a sense of control, and eases emotional or psychic distress.

- **Turquoise**—Promotes general good fortune and protects against negative energy.

Ley Lines

Ley lines are alignments of ancient sites or holy places, such as stone circles, standing stones, cairns, and churches. Interest in ley lines began with the publication in 1922 of *Early British Trackways* by Alfred Watkins (1855–1935), a self-taught amateur archaeologist and antiquarian. Based upon an ancient map in England, it was possible to link a number of landmarks by a series of straight lines, so Watkins became convinced that he had discovered an ancient trade route. Interest in these trade routes as sources of mystical energy has become very popular.

Today ley lines have been adopted by Natural Magicians everywhere as sources of power or energy, and they can be detected by dowsing rods (see Chapter 6). Natural Magicians believe that certain sites on Earth are filled with special "energy." Stonehenge, Mt. Everest, Ayers Rock in Australia, Nazca in Peru, the Great Pyramid at Giza, Sedona in Arizona, and Mutiny Bay, among other places, are believed to be places of special energy. Wizards claim that the energy is connected to changes in magnetic fields.

Cooking Root Vegetables: Vegetable Soup

Although all food is given to us from Mother Earth, root vegetables grow in the Mother's bosom, so they are the Earth food above all others. Carrots, beets, potatoes, turnips—they connect the Natural Magician to the Earth on the dining room table.

Here's a soup that honors Earth and can be used in a ritual to give reverence to the Lady and to the Earth's gnomes.

¼ cup ghee (or 6 TB. of olive oil)

½ green pepper, coarsely chopped

4 cups broccoli, coarsely chopped

½ cup sweet onion, coarsely chopped

3 medium potatoes, peeled and cut into chunks

5 cups spring water or vegetable stock

Salt and pepper to taste

Sour cream (optional)

> **Cauldron Bubble**
>
> A raw, whole potato can be used to make a sort of Ms. Potato Head poppet. (Remember, only positive magick—do *not* send out ill wishes to another person.) Pin something of the person, such as a strand of hair, on the "doll," state your intentions, place the potato on a northern windowsill, and leave it for one full month. Your blessing should come to pass.

In a large soup pot, heat the ghee or olive oil over low heat. Sautée the green pepper, broccoli, and onion for 10 minutes, stirring frequently. Add the potatoes and water or stock, and bring to a boil. Cover and reduce the heat. Simmer until the vegetables are tender—about 30 minutes.

Blend half of the soup in a blender until puréed. Stir back into the remaining soup. Season to taste with the salt and pepper. Serve with a dollop of sour cream, if desired. Serves 4 to 6.

Serve the soup with a crusty loaf of French bread, which also invokes the Earth Elements because of the grains used. Offer the following blessing:

> *Mother Earth, bless us with your bounty,*
> *Feed our bodies and our spirits.*
> *We honor you and respect you.*
> *Thank you for nourishing us*
> *And being with us in this time and place.*

If you need to balance pitta, replace 2 cups of water with coconut milk. For more balance to vatta, stir in ½ cup of crème fraîche and garnish with fresh tarragon.

Earth is a stabilizing Element that grounds us in reality and reminds us that the Mother is with us daily in the plants, soil, and animals we enjoy.

The Least You Need to Know

- ◆ Earth is an Element closely tied to stability and common sense.

- ◆ Gnomes are the spirits most closely associated with the Element of Earth.

- ◆ Earth connects you to the Mother and to the world around us.

- ◆ Eating pungent, bitter, and astringent food can help balance your kapha dosha, according to ayurvedic principles.

- ◆ Root vegetables on your table put you in touch with the Earth Element, bringing it into your body in grounding harmony and balance.

Chapter 8

Call to Spirit

In This Chapter

- ◆ The Akasha Spirit in all things
- ◆ Meditation to connect to Spirit
- ◆ Finding your spiritual guide
- ◆ A recipe to honor Spirit

Spirit is the creative force from which all the other Elements arise. Because we cannot see or feel a piece of Spirit, it is a difficult thing to define. Spirit is in all things. It is what connects everything on this planet—maybe other planets as well.

Some sense Spirit as a guiding force. It allows things to occur in a way that teaches or heals. It can be understood by remembering cause and effect, the Wiccan law of three, and karma. All these can be seen as aspects of Spirit.

The Akasha Connection

Spirit is considered the fifth Element and is sometimes referred to as Akasha. Spirit is the binding force of the other elements, the part that runs through all matter, and it is also the collective unconscious of life forms.

Sources don't agree on the original meaning of Akasha. Some say the word is Persian or East Indian and means "inner space." Others say it's a Sanskrit word that means "hidden library." Liguana learned it as coming from the Sanskrit word *kash*, which means "to radiate." Despite its elusive origins, all Magicians know it as Spirit.

Spirit Qualities

Because the Elements emerge from Akasha, the undeniable, changeless Source of all energy, it is the realm of potential, of promise, of paths not yet taken, of the unforeseen, and of the unknowable. It exists in every living creature, every plant and rock, every running stream and puddle of water.

And, of course, Akasha is present within our bodies. Some believe that the spark of life, that force that we sometimes call the soul, is a bit of Akashic energy housed in our physical bodies.

> ### Liguana's Grimoire
>
> The Sioux Indians call Spirit Skan, or something that is always in motion. Their creation story says the Great Spirit Skan made them with bones from stone, bodies from Earth, and souls from himself, Wind, and Thunders. The gifts of Sun, wisdom, Moon, and revealer gave them life. A council of the Spirits named the Sioux "Buffalo Nation" and instructed them to care for the Earth's spirits.

Akasha is not used by itself in Natural Magick; rather, it's the primal source of energy that creates and fuels the Elements. When a magickal practitioner raises power, he or she pulls up power from within the body and merges it with Spirit energy, which can then be sent forth to affect Elements outside of the body. This is how a magickal wizard connects with the Spirit force of those Elements. There are three sources of magickal energy flow: the etheric body of each person, the Earth itself, and the Divine. All magickal sources are elements of Spirit.

Akashic Records

Many Natural Magicians believe in an ethereal field of knowledge, which can be accessed by those who train or have the natural ability to do so, called the *Akashic Records*. The Akashic Records are a spiritual realm, supposedly holding a record of all events, actions, thoughts, and feelings that have ever occurred or will ever occur.

Clairvoyance, spiritual insight, prophecy, and many other metaphysical and religious notions are made possible by tapping into the Akasha. The records have been referred to by different names, including the Cosmic Mind, the Universal Mind, the collective unconscious, and the collective subconscious.

Information about the Akashic Records, or Book of Life, can be found in folklore, in myth, and throughout the Old and New Testaments. Among all of these references is the belief that there is in existence some kind of celestial tablets that contained the history of humankind and all manner of spiritual information.

Some believe that the events recorded upon the Akashic Records can be read in some states of consciousness. Such states of consciousness can be induced by certain stages of sleep, weakness, illness, and meditation, so not only mystics but ordinary people can and do perceive the Akashic Records. Some mystics claim to be able to reanimate their contents like they were turning on a celestial computer. Yogis also believe that these records can be perceived in certain psychic states.

Spirit Meditation

Learning how to quiet your inner voice and stop talking to yourself is how you begin to hear the voices of all other things connected to Spirit. A few really good meditation techniques can help with this.

Begin by picking a time when the house is quiet. Be sure you're wearing comfortable clothes and sit in a comfortable position. Liguana finds it most effective to gaze at a blank wall to open her mind to the voice of the Goddess. Or you might stare at a candle flame. Empty your mind of all your mundane thoughts and worries. How can you hear the voices of gods and other entities if you fill your silences with your own internal chatter?

Connecting to Spirit through meditation takes some practice. Be patient and listen for the voices to come to you. The more you meditate, the easier it will be to hear the Goddess. Liguana is often "spoken to" when she's in the shower. She isn't sure if it's the negative ions, the white noise of the water, or the fact that she's skyclad (naked). Use whatever works for you.

> **Liguana's Grimoire**
>
> In the early 1970s, a psychic researcher experimented by having his subjects meditate in a solid field of color. The Ganzfeld experiments were really an experiment with sensory deprivation. The results after a few hours were most interesting. Nearly all the test subjects reported hearing voices and seeing visions.

A Natural Magician might find meditating in a garden or near running water a place of Spiritual connection. There is no wrong place to meditate. Pick a place where you feel safe and connected, where you will be undisturbed. Spirit will speak to you if you listen.

Magickal Correspondence and Spirit

The problem with connecting Spirit to the mundane world is that there is so much crossover correspondence, with Spirit being part of all things.

Mistletoe and almond almost always correspond with Spirit. All time and all space is Spirit. In Wicca tradition and Native American tradition, center, above, and below are the directions most closely linked to Spirit. Other correspondences are myrrh incense, diamond, yarrow, vervain, white, gold, violet, mescal, marigold, wormwood, and electricity.

Using Magickal Will to Connect to Spirit

Magickal Will is often represented as the fifth point on a pentacle, with Spirit residing in the center. A pentacle is a five-pointed star often used in Wiccan spells and rituals. A Natural Magician uses Magickal Will to focus Spirit.

An old proverb says, "If wishes were horses, then beggars would ride." This implies that wishing can't bring about the results a Natural Magician wants. On the other hand, we've all wished upon a star and listened to *Pinocchio*'s Jiminy Cricket sing, "When you wish upon a star, your dreams come true." Modern child psychology experts discourage magical thinking or making a child believe he or she caused something to happen just by thinking about it. But in rare instances, Natural Magick does happen because someone wishes hard enough. Most of the time, affecting an outcome requires Magickal Will.

Magickal Will is a sense of determination and focus on a result. It is the push to get the job done. This is one of the safeguards of your magickal practice. You can think impulsively, but focusing on your intent and pushing your spell into the world takes a little more time and energy. Liguana may think about making the flowers in her yard grow and bloom in February, but she won't will this to happen; she leaves it to the Goddess to decide the best time.

Spiritual Beings

Natural Magicians tend to connect to the Spirit world through beings whose role it is to guide and support them in both the spiritual and earthly realms. Different religions refer to these beings in different ways, but all of them are depicted as benevolent and protective.

Day of the Dead

Traditionally a Mexican festival, the Day of the Dead honors ancestors who have moved on to the Spirit Realm and recognizes the continuity of life. It is not a morbid occasion, but rather a festive time of celebration that welcomes the souls of the dead back into the home.

Mexicans celebrate the Day of the Dead during the first two days of November. Celebrants believe that the souls of the dead return and are all around them. Families remember the departed by telling stories about them. Generally, the holiday's activities consist of families welcoming their dead back into their homes and visiting the graves of their close kin. At the cemetery, family members decorate the gravesites with large, bright flowers such as marigolds and chrysanthemums, and small trinkets. Traditionally, families bring a picnic lunch to eat in the cemetery along with other family and community members who gather there.

The meals prepared for these picnics are sumptuous, usually featuring meat dishes in spicy sauces, chocolate beverages, cookies, sugary confections in a variety of animal or skull shapes, and a special egg-batter bread called pan de muerto, or "bread of the dead" (see the following recipe). The festive interaction with both the living and the dead in an important social ritual is a way of recognizing the cycle of life and death that is human existence.

> **Liguana's Grimoire**
>
> The original celebration can be traced to many Mesoamerican native traditions, such as the festivities held during the Aztec month of Miccailhuitontli, ritually presided over by the "Lady of the Dead" (Mictecacihuatl) and dedicated to children and the dead.

In homes, observant families create an altar and decorate it with items that they believe are beautiful and attractive to the souls of their departed ones. Family altars are profusely decorated with flowers and adorned with religious amulets and offerings of food and alcoholic beverages. They also include items that will remind the living of the departed, such as photographs, jewelry, or an article of clothing. This is done to entice the dead and ensure that their souls actually return to take part in the remembrance.

Honoring the Dead: Pan de Muerto

There are numerous variations of this recipe, but most include anise seed, which attracts Spirit; orange, which attracts wisdom and luck; and eggs, the Mother symbol. Yeast breads in general are good for attracting Spirit because they rise to a light dough rather than a dense, quick bread dough.

This bread is often shaped into skulls or round loaves with strips of dough rolled out and attached to resemble bones. In southern Mexico, it is considered good luck to be the one who bites into the plastic toy skeleton hidden by the baker in each rounded loaf of pan de muerto. Try this in your own celebration of your ancestors—but warn your family and friends first!

½ cup butter

½ cup milk

½ cup water

5 to 5½ cups flour

2 packages dry yeast

1 tsp. salt

1 TB. whole anise seed

½ cup sugar

4 eggs

In a saucepan over medium heat, stir together the butter, milk, and water until very warm but not boiling.

Meanwhile, measure out 1½ cups of the flour and set aside the rest. In a large mixing bowl, combine the 1½ cups flour, yeast, salt, anise seed, and sugar.

With an electric mixer, beat in the warm liquid until well combined. Add eggs and beat in another 1 cup of flour. Continue adding more flour until the dough is soft but not sticky.

Turn out onto a lightly floured board and knead for 10 minutes or until smooth and elastic. Resist the temptation to add more flour; it will result in a lighter bread if you keep the flour to a minimum. The dough will become less sticky as you knead.

Place dough into a lightly greased bowl, cover with a damp towel, and let it rise in a warm place until doubled in bulk, about 1½ hours.

Punch down the dough and shape into two round loaves with "bones" placed ornamentally around the top. Tuck a small plastic skeleton into each loaf. Place on a cookie sheet and let the loaves rise for 1 hour or until doubled in bulk.

Bake the loaves in a preheated 350°F oven for 40 minutes. Remove from oven and paint on the glaze.

For the glaze:

> ½ cup sugar
>
> ½ cup fresh orange juice
>
> 2 TB. grated orange zest

Combine all the ingredients and bring to a boil for 2 minutes. Apply to the top of the bread with a pastry brush. Sprinkle on red colored sugar while the glaze is still damp.

As you pass the bread at your Day of the Dead celebration, set out a plate for the Spirits you're entertaining. Thank them for coming home and ask them to guide your steps in the coming year.

Animal Totems

In earlier days, humans believed themselves simply one of many animals on Earth. Now too many humans believe they are the greatest and most important species. But Natural Magicians know that humans are only a small part of Earth, only a part of Nature—a child of Mother, a sliver of Spirit.

We used to respect Nature, honoring and thanking animals for providing us with life, nourishment, and comfort. In earlier days, humans gave recognition to the power of the animal spirits by wearing skins and masks, singing praise, and offering prayers to specific animals. People painted animal images on their homes, caves, and death chambers, and asked the Spirit to guide them to the animal that they consumed. These acts allowed people to remain linked to the animal guides and to accept the power they offered in lessons, in life, and in death. It was a reminder that all animals are our sisters, brothers, cousins, and, most important, our teachers and our friends. It reminded us that we, too, are animals with Spirit.

Because of this, it is important to reconnect to Nature's language through the animal realm. Early societies thought the only way for Spirit or the Divine to connect to Natural Magicians was through Nature—especially animals.

In every tradition, there are teachings about the sacred wisdom of animals. Animal teachers, animal guides, power animals, animal totems—all of these are just a few terms applied to the mystical teachings of animals. The Spirit—or Mother Nature, if you will—is very wise and brings into our lives the animals that have a message for us. If we learn to listen to Nature, we can more easily reconnect to Animal Spirit.

Connecting to Spirit makes life run more smoothly. What wasn't working will work. What was blocked will flow. What was irritating will drop away. What seemed out of reach will be accessible.

Familiars

Many Natural Magicians have pets, but not all of them are familiars. Familiars can fill many different roles in your life, including that of teacher, friend, healer, or assistant. Any animal of any species can present itself as the familiar of a Natural Magician. The form your familiar chooses to take may be a message in itself and may be completely unexpected. A familiar may arrive in the form of a family pet, but it should not be treated that simply. They are independent spirits that must be respected and honored.

If the animal is a familiar, you may develop a strong psychic bond and it will likely show a clear interest in your ritual work. Each person's relationship with his or her familiar is special, unique, and individual.

Of course, your familiar might not even be a physical being. Having an astral familiar is also a possibility. Astral familiars usually take the form of regular animals, but they also may take the form of more exotic beasts, such as a dragon. Working with astral familiars usually takes place during dreams or meditation.

Sometimes you need to search out your familiar, but other times it will find you. You can't summon a familiar; you can only invite one into your life. Familiars may arrive in your life when you call or just when you are in need of them. They can also disappear from your life if you no longer need their help or guidance. Most familiars stay with a person for a good many years, typically the life span of their animal hosts, but don't be surprised if they move on unexpectedly once their work is done.

Angels on Earth

Some Spirit guides take human form. We teach small children that they have a guardian angel watching out for them, but Natural Magicians believe in angels, too. Ethereal creatures, angels can be benevolent guardians or fierce defenders. Depicted as white-robed, winged creatures in most religious paintings, angels rarely appear on the physical plane, preferring to do their work from the angelic realms (higher energy realms).

Angels are without gender. They may appear to us as more masculine or feminine if they agree to appear to us at all, but they are generally androgynous. Angels function on a higher vibration than Spirit guides. Angels are such beautiful beings with such love that their energy itself can bring truth to a Natural Magician. They are the essence of purity.

Too much truth can be terrifying, which is why angels usually take on a form of lower stature when we encounter them—someone on our level so we can interact with them. They are excellent conveyors of universal love, but they are not always equipped to deal with earthly problems. Spirit guides, on the other hand, have a lower energy and aren't nearly as intimidating in their full form. To put it simply, angels are of the heavens and Spirit guides are of Earth. To read more about angels, we suggest *Empowering Your Life with Angels*, by Rita Berkowitz with Deborah Romaine (Alpha Books, 2004).

Connecting to Spirit can be both calming and enlightening. Listening to the voices of the Deities, practicing connecting to the energy of Spirit, can make it easier for Natural Magicians to use the power of the other four Elements as well.

The Least You Need to Know

- Spirit both teaches and heals, and can enlighten us about what path we should be taking.
- One way to connect to Spirit is by quieting your inner voice and meditating.
- Honoring your ancestors celebrates the cycle of life.
- When an animal totem or familiar is needed, they often show up on their own accord, either in a dream or on your doorstep.

Chapter **9**

Stirring Powerful Dragons and Watchtowers

In This Chapter

◆ Who are the Guardians?

◆ Inviting the Guardians to ritual

◆ Stirring up a dragon or two

◆ Knowing how and when to call a dragon

◆ Using power wisely

Guardians or Watchers are very old beings that exist on the astral plane or between the worlds. Sometimes only four of them are identified in ritual as beings guarding the use of the elemental energies. Sometimes they are perceived as many.

In some spiritual traditions, the Guardians are thought to be a very old type of being, advanced in thought and energy use to the point of no longer needing a physical body. They are made of light or energy.

Getting to Know the Guardians

Remember the three sources of magickal energy? (See Chapter 8.) They were the etheric body, Earth's energies, and the Divine. Guardians exist somewhere between Earth's etheric realms and the realm of the Divine. They are said to guard the doorways to other dimensions. Some traditions recognize these beings as angels.

Their job is to safeguard all people making magick if called upon to do so. We humans can make magick with the best of all intentions, calling Elemental beings to assist us and yet not having full control over these beings. The Guardians of the Watchtowers of the four directions are charged with monitoring the magickal currents flowing out from us and the energies we open up to when we do our magick. They are protectors of all magickal people.

Meditation for Meeting the Guardians

Meeting up with any spirit on the astral plane is usually accomplished through meditation or, in some cases, through dreams. Here is one purposeful way to invoke the Watchers.

Do these meditations at the time of the *Waxing Moon*. It's all right to meditate and call for each one a day or two apart. Never do two in the same day. These are powerful energies you are invoking.

> **Magickal Bounty**
>
> A **Waxing Moon** is one that is getting bigger—heading to Full Moon—as opposed to a **Waning Moon**, which is getting smaller. If it is visible in the evening sky, the Moon is waxing. If the moon is visible at dawn or in the early morning, it is waning:
>
> *If you see the Moon at the end of the day,*
> *A bright Full Moon is on its way.*
> *If you see the Moon in the early dawn,*
> *Look real quick; it will soon be gone.*

Sit or lie comfortably, orienting yourself toward the direction of the Elemental Guardian you are seeking (North for Earth, South for Fire, East for Air, West for Water). Close your eyes and breathe in deeply, listening to your breath and the noises around you. Let yourself relax, breathing slowly.

Visualize yourself in a white, shimmering room. All around you it looks like brilliant sunlight on fresh snow. You are warm and comfortable.

In the center of the room there is a small, white, circular table with two shimmering chairs next to it. Move to the chair closest to you and sit down, resting your hands on the table. Now say out loud, "I am here to stir the Guardian of the Watchtower of the East (or whichever one you are calling) and to learn who you are. I invite you to tell me of your mission at the Eastern Watchtower and teach me of my own mission there."

After a time, you become aware of another presence at your table. The being is bright, its form difficult to distinguish from the sparkling atmosphere around you both. It may speak to you in words or pictures or telepathically. Listen with an open mind and heart until the Watcher chooses to leave or tells you it is time to go. Think hard about your physical body and you will return there. Slowly become aware of your surroundings in the mundane world. Breathe deeply and slowly several times and think about the wisdom given to you.

Repeat this process for each of the Elemental Watchers. Remember, only one per day.

Liguana has an astral plane friend Questle. (She isn't sure of the spelling or pronunciation.) She believes *Q* is one of these beings, from all he has told her. He can manifest as a human but is actually a being of light, without corporeal form. He says his kind are genderless, though we might classify them individually as more masculine or feminine, based on our own gender understanding.

Creating Sacred Space

Because these Guardians are protectors, they are usually invoked when casting a circle or creating sacred space in some way. Inviting them to join you during a ritual helps ensure your safety as well as the safety of others who may be participating. Always keep in mind that these are powerful energies and they will be watching to make sure your intentions are pure. If your intent is to do harm, remember the *Wiccan Rede* or the Golden Rule. If you don't, you might find yourself in serious trouble with the Guardians.

> **Magickal Bounty**
>
> The **Wiccan Rede** says, "An it harm none, do what ye will." *Rede* is an archaic word that means "advice" or "counsel." Wiccans believe that whatever Magickal Will you send out, you will receive back threefold. In other words, if you wish somebody warts, expect to end up with three times as many as they do!

Natural Magicians create a sacred space in various ways. They might kneel in front of an altar, they might cast a circle, they might outline a space around them with an *athame* or wand, or they might simply have a quiet place they go to light candles and meditate. The key is to temporarily turn a mundane space into something sacred. In other words, you are creating a temple that exists in both the physical world and the astral realm.

Inviting the Guardians to join you in that space can be done as a formal ritual or as a simple invitation. If you want to keep it simple, you can invite them with something like this:

> *I call upon the Guardians of the Watchtowers of the East, South, West, and North. Join me in this sacred space. Guide my hand and my Spirit, that everything I do here be for the good of all. Blessed be!*

Wait a few moments until you feel their presence. Perform the ritual you had planned and then release them:

> *Hail and farewell, Watchers. Go peacefully from my presence as I thank you for yours.*

A More Formal Ceremony

If you're hosting a gathering and want to invite the Guardians in a more formal way, there are endless possibilities. We'll share one with you here, but remember that being a Natural Magician isn't about following someone else's rituals. Sit quietly and see if your own invitation ritual comes to you naturally. The Watchtower Guardians aren't impressed with pompous ceremony. They want sincerity and good intentions.

Begin by outlining the sacred space with two fingers, a wand, or an *athame*. Common to most Natural Magicians is a sacred circle, the symbol of the Goddess. Facing each direction as you invoke it, hold up your hand or the tool you used and say:

Magickal Bounty

An **athame** (pronounced *a-tha-may*) is a two-edged knife used by Natural Magicians to cut or outline a space on a spiritual plane, among other things. It generally has a wooden or silver handle.

Hail, Guardians of the Watchtowers of the East, powers of Air. We call you and invoke you. Guardian of breath, keeper of soft breeze and mighty wind, join us!

Hail, Guardians of the Watchtowers of the South, powers of Fire. We call you and invoke you. Guardian of passion, keeper of spark and flame, join us!

Hail, Guardians of the Watchtowers of the West, powers of Water. We call you and invoke you. Guardian of intuition, keeper of healing rain and flood, join us!

> *Hail, Guardians of the Watchtowers of the North, powers of Earth. We call you and invoke you. Guardian of body, keeper of fertile soil and earthquake, join us!*

Once the circle is cast, you can perform whatever ritual you had in mind under the watchful eyes and guidance of the Guardians. Begin with an invocation:

> *As above, so below.*
> *As the universe, so the soul.*
> *As without, so within.*
> *Blessed and gracious ones,*
> *We consecrate ourselves to you*
> *In body, mind, and spirit.*

Once you have completed the ritual, be sure to release the Guardians:

> *Guardians of the East, Powers of Air, we thank you for joining in our circle, and we ask for your blessing as you depart in peace. Blessed Be!*

> *Guardians of the South, Powers of Fire, we thank you for joining in our circle, and we ask for your blessing as you depart in peace. Blessed Be!*

> *Guardians of the West, Powers of Water, we thank you for joining in our circle, and we ask for your blessing as you depart in peace. Blessed Be!*

> *Guardians of the North, Powers of Earth, we thank you for joining in our circle, and we ask for your blessing as you depart in peace. Blessed Be!*

Cakes and Ale: Buttercup Cake

After a ritual, it is often customary to serve "cakes and ale." We will have more recipes for you later in the book (see Chapter 23), but here's a quick cake recipe to get you started. This buttercup cake is a thick, dense cake flavored with citrus that helps clarify thoughts and topped with a nutty streusel that invokes Earth. Served to guests, this cake will help them more clearly touch base with their practical sides.

2¼ cups flour

1½ cups sugar

1½ tsp. baking powder

½ tsp. salt

½ cup shortening, softened

1 cup buttermilk

½ tsp. vanilla

½ tsp. orange extract

½ tsp. lemon extract

2 eggs

For the streusel:

½ cup sugar

⅓ cup flour

4 TB butter or margarine, softened

1 cup walnuts or pecans

Mix together the flour, sugar, baking powder, and salt. Cut in the shortening until the mixture is crumbly. Add the buttermilk, the orange and lemon extracts, and the eggs. Beat with an electric mixer until smooth. Pour the batter into a greased and floured 13×9–inch baking pan.

Cauldron Bubble

If you're feeling decadent, double the streusel recipe. Serve the cake with a light fruit punch that has citrus overtones.

Next, mix together the sugar and flour for the streusel. Cut in the softened butter until the mixture is crumbly. Fold in the nuts. Sprinkle the mixture evenly over the batter.

Bake at 350°F for 35 to 40 minutes.

Stirring Dragons

Dragons have been feared and revered as long as there have been people. But what are they, really? Natural Magicians know that dragons are beings who live in the astral plane and can be contacted and communicated with through meditation and trance work. They can cross over to the physical plane at will but seldom choose to do this, preferring instead their solitude or the company of other dragons. When a Natural Wizard knows enough to find the astral realms, he or she may well catch the attention of the dragons who live there. Be sure this is what you want to do.

Dragons are *invoked* or *evoked* during Sabbats and only in times when great magick is needed—not when you cannot find your keys, but in times of great crisis.

When you evoke something—that is, call it to you—you are asking the being (dragon, faerie, deity …) to join you while you are working and to lend you not only their presence, but also their power. Evoking is a powerful magick. You must be sure of what you are doing and must remember to be respectful of those you call to you. When you evoke a dragon, you are asking a very powerful creature for a favor.

Magickal Bounty

Although not all traditions make the distinction, for some Natural Magicians, **invoking** means to call into you, literally into your spiritual body, while **evoking** means to call a spirit to you, to join alongside you in your magickal workings.

Now invoking, calling into you, is a different story. To call a being into you is very tricky. The dragon that you beckon is being asked to join into you and work with you as one. That is, you and the dragon are the same creature during your magickal workings. This is not for beginners to attempt because it is very easy to lose yourself in the dragon. The dragons are by no means malevolent; it is just that they are so powerful that it is very enticing to give yourself over to them.

We recommend evoking many times until you are comfortable with the dragons and they are comfortable with you. Dragons are drawn to many things that they like, and if you show respect, they may be drawn to you.

In addition to helping you, dragons perform their own brand of magick. The form they use is something of a mystery, but many legends have them holding pearls or crystals or other jewels as a source of their energy and potency. Dragons also influence and change natural patterns of cause and effect. In their own way, dragons are wizards.

Stir Gently …!

Know your dragon well before you start asking favors. Not every dragon cares to serve humanity. Dragons don't appreciate being stirred around for frivolous reasons. Keep in mind that just because you have gained the attention of a dragon doesn't mean the dragon will let itself be commanded by you. A dragon is a free being.

When Should You Call a Dragon?

Why would a Natural Magician seek out dragons? Dragons can easily manipulate energies on both the physical and astral planes. Because of this, a good relationship with a dragon or two is most beneficial to a magickal person.

In the Asian world, dragons are considered lucky. They bring material wealth and wisdom to those who successfully connect with them. Though Western mythology often portrays dragons as bloodthirsty and greedy, they have also been used to represent powerful governments and leaders. It is possible that a dragon could influence the course of history, assisting a favored king or government. A wise sorcerer understands that dragons can be valuable allies in any endeavor.

Because they can be fearsome protectors of any magickal person they like, dragons should be called upon only when you feel the need for a powerful ally. Remember, you are not asking them to do someone harm, only to stand beside you in a crisis. Believe us! You will feel their strength and be able to lean upon it in your time of need.

Attracting Dragons

In actuality, it is not hard to attract a dragon or even several dragons. One thing in common with all dragons is their love of the flow of power. Your magickal workspace is really all that you need to attract them. It does not matter if you are there just trying to center yourself and feel the magick about you; dragons will be there if they feel welcome.

Dragons are, on the whole, mistrustful of humans, at least at first. They live for thousands of years and have seen many humans come and go. They have also seen the destruction that we have caused to Earth and to each other. It's no wonder dragons are skeptical.

> **Liguana's Grimoire**
>
> Names commonly used for the ruler of all the dragons of its Element are as follows:
>
> - Ruler of the Air or Sky dragons—Sairys
> - Ruler of the Fire dragons—Fafnir
> - Ruler of the Water dragons—Naelyon
> - Ruler of the Earth dragons—Grael

Stirring a dragon requires concentration and strong Magickal Will. Incense, especially dragon's blood, will help attract dragons. A simple ritual is to wave a sword or a staff over your head three times and then plunge it into the earth as you say something like the following:

> *Oh mighty dragon, please come stand beside me. I am so small and your power is so great. Let me lean on you and keep me safe.*

Don't be surprised if you feel the earth tremble slightly or if the wind picks up. You will be aware of the dragon's presence.

The two most important factors in attracting dragons are respect and making them feel welcome. Always keep in mind that these beautiful creatures are extremely powerful beings and deserve our respect. Reach out to the dragons with your heart and mind, and welcome them into your life; the dragons will come.

Dragon Lore

In the creative imaginations of humanity, dragons have existed side by side with people since before written history. In Babylonian legends, the primal goddess mother was the dragon Tiamot, who gave birth to the Earth and the Sky when her body was split in two by the younger god, Marduk. Tiamot was said to be made from the energies of salt water and the emptiness of chaos.

In an older Sumerian legend, the plans for the natural patterns of the Universe were stolen by the dragon Zu, who was attempting to bring back the void, the chaotic realm where dragons and gods are born.

From the Greek word meaning "she-goat," the Chimera was a fire-breathing creature with the body of a goat, the head of a lion, and the tail of a serpent. Although more of a hybrid than a pure dragon, this fire-breathing creature was feared for its power and destruction.

Some believe there are dragon personalities living among us on the physical plane. These are people who have been born with dragon energy as well as human energy. Their connections with Spirit come easier. They tend not to do magick often, but when they do it, it works.

All of these legends and stories, existing across different eras and cultures, lends some credence to the existence of these astral creatures. Use them wisely.

> **Liguana's Grimoire**
>
> Liguana's friend Jessadriel claims to know several people who are dragonkin. Mostly they are loners, very wise, powerful, and passionate.

Growing Your Natural Power

In this chapter, we have talked about invoking and evoking some fairly high-level beings to assist you in your magickal workings. We can't stress enough that as your Natural Magick grows stronger with practice, it is easy to do accidental harm. This is especially true when you are stomping around with beings on an astral plane.

Always stop to think what your intentions are before you contact a Guardian or a dragon. If you have even the slightest thought of hurting someone or trying to bend someone's Will to your own, don't go there! Is there the hint of jealousy or envy in your heart? Although these are certainly normal human emotions, when mixed up with magick, it can be to everyone's detriment. These beings will not look upon you kindly if you contact them for frivolous or nasty purposes.

Keep in mind always that whether you are casting a circle or kneeling before an altar, your magick should be performed in perfect love and perfect trust—*naturally*.

The Least You Need to Know

- Guardians or Watchers exist between worlds on an astral plane. Their job is to guard all magickal people.

- You can contact a Guardian through meditation to assist you in understanding your mission at his Watchtower.

- In some traditions, evoking a being means to work side by side; invoking a being means asking it to join with your Spirit to work as one.

- Contact dragons only in times of crisis or when powerful magick is needed—not for frivolous purposes.

Part 3

Wildcrafting

Wildcrafting means connecting to the Earth in mundane ways that become magickal. It means planting, harvesting, hiking, camping, sunbathing, skiing, and reveling in all of the seasons. As a Natural Magician, you accept what the Earth hands out and use it for the benefit of everyone in your life.

10

The Craft of Gathering and Planting

In This Chapter

◆ What is ethical wildcrafting?

◆ Searching for useable items

◆ Planting herbs to use in spellcrafting

◆ Crab apple jelly for love and luck

◆ Planting a container garden

Wildcrafting is the age-old practice of harvesting and using wild materials from their natural habitat for food, decoration, rituals, construction, and craft. Originally, such activity was the only grocery store, medicine chest, and hardware store available.

A Natural Magician keeps the value of the Earth in mind when planting and gathering. Ethical wildcrafting is about sustainability. We must not only seek to do no harm in our gathering, but we must also look to the future of the land we walk upon. Using "found" materials is a good way to enjoy the outdoors while taking advantage of the Goddess's bounty with humility and thankfulness.

Gathering Ethically

What kinds of things do Natural Magicians gather during wildcrafting? The possibilities are endless: mushrooms, driftwood, flowers, feathers, rocks, shells, grains, quills, clay, wicker, burls, seaweed, weeds, nuts, food, herbs, berries, seeds, cones, roots, bark, dye, antlers, fur, bones, leather, teeth, mosses, ferns, and saps such as maple and pine. And that list is just a good start!

Stir Gently ...!

Do not eat wild mushrooms you've picked unless you are absolutely sure they're edible! Many species are poisonous and can cause severe liver damage or even death if eaten. Know your berries, too. If you aren't positive they're safe to eat, leave them alone.

Many Natural Magicians prefer wild herbs to cultivated ones because they believe that plants gathered from the wild have more power and inherent healing qualities. Although it is true that wildcrafting is perhaps the most direct way of getting in touch with the healing powers of Mother Earth, if we simply take for greed's sake without regard for the well-being of the greater whole, we ultimately damage the Earth and, therefore, ourselves. It is important to undertake this task in harmony with nature, to avoid further damaging our already suffering ecosystems.

Make wildcrafting a spiritual activity. Ask the Elements for permission before you take anything, and always give something back when you can. You can sow some seeds, for example, so that the next person to come along can also find some plants to harvest. Never take *all* of everything; collect in swatches and leave the best seed stock for the future. "Waste not, want not" should be every Natural Magician's motto. Never take more than you need. Remember that others may also need some of the plants that you are gathering. Most important, give consideration to animals and insects, who may not only depend on the plants you are harvesting, but who also help with pollination and seed distribution.

Before gathering any gifts from Nature, study the environment from which they come. Is it healthy or diseased? Has it been sprayed with chemicals? Do not take from diseased habitats, from the sides of roads, or in the vicinity of factories that may have polluted the earth.

Planting the Future

Wildcrafting does not have to wait for something useful to grow in an area. You can add trees or plants that will become productive over time. Fruit or nut trees can be introduced to grow in wild areas, as can herbs and flowers. (The honeybees will love you!) Any area of marginal land has the potential to grow things that are suitable for wildcrafting. Although you may not necessarily want to cultivate or farm these areas, scattering seeds of things you might want to harvest to see if they will take advantage of a location is certainly permissible.

Be sure you aren't planting or gathering on private land. Asking permission before you take anything is not only ethical, but it potentially sends positive energy out into the Universe by utilizing something someone else may not be using.

Also be sure to take into consideration the other plants in the vicinity before you sow any seeds. You don't want to plant an invasive plant that will choke out the area's natural vegetation. Realize, for example, that planting a tree will eventually shade an area that may need sunlight to thrive.

If you take large rocks or stones, don't leave gaping holes in the earth. Smooth over the dirt and scatter some seeds over the area so grasses or herbs will fill in the space. Be aware that taking too many plants from hillsides can start erosion that may seriously damage the earth and the surrounding plants. And, of course, don't leave the remains of your lunch scattered around. When a Natural Magician leaves a wild area, it should look undisturbed for the next person who comes along.

> **Stir Gently ...!**
>
> Never remove a wild animal from its habitat. A baby bird or fawn may look abandoned, when, in fact, its mother may be hovering nearby. Remember that death is a natural cycle of life, and trying to "rescue" an animal may just be interfering with Nature's larger plan.

Urban Wildcrafting

Wildcrafting does not always have to be done in the wild. There are opportunities for wildcrafting in urban and suburban areas as well. Many "wild" patches in the city may have useful items growing in them—although be careful you aren't picking purposefully planted flowers or shrubs.

Adopt an empty lot, if there's one in your neighborhood. Once you've cleaned out any litter, wild grasses or hearty flowers may thrive there. Even poor, rocky soil can support life if encouraged a little. For example, an easy-to-grow and attractive ornamental grass is Chinese silvergrass. It makes an excellent ground cover and can grow up to 8 feet tall. It is a strong growing plant and is tolerant of both wet and dry sites and sun or shade. Silvergrass has feathery plumes at the top of the plant, which a

Natural Magician can use to direct smoke during smudging (see Chapter 4). Recite something like the following blessing as you fan the smoke with your living fan into every corner of a room:

Cauldron Bubble

In general, roots should always be harvested during a Waning Moon or at the dark of the moon. Leaves and bark should be collected during a Waxing Moon. Flowers and fruit should be picked during Full Moon. This ensures the maximum amount of chi or Spirit energy.

Guardians of Earth and Air,
Protect this space,
Cleanse it of negative energy,
And let it be used for good purposes.

Another approach to urban wildcrafting might be to see what people have growing in their yards. For example, often people plant crab apple or cherry trees for their flowers and never harvest the fruit. Or some people may have a fruit tree or bush they just don't have time to harvest. This is an opportunity to offer to harvest for a share of the crop or a portion of the jelly you're going to make. Just make certain you have permission!

Crab Apple Jelly

Crab apples make a delightfully tart jelly. Fruit of the Mother, apples attract psychic energy and strengthen relationships. Crab apples are often overlooked when cooks select apples to use in a recipe. The trees are ornamental but also produce useable fruit. Just be sure to leave a few apples for the squirrels.

You'll need as many whole crab apples as you can harvest, enough water to just cover the apples in a large pot, lots of white sugar, and several blocks of paraffin. (Don't worry, the directions get more specific as we go!)

Wash the apples and remove the blossom ends. Leave the crab apples whole—do not peel or core. Add enough water to the apples to just cover them, and simmer for 15 minutes. Crush the apples with a masher and simmer for five minutes longer. Line a strainer or a colander with several layers of cheese cloth. You may use clothespins to secure the material to the colander. Pour the apples into the colander with a large pan beneath it to catch the juice. Let it drain overnight.

Measure the amount of juice you have by cup. If the last cup is short, add enough water to make it a full cup. Bring the juice to a full, rolling boil that cannot be stirred down, stirring occasionally. Add ⅔ cup sugar for each cup of juice, and bring back to a full rolling boil, stirring constantly. Boil until the jelly sheets off the spoon—in other words, it is thick enough to drip off the spoon like syrup rather than like juice.

Melt the paraffin in a heavy glass jar by placing the jar in boiling water.

Pour the jelly into sterilized jelly glasses, leaving ½ inch space at top, and cover with melted paraffin. Store the jars in a cool, dark place and use within 12 months. (Jelly will keep in the refrigerator for up to two months without paraffin but sealed with a lid.) Allow jelly to sit for 24 hours before moving to storage. Five pounds of apples yields 12 or 13 half pints of jelly.

Wildcrafting for Inedibles

Wildcrafting for nuts and berries and other foodstuffs may be the most practical form of gathering, but searching for items to use in crafts or ritual is equally satisfying. No matter where you live, there are places to look for useable items.

If you live near the beach, for example, the right piece of driftwood can be turned into a staff or wand and will put you in close touch with the Water Element during rituals. A feather or an animal bone can be used during meditation to call up an animal totem. Keep your eyes open for unusual stones or shells, empty birds' eggs, oddly shaped branches, pine cones—almost anything can be incorporated into a centerpiece for a Sabbat table.

Plants and roots make excellent natural dyes. Try gathering up all those pesky dandelions in the spring and summer. Chop the flowers into small pieces and place in a pot. Double the amount of water to plant material. Bring to a boil, then simmer for about an hour. Strain. Now you can add your fabric or yarn to be dyed a cheerful yellow. Since dandelions bring courage and wealth, a Natural Magician can knit up a blessing for every member of the family! Experiment with dyes made from nuts, berries, bark, and leaves, too.

If you see a plant you especially like while you're out on your wildcrafting adventure, carefully transplanting it to your own garden is a way to continue to enjoy it. Try any of these plants in your own backyard.

Flower	Magickal Correspondence
Asters	Variety, patience
Black-eyed Susans	Justice
Borage	Courage
Chrysanthemums	Protection, happy home
Clover	Good luck, clairvoyance

continues

continued

Flower	Magickal Correspondence
Coneflowers	Good health, strengthens spells
Daisies	Innocence, love
Heather	Luck
Honeysuckle	Fidelity, attraction
Jasmine	Attraction
Lavender	Relaxing
Lilac	Luck, love
Lilies of the valley	Counters spells, attracts faeries
Morning glories	Love, peace, mental health
Poppies	Charm for someone bewitched by love
Roses	Love, passion, friendship
Sunflowers	Truth, fame, recognition, granting wishes
Violets	Love, honesty, virtue

Magickal Bounty

A **tussy-mussy** is a cone-shape holder often made of silver that was used in the Victorian era to hold a small bouquet that was meant to be carried. That way, a lady's hands didn't become soiled or sticky.

You can offer a blessing to your newly planted flower garden:

> *Heed ye, flower, bush, and tree*
> *By the Lady blessed be!*

Bring a few flowers indoors each week, but be sure to remove them once they've faded. It's bad Feng Shui energy to have dead flowers sitting around (and they can start to attract gnats). If you're involved in wedding plans, creating your own bouquets or *tussy-mussies* is a lovely spiritual gift to give the bride (even if the bride is you!).

Gardening with Natural Magick

Whether your garden covers half an acre in your back yard or five large pots on your city balcony, Natural Magicians try to plant responsibly using no chemicals and taking advantage of Nature's cycles to be successful.

Planting should be done when the Moon is in an Earth or Water sign of the Zodiac, preferably Earth. The aerial parts of plants, the leaves and flowers, should be harvested when the Moon is in a Water or Air sign. Stems and bark should be gathered when the Moon is in an Earth sign. Weeding will be more successful and less work if done when the Moon is in a Fire sign. Paying attention to your timing is a way to take full advantage of natural patterns of energy. One old planting saying is, "If you can sit on the ground with your trousers down, it's safe to sow your seeds."

The Native American Squanto was a master Natural Magician and Healer. It was Squanto who taught the Pilgrims how to tap the maple trees for sap. He taught them which plants were poisonous and which had medicinal powers. He taught them how to plant Indian corn by heaping the earth into low mounds with several seeds and fish in each mound. The decaying fish fertilized the corn.

A Natural Magician tries to mix a little Natural Magick with common sense. Adding a handful of nails into the planting hole for a tree might boost the iron content of the soil, but the last thing you need is to be littering your soil with rusty nails. Some natural remedies actually do work, though. Placing several banana peels in the planting hole for roses does yield healthier roses. The decaying peel releases magnesium, calcium, potassium, sulfur, phosphates, and sodium, all of which the plant uses.

Before commercial fertilizers, gardeners used all sorts of things to boost their garden's yield, from animal carcasses to beer and milk. Diluted milk is still used by some gardeners who grow pumpkins, which seem to benefit from the milk's protein. Today a Natural Magician can just be careful about buying natural fertilizer. Fertilizers made of blood meal and bone as well as barnyard manure are readily available. Using natural gardening techniques rather than chemicals is the Natural Magician's way to honor the Earth and protect Nature.

Liguana's Grimoire

Liguana's partner weaves and sells cedar garlands every Yuletime. He is careful to harvest in a way that will be beneficial to the tree in the coming year, thinning overgrown areas and large, sagging branches that are encroaching on new growth or in danger of snapping off with the first snowfall. People are happy to let him harvest on their land because he has a reputation of caring for the trees. The trees themselves seem to respond well to his presence in their lives, becoming fuller and healthier every year.

Willow Tea

Note: Not for human consumption!

For indoor gardeners (or gardeners who start plants indoors to be moved outdoors in the spring) who are having trouble getting cuttings to root, a brew of willow tea can help. Ask the tree's permission (and that of its owner) to take a few branches, and thank the tree for its cooperation. Place the twigs in a container and cover them with warm water. After a few days, remove the stems and dip your cuttings in the tea before planting. The willow produces a growth hormone called indolebutyric acid. It promotes root growth, and plants seem to thrive on it. Because willow trees are often used as a symbol of the Lord, this technique combines the Lord's nourishment with the Lady's comforting bosom. It's a marriage guaranteed to produce results!

Herbs and Magick

Planting an herb garden, either inside on a sunny windowsill or outside in your backyard, can provide a Natural Magician with fresh herbs to use in both cooking and spellcrafting.

Here are some common, easily grown herbs and how they might be used in Natural Magick.

Herb	Magical Correspondence
Basil	Money, success, prosperity, love
Chives	Wards off diseases, protection
Coriander	Alleviates pain
Dill	Wealth, protection
Fennel	Good luck, protection
Marjorum	Love, happiness
Mint	Passion, romance
Oregano	Honor, peace
Parsley	Rebirth, new beginnings
Rosemary	Fidelity, good luck, protection
Sage	Memory, wealth, long life
Tarragon	Money, success, protection
Thyme	Honor, courage

Always remember to ultimately use your own intuition when choosing herbs for a recipe or in spellcrafting. Use these suggestions as a starting point, but know there are no "wrong" herbs you can choose. The herbs only enhance your own magickal intentions. If an herb speaks out to you, use it. (For more herb correspondences, see Chapter 3.)

A Snack for Good Luck: Pita Crisps

The next time you're hosting a gathering for family or friends, make this quick treat to ensure that everyone has good luck and protection from anyone wishing them harm.

You will need the following:

>   Pita bread
>
>   Olive oil
>
>   Salt
>
>   Fresh rosemary

Slice each pita round into six pie-shape triangles and place them on a cookie sheet or broiling pan. Brush lightly with olive oil and sprinkle with salt and the rosemary leaves. Place under a broiler until crisp.

> **Liguana's Grimoire**
>
> Students in ancient Greece wore garlands of rosemary around their necks or braided rosemary into their hair to improve their memory during exams. In medieval times, rosemary was braided into a bride's hair or placed in her bouquet to ensure a long-lasting, faithful marriage.

Indoor Gardening

There are several options for a Natural Magician who wants to grow herbs, flowers, small shrubs, or even some vegetables indoors or on a balcony. If you don't have a big backyard, don't despair; container gardening may be just the thing for you. All you need is a little ingenuity.

Start first with obtaining your containers. A frugal purchase of containers means more cash to purchase the variety of bulbs, plants, and flowering bushes you want. Try first at garage and yard sales. The containers don't have to be beautiful. Once your plants start growing, the containers will be barely visible. By strategically placing a few pretty pots in front of your found ones, no one will be the wiser. Almost anything can be used for a container garden, as long as drainage holes can be placed in the container. Try using wooden boxes, hydraulic oil buckets, old pails, or even wash tubs.

First of all, be sure to clean your containers, especially anything that had been used for oil storage. Just a little soap, water, and elbow grease will prepare your containers for planting. Next drill some drainage holes in the bottom of your container. (If you're using old crocks or pottery, use a masonry drill bit to drill the holes.) Then place some small stones or broken pieces of pottery in the bottom of your container over the drainage holes. This will keep the dirt from running out of the holes during watering, which can plug them up.

Fill the containers with good potting soil, and you're ready to plant. Gather seeds in the fall or dig up small plants in the spring for transplanting. Of course, you can buy seeds or plants, too. We've already looked at some common herbs and flowers you might want to use in spellcrafting, but here are a few suggestions for what color of flower to plant for magickal purposes.

Color	Magical Correspondence
Red or pink	Love, affection
White	Truth, purity
Yellow	Happiness, friendship
Orange	Energy, bounty
Bronze	Happy home
Purple	Power, protection
Blue	Peace, mental health

Incorporate the appropriate-color flower into spells and charms to enhance your Natural Magick. For example, a potpourri of dried red and white roses placed in your bedroom will encourage a pure and honest love to develop. Toss in a handful of yellow chrysanthemum petals so that you and your romantic partner also stay friends. Experiment with different combinations of flowers and herbs that you've gathered during wildcrafting—even if it was just into your own backyard.

The Least You Need to Know

- Wildcrafting should be approached ethically with an eye to sustaining the land you're on.

- Be on the lookout for unusual objects that might be used on an altar or in a ritual to represent a Deity or an Element.

◆ Most herbs and flowers have a magickal correspondence and can be incorporated into a spell or ritual to enhance your magickal intent.

◆ Container gardening is a great way to grow your own ingredients if you live in an apartment or a small space with no yard.

◆ Always listen to your own intuition when choosing flowers and herbs to use in spellcrafting; nothing is written in stone for a Natural Magician.

The Four Winds

In This Chapter

- Utilizing the Four Winds in your magick
- Weather working
- Weather by Liguana
- A windy treat
- The Holy wind

On the physical plane, we know Wind very well. It brings the rain and snow, makes our sailboats move, and carries kites high up into the sky. It can come in the guise of a warm summer breeze or a fierce wintry gale. It can be beneficial, scattering seeds and pollen to replenish the Earth, or it can be a terrifyingly destructive force that wipes out whole towns in one giant breath.

On a spiritual plane, the Winds are governed by the four Gods and Goddesses of the Directions. Each pair of Deities has its own temperament and purpose. They can be passionate, gentle, healing, and invigorating. Connecting to Wind energy is calling on powerful Natural Magick.

Getting to Know the Winds

A Natural Magician will want to get to know the Four Winds to utilize them in spell-crafting. Just like the phases of the Moon, the direction of the Wind can influence the outcome of a spell or ritual. Asking the Wind to assist you utilizes Nature's positive energies and makes your job easier.

> **Cauldron Bubble**
>
> You can introduce young children to the Wind by giving them a pinwheel. Being able to play with the Wind and to see its movement through the turning of the wheel helps them to begin thinking of Wind as more than an invisible force.

It's best not to try to compete with Wind. Timing your spell work to evoke the Wind's cooperation in working alongside you is a smart plan. Wind can be a powerful ally, but it can also interfere with an outcome if it believes your intentions are questionable.

A Cold North Wind

An old nursery rhyme begins, "The North Wind doth blow, and we shall have snow," which isn't a bad piece of folklore to keep in mind. Magickally, a North Wind is a cold, dry wind—the Wind of change, letting go, and endings. When the wind is from the North, focus on spells and rituals that involve stabilizing a situation or becoming comfortable with the changes that are occurring in your life. If you have problems with jealousy, anger, depression, or anxiety, face into the North Wind and it will help to drive them away.

The God of the North Wind is Boreus, the bringer of storms. His Lady is Boreana, the primary mover—all things move when she pushes them. She even has the power to move stationary objects such as rocks and trees. If you want the North Wind's help, you must ask for it. Stand facing the North (outside, if possible), raise your hands to the sky in supplication, and say something like the following:

> *Boreana, mighty Lady of the North Wind, Mistress of changes, I welcome you. Boreus, Lord of power and storms, join me in this place. Direction of the Element Earth, help me to be patient during this time of change and release me from my negative feelings.*

Magickal correspondences for the North Wind are midnight and the color black. It is represented in the tarot cards as Death and the Tower. In the long version of the Wiccan Rede, the couplet concerning the North Wind reads:

> *Heed the North Wind's mighty gale,*
> *Lock the door and drop the sail.*

An Easterly Breeze

Winds out of the East bring freshness, strength, and power. This is the Wind of creation and celebration—a warm, bracing wind. Eastern winds encourage new beginnings, dramatic improvements, and optimism. This is the time to perform rituals to bless new projects or endeavors. If you find yourself procrastinating or unmotivated to start a new project, stand facing an Easterly breeze to help refresh your Spirit.

Cauldron Bubble

The Wind loves to play occasionally. Buy a kite, go to an open space, and have a tug-of-war with the Wind. Or blow some bubbles and watch them dance away on the breeze.

The God of the East Wind is Euros, the bringer of rain. His Lady is Eurana. She brings the breath of life and clear thinking, as well as the torment of the harpy wind to those who have displeased her. She offers the unfettered freedom of movement of the tumbleweed, but her wrath is as terrible as an unleashed tornado. It is easy to ask for help from the East Wind because it is generally benevolent unless angered. Stand facing the East, arms open wide, and say this:

> Eurana, merciful Lady of the East Wind, Mistress of clarity, I welcome you. Euros, Lord of freedom and rain, join me in this place. Direction of the Element Air, rejoice with me and assist me in succeeding in my new endeavor.

Magickal correspondences for the East Wind are early morning and the color white. It is represented in the tarot cards as the Star and the Fool. In the long version of the Wiccan Rede, the couplet concerning the East Wind reads:

> When the wind blows from the east,
> Expect the new and set the feast.

A Southern Gust of Wind

A Southern wind is the Wind of passion, love, excitement, and obsession. A hot, dry wind, Southern winds can help banish bad influences as well as attract new relationships and strengthen your resolve. If you have a bad habit you're trying to break or find yourself unable to get over an unhealthy obsession, facing a hot Southern breeze can take away those Spirit-crushing feelings.

Cauldron Bubble

Some winds are mischievous, snatching hats off people's heads and scattering your paper plates across the park. Let the wind mess up your hair now and then to satisfy this impish urge.

The God of the South Wind is Notus, the bringer of heat. His Lady is Nona, Mistress of ardor, dedication, and eagerness. She rules the winds of passion and love. She is the breeze that carries pollen to rejuvenate life as well as the bone-scourging Sirocco. Slightly flirtatious, the South Wind can be coaxed to help you if you ask with praise and gifts. Lay a few yellow flowers at your feet, stand facing the south, cross your arms across your chest as though embracing a loved one, and say:

> *Nona, beautiful Lady of the South Wind, Mistress of ardor, I welcome you. Notus, Lord of zeal and heat, join me in this place. Direction of the Element Fire, blow new companions toward me and help me banish all the negative relationships currently in my life.*

Magickal correspondences for the South Wind are the middle of the day and the color yellow. It is represented in the tarot cards as the Sun and Strength. In the long version of the Wiccan Rede, the couplet concerning the South Wind reads:

> *When the wind comes from the south,*
> *Love will kiss thee on the mouth.*

Gentle Westerly Zephyrs

A Western wind is the Wind of gentle healing, love, and fertility. A cool, moist wind, it can help bring you comfort in times of stress as it caresses your Spirit with healing fingers. During a West Wind, perform protection rituals or rituals to assist you in divination. If you feel tired, despondent, ill, or anxious, facing a West Wind can help you feel cared for and rejuvenated.

The God of the West Wind is Zephyrus, the bringer of gentle ways. His Lady is Zephrina. She offers protection during times of chaos, much like the eye of a hurricane exists within the storm. She carries the sounds of Nature on soft breezes and nourishes the seeds that replenish the Earth. The West Wind will, like a loving parent, willingly embrace you, so asking for help is barely a requirement—but the polite thing to do. Facing the west, stand with your hands facing palm up in front of you about waist high and say this:

> *Zephrina, gentle Lady of the West Wind, Mistress of protection, I welcome you. Zephyrus, Lord of comfort and warmth, join me in this place. Direction of the Element Water, strengthen my intuition and ease my damaged Spirit, that I might find peace.*

Cauldron Bubble

When it isn't too hot or too cold, sleep with the windows open and let the wind bring the night sounds and fragrances into your dreams. Embracing Wind in your everyday life will make it easier to call for the Goddess's help when you need it.

Magickal correspondences for the West Wind are the evening and the color blue. It is represented in the tarot cards as the Lovers and the Hermit. In the long version of the Wiccan Rede, the couplet concerning the West Wind reads:

> *When the West Wind blows o'er thee,*
> *Departed spirits restless be.*

Remember that these invocations are only suggestions of ways to call out to the Four Winds. Natural Magicians will find their own ways of talking to the Gods and Goddesses of the Directions. A ritual you write yourself carries your own special energy to join with the energy of the Deities. And, as always, if you feel a special connection to one direction, there is no reason you can't go to that God and Goddess for any help that you require.

Calling Up a Little Weather

Not every cloud holds a storm, but every cloud holds the essence of rain. Not every breeze that blows teaches us the lessons of the Wind, but the lessons are there if we seek to discover them. To successfully do Weather Magick, you must first learn all you can about weather patterns—prevailing winds, types of clouds (*stratus, cumulus, cirrus*), and weather patterns that precipitate storms. Remember this basic magickal tenet: Knowledge is power. Understanding a thing gives you the power to interact with it on a magickal level. A wise Natural Magician is a scholar first.

Magickal Bounty ___

Stratus clouds are horizontal, layered clouds that stretch out across the sky like a blanket. **Cumulus** clouds are puffy in appearance; they look like large cotton balls. **Cirrus** clouds are very wispy and feathery looking.

A great advantage you have when doing Weather Magick is that you have already experienced many forms of weather. Just living on this planet has probably exposed you to winds and rain and hail and snow, as well as thunder and lightning. If you can't call to mind some good, strong weather memories, you need to get back out there and feel the power of Mother Nature in her guise as Mother of Winds and Storms.

We do not advocate putting yourself in dangerous positions, however. Tornado chasing is for scientists and fools. You can stand under the eaves of a house or under a carport during a thunderstorm, though, and experience exhilaration as lightning flashes and thunder booms. If hail the size of golf balls is falling from the sky, watch it and listen to it from inside your home. You can get the idea and feel of the Air and the Earth Elements during a hailstorm just by standing in an open doorway when it's happening. If the hail is pea size or smaller, it's probably safe to put on a hat and boots and walk around outside listening to the hail as it hits the roofs and trees and crunches under foot. It's easy to connect to weather just by taking a walk. Pay special attention to what you're feeling, and don't let the Elements stop you. Buy a big (non-metal) umbrella and head out into the storm!

When you go out to expose yourself to different types of weather, remember that you are trying to experience everything you can about what is happening. How does it feel on your skin? What do you hear when it's happening? What does it look and smell like? How does it make you feel on an emotional level? You are going to want to re-create these feelings in your mind when you call the Wind or conjure storms.

Some people believe that influencing the weather is working against Nature and is unethical. We believe that we are an integral part of Nature. If we as Natural Magicians cause an effect and a change in the prevailing weather, that change was meant to be.

Influencing the Weather Through Meditation

From the ancient Egyptians to the twentieth-century Balkans, people have tried to influence the weather, usually to evoke rain and ensure an abundant harvest. Natural Magicians can do the same thing with meditation.

Examine your reasons for wanting to influence the weather, keeping in mind they shouldn't be frivolous or mean-spirited. If you just want to ruin the outdoor wedding to which you were not invited, don't do it! Not only will the Goddess ignore your request, but you might find all of your outdoor plans rained out for the next year.

> **Liguana's Grimoire**
>
> The Native American Hopi tribe still performs a traditional snake dance that originates from their earliest beliefs. The Hopi regard the snakes as their "brothers" and believe they will carry their prayers for rain to the under-world, where the gods and the spirits of their ancestors live.

Face the Wind direction based on what type of weather changes you're attempting to make. A North Wind most likely governs snow. A West Wind brings rain. A South Wind brings heat. And an East Wind clears away storm clouds.

Weather work is best done outdoors, if possible. Let's say you're eager for a little rain for your garden. Sit comfortably facing the West, close your eyes, and breathe slowly. Focus on the weather that surrounds you now. If it's sunny, concentrate on the sun's warmth on your skin. Feel the warm breeze ruffle through your hair.

When you feel ready, visualize in your mind's eye the change you want to make. Picture a bright blue sky slowly filling up with clouds. The clouds get bigger and darker. Hear the low rumble of thunder in the distance. Hold the picture in your mind as long as you can. You might even begin to "see" the rain falling.

Once you are satisfied that your request has been heard, think about coming back into the present. When you are fully back into the moment, thank the Goddess for listening—and keep your umbrella handy.

If it's raining and you want to bring out the sunshine, just reverse the process. Picture the clouds leaving one by one until there is nothing but bright blue sky above your head. Eager for snow? Visualize a dark winter sky and large fluffy flakes drifting down to Earth. You get the idea.

> **Stir Gently …!**
>
> Remember that you cannot bend Nature to your Will. Unless your purpose is to "recharge" the spell, don't keep repeating the meditation until the weather changes, or you could be calling up floods or droughts or blizzards. Ask once and let Nature take it under consideration. If it doesn't change, it isn't meant to.

Liguana's Weather Rituals

Liguana has conjured storms, but only twice and only when it was already cloudy. She visualized the clouds rolling closer and getting darker. She felt the wind and rain before it occurred because she brought up a strong memory, so strong she could feel it. Body and mind were aligned to accept the effect. When she felt this happen, she reached down into the Earth with her consciousness, first feeling herself grounded, then feeling Earth energy pulled up and flowing through her body and into the ether. With this flow, she poured forth thought and memory of storm. Concentrating on the intention and the feel of storm, she built up a feeling of pressure; when it seemed it could no longer be contained, she released the storm energy flow into the air. After that was done, she grounded excess energy and tried very hard to think of other things, not the storm she was calling. In this way, she cast a spell, totally releasing it to cause an effect. When all that was done, she had but to wait and watch for the dark clouds and the lightning to appear, just as envisioned.

What Liguana has done a lot of is parting clouds and keeping the rain at bay. First, she grounds and centers herself. Then she opens to Spirit, going into a light trance state. She pulls energy up through her body, lifting her arms above her head. Visualizing the clouds overhead, she sees herself reaching hands into the vapors, spreading them apart and opening an area large enough to see clear sky through. She keeps pushing clouds outward and widening the opening until she can visualize the clouds widening on their own. Usually she finds this is best done a week before the clearing is needed and then reinforced several times. It is helpful at some time in the visualization process to also imagine and visualize the place where you want the weather to be nice.

Liguana's Grimoire

Liguana has been called upon twice to ensure clear weather for her local lantern festival. Last year it rained three days before the festival and two days after the festival. It rained the morning of the festival, too, but when it was time for fire and lanterns, the sky was clear and the stars were brilliant. The event coordinator credited her in a video he made of the event: "Weather by Liguana."

Food for the Wind: Spicy Popcorn

"Wind food" is, of course, light and airy. Popcorn is the perfect Wind treat. Although you can use microwave popcorn, a Natural Wizard would most likely use "real" kernels popped in vegetable oil to avoid eating all the chemicals added to the microwave varieties. Remember, eat as close to the Earth as possible, to more easily connect to its energy.

> 3 TB. vegetable oil
>
> 1 tsp. cumin
>
> ½ tsp. cayenne pepper
>
> 1 tsp. chili powder
>
> ¼ tsp. cinnamon
>
> ½ cup popcorn kernels
>
> Salt

Heat oil in a large, heavy pot over medium-high heat and stir in spices. Add one kernel to the pan and cover. When the kernel pops, pour in the remaining kernels. Shake the pan until popping ends. Season with salt and serve immediately. This recipe will add passion to a relationship and enthusiasm to a family gathering, and is a good recipe for attracting the Lady of the South Wind.

This recipe doesn't work as well with air-popped popcorn because the spices don't stick to the dry kernels. If you prefer air-popped popcorn, try spreading it out on a cookie sheet and spraying it lightly with butter-flavored cooking spray before tossing on the spices.

Following are two variations of this recipe. For confidence, joy, and new beginnings, celebrate with this spice combination:

> ½ tsp. curry powder
>
> ½ tsp. garam masala (available in Asian markets or most health-food stores)
>
> ¼ tsp. ground turmeric
>
> ¼ tsp. black pepper

For protection and added wealth, substitute these spices in the basic recipe:

> ½ tsp. basil
>
> ½ tsp. rosemary
>
> ½ tsp. dill
>
> ¼ tsp. lemon pepper

Experiment with your own combination of spices, depending on your tastes and the results you are looking for in your spellcrafting.

Some Other Windy Traditions

People down through the ages have celebrated and worshipped Wind in literally thousands of ways. It is especially a tradition in many Native American cultures. The Incas, Hopi, Choctaw, Shawnee—all of them include the Wind Spirits in their spiritual beliefs. We haven't time to explore them all fully, but the Navajo beliefs will help give you an idea of Sacred Wind in other Nature-based religions.

The Navajo word for Wind is Nítch'i, although that translation does not fully cover what the word means to them. Nítch'i refers to the air, the atmosphere in its entirety, when still and when in motion. It is considered holy, with powers that are not acknowledged by European-based cultures. The term most closely relates to the Christian concept of Holy Spirit.

Liguana's Grimoire

A Medicine Wheel is an ancient place of prayer sacred to Native Americans, symbolizing the totality of existence. The traditional design of the Medicine Wheel uses six colors: yellow, white, black, red, green, and blue. The first four colors symbolize the four directions: East (yellow nation, Earth, food, heart), South (white nation, Fire, mind, respect), West (black nation, Water, trust, honesty), and North (red nation, Wind, patience, endurance, courage).

Because Wind permeates all of nature, it is responsible for giving life, thought, speech, and the power of motion to all living things. Wind is also the means of communication between all Elements of the living world. It sits on the tip of your tongue, allowing speech. It whispers into the ears of the Navajo people, advising them on the proper actions. Those who repeatedly ignore its advice are abandoned by the Spirits.

Rather than being isolated within each individual, like the Western notion of the soul, Holy Wind is a single entity that exists everywhere and in which all living creatures participate. This means that all living beings are related and that nothing exists in isolation. Furthermore, the act of breathing is believed to be a sacred act through which the individual participates in an ongoing relationship with all other living things. Thus, by breathing, one has direct access to the thought and speech of the Spirits and the animal world, as well as every other human.

As we said earlier, the Gods and Goddesses of the Four Winds can be powerful allies if you approach them with reverence and humility. Call out to the Winds in your time of need and let your words be carried to them on a current of Air.

The Least You Need to Know

- The Four Winds signify the directions, with each direction linked to one of the Elements: Air, Fire, Water, Earth.

- Get to know the Four Winds so that you can call on the appropriate God and Goddess when it's time.

- A Natural Magician never attempts to influence the weather for trivial or vengeful reasons.

- People have been holding the Wind sacred for centuries, and it is an essential part of many Native American spiritual beliefs.

Chapter 12

Sun Shine

In This Chapter

- The history of Sun worship
- Celebrating the solar cycle
- Magickal Sun correspondence
- Sun rituals for some daily magick
- Herbs in a recipe to honor the Sun

The Sun, the bringer of light, heat, and fire, is crucial for life on Earth. Without the Sun, there would be no plants or animals, life would perish rapidly, and existence would end. It is, therefore, not surprising that many human cultures have worshipped the Sun, acknowledging its importance and magnificent power.

On the physical plane, the Sun can lift our spirits, tease open the budding trees and flowers, and encourage our fruits and vegetables to grow. On a spiritual plane, the Sun is perhaps the most powerful Deity of all. It is no wonder that hundreds of songs and poems in all languages celebrate the Sun.

Here Comes the Sun

Throughout the thousands of religions around the world, the Sun has been depicted as a range of entities, from the eyes of a giant in Chinese mythology, to sparks of fire tossed into the air, according to the Norse belief. More often, however, the Sun is personified as a god.

Frequently, the Sun is associated with masculine qualities, or yang, whereas the Moon is portrayed as a woman. However, there are exceptions. The oldest Japanese religion, Shintoism, tells us that the Sun is female, the shy but extraordinarily beautiful Sun goddess Amaterasu.

The ancient Egyptians, renowned for their Sun worship, knew the Sun as their chief god, Ra, who rides across the sky in a boat called Sektet and is often represented by the hawk. During his trip across the sky, Ra has to defeat his chief enemy, a serpent or snake named Apep. A great battle is fought daily between Ra and Apep, and Ra is usually victorious. However, on stormy days or during an eclipse, the Egyptians believed that Apep was victorious and swallowed the Sun.

Both the Greeks and the Romans believed in the Sun god Apollo, who rode across the sky on a fiery chariot drawn by wild horses. Apollo, also the god of love, hunting, and music, was said to be favored among women for his handsome features and immortal strength.

Strikingly similar to Apollo is Tsohanoai, the god of the Sun to the Navajo tribe. Tsohanoai is said to carry the Sun on his back and hang it on the west wall of his house before unraveling the dark rug of Night. The Incas believed in the Sun god Inti. Inti was depicted as a formidable face surrounded by blazing rays. The Aztecs, a tribe similar to the Incas in many ways, told that the Sun was home to the great god Quetzalcoatl and moved in his breath.

> **Liguana's Grimoire**
>
> Although no one knows for certain, Stonehenge, the world-famous megalithic monument in Wiltshire, England, was most likely erected to honor the Sun.

The Sun and its various deities are usually attributed with positive forces such as goodness, love, warmth, and joy.

Today many cultures still honor the Sun in some form. During special occasions, the Amazon Indians wear headdresses made from feathers that represent the Sun's rays. The written religious traditions also honor the light and fire brought by the Sun. Christianity and Judaism speak of "the Light of God," and candles are lit to represent God's divine presence. Hinduism describes the Fire god Agnee and celebrates the Festival of Light, while in Buddhism, fire is regarded as a sacred and purifying element.

The Season of the Witch

In Natural Magick, Wicca, and other pagan religions, we celebrate the natural cycle of the solar year through ritual, thus attuning ourselves to Nature and the Divine that is inherent in all things. The God archetype changes during the course of a year, and learning to tap into his changing roles and power can give Natural Magicians more power themselves.

December

Around December 21, pagans celebrate the Winter Solstice, Wiccans celebrate Yule, and Christians and Jews prepare for Christmas and Hanukah. All four holidays represent the rebirth of light. We light advent wreaths and menorahs and luminaries. Here, on the longest night of the year, the Goddess gives birth to the Sun Child, and hope for new light is reborn. This is the time to awaken to new goals (New Year resolutions, for example) and to leave behind old regrets.

February

February 2 is Candlemas, Imbolic, or Groundhog Day. These celebrations involve banishing the winter and looking forward to spring. At this time, the newborn Sun God is seen as a small child nursing from his Mother. It is traditional at Candlemas to light every lamp or candle in the house for a few minutes, in honor of the Sun's rebirth. We search for the Sun God in the groundhog's shadow and patiently wait for spring.

March

Around March 21, pagans celebrate the Spring *Equinox*, Wiccans plan for Ostara, and Christians prepare for Easter. This is the point of equilibrium—the balance is suspended just before spring bursts forth from winter. The Sun God and his Goddess are young children at play, and holiday festivals use brightly colored eggs to represent the child within. This is the time for rituals that free you from anything in the past that is holding you back.

> **Magickal Bounty**
>
> The word **equinox** is derived from the Latin term *aequinoctium*, which, in turn, came from *aequus* (equal) and *nox* (night). It refers to the time that occurs twice a year when the nighttime is equal to the daytime—each being 12 hours long.

April

On April 30, Wiccans celebrate the sacred marriage of the young Sun God and Goddess with Beltane. And, of course, the pagan holiday May Day follows after. Beltane honors the fertility of the Earth, the divine union of the Lord and Lady. Celebrations include weaving a web of life around the Maypole and leaping the Beltane fire for luck. This is a time of self-discovery, love, and union, as well as developing your potential for personal growth.

Liguana's Grimoire

Shakespeare may have been the first writer to portray the faerie folk as tiny or cute in his play *A Midsummer Night's Dream*. Many of the playwright's contemporaries, including Samuel Pepys, found the play ridiculous, bordering on the occult. Maybe he'd never seen a faerie!

June

Around June 21 is Midsummer or the Summer Solstice. This is the longest day of the year, a time of triumph for the light. This holiday represents the Sun King in all of his glory. In many Wiccan celebrations, this is when the Oak King, who represents the waxing year, is triumphed over by the Holly King, who represents the waning year. The two are one: the Oak King is the growing youth, while the Holly King is the mature man. Healings and love magick are especially suitable at this time. Midsummer Night's Eve is a good time to commune with field and forest sprites and faeries (see Chapter 15).

August

Lammas on August 2 is the celebration of the first fruits of the harvest. The Sun King, now the Dark Lord, gives his energy to the crops to ensure life, while the Goddess prepares to give way to her aspect as the Crone. Now is the time to teach what you have learned, to share the fruits of your achievements with the world. Fruits and vegetables are canned and frozen, bread is baked, and grains are harvested.

September

At the Autumn Equinox, around September 21 (or Mabon, as Wiccans call it), the days and nights are again equal. It is a time of balance, but light gives way to increased darkness. It is the second harvest, and the Goddess mourns her fallen Sun God as he dies. But the emphasis is on the message of rebirth that can be found in the harvest seeds. It is a good time to walk the forests, wildcrafting dried plants for use in rituals or to gather herbs for herbal magick (See Chapter 10).

October

Samhain, October 31, or Halloween, is said to be the time when the veil between the worlds is very thin, when souls that are leaving this physical plane can pass out and souls that are reincarnating can pass in. Darkness increases and the Goddess reigns as the Crone while the God, the Dark Lord, passes into the underworld to become the seed of his own rebirth (which will occur again at Yule). Many Pagans prepare a Feast for the Dead on Samhain night, when they leave offerings of food and drink for the spirits. Divination is heightened at this time.

Identifying Samhain as the celebration of a Celtic Death God is one of the most persistent errors associated with Halloween. No such God ever existed. Samhain is the day when Wiccans believe that their God dies, later to be reborn. Thus, Samhain is not *a God of death*; it is actually a yearly observance of *the death of a God*.

Sun Correspondences

Channeling the Sun in his various aspects is invigorating and energizing. A Natural Magician can draw closer to the Sun God by using herbs and crystals sacred to him during meditation and in spellcrafting and cooking. Use this table as a guideline in selecting what to use for the season's Sun cycle.

Sun Cycle	Crystals	Herbs and Flowers
Samhain: The Dark Lord enters the underworld.	Obsidian, black onyx, bloodstone, amethyst, opal	Bay leaf, lavender, nutmeg, sage
Yule: The Sun God is born.	Quartz, blue sunstone, emerald, ruby, sapphire	Chamomile, rosemary, ginger, sage, cinnamon, mistletoe
Candlemas: The Sun God is a nursing infant.	Quartz, opal, moonstone, aventurine, sunstone	Angelica, basil, bay leaves, myrrh

continues

continued

Sun Cycle	Crystals	Herbs and Flowers
Ostara: The Sun God is a small child.	Moss agate, green moonstone, orange calcite, rose quartz	Jasmine, rose, violet
Beltane: The Sun God is a young groom marrying the Goddess.	Quartz, sunstone, orange calcite, malachite	Frankincense, lemon balm, lemon thyme, saffron
Midsummer: The Sun God reigns supreme.	Amethyst, malachite, golden topaz, opal, quartz, azurite-malachite, lapis lazuli, diamonds	St. John's wort, chamomile, lavender, trefoil, vervain
Lammas: The Sun God becomes the Dark Lord and becomes an old man.	Tiger-eye, golden topaz, opal, citrine, ametrine	All herbs and grains
Mabon: The Dark Lord lays dying.	Amber, quartz, tiger-eye, citrine	Myrrh, hibiscus, marigold, sunflowers, rose petals

Splendid in recipes, herbs can be used in all kinds of spellcrafting. Creating a rosemary wreath for the doorway, for example, gives protection to a home and honors the masculine aspect of the Divine. Or hang crystals in a sunny window to draw the Sun's energy into the home.

Sun God Rituals

This ritual is the counterpart to the Drawing Down the Moon ritual, which is perhaps better known (see Chapter 13). It is used to bring the participants closer to the essence of the Sun Deity, especially at the Solar Festivals, and to replenish the energies of those present. Drawing Down the Sun is a way to connect with the masculine energies of the Deity to enhance your life.

Ideally, the ritual is performed outside during full sunlight. You might light some incense—frankincense is a good choice because it is sacred to the Sun. Frankincense is a golden resin that has been used throughout the ages to honor and attract the attention of the male aspect of the universe. Many masculine gods have been so honored. Frankincense has a bright, sweet smell. Magickally, it is used to dispel negativity, purify an area, and promote meditative focus. It is also used to consecrate magickal tools by bathing them in the smoke of the melting resin.

Stand with your arms folded across your chest, hands on opposite shoulders. Ground and center yourself, letting your feet tap into the fiery energy of the Earth's core. Pull that energy up and feel it rushing to the top of your head. Now visualize the power of the Sun God entering your head and filling you down to your toes, combining with the energy surging through your body. Breathe deeply and let the warmth of the Sun wash over you until the feeling of being replenished within fills your Spirit.

Hold the feeling as long as you can, and then release the energy, letting the excess drain away back into the earth. This is a great ritual when you have to face a long day ahead or are feeling drained of your own energy.

Greeting the Dawn

The yearly solar cycle dictates greeting the newborn Lord at Yule, but you can greet him daily with a dawn ritual to charge your inner battery for the day. It is important to know exactly what time sunrise is where you live. You want to start this ritual about 10 minutes earlier, when the world is still dark.

Stand facing the east, preferably where you can see an uncluttered horizon. You might bring gifts for the "newly born" Sun. Place on an altar or on the ground in front of you any combination of the stones and herbs that are sacred to the Lord from our chart. You might present them in a cornucopia, which is often used as a God symbol. Add any other God symbols you like—an athame, for example.

Take a quartz crystal with you, and let the first rays of the morning Sun reflect off your crystal and into your eyes. Feel and see the intensity of the light. This is energy of a very high vibration. In as many ways as you can, experience

Liguana's Grimoire
The tale of the cornucopia is originally Greek. The infant god Zeus was nursed by a she-goat named Amalthea. In his exuberance one day, Zeus pulled off one of his nursemaid's horns. She became upset about this until the young god made the horn grow large and filled it with Earth's bounty, promising that it would be a horn of plenty that would always be full of fruits and vegetables of the harvest.

the sunrise. Listen for the morning sounds. Feel the temperature change as the Sun climbs higher into the sky. See the colors in the sky. The object is to learn and experience so much about the sunlight that you almost feel you are a fragment of that energy. You are.

If the mood strikes you, add an incantation:

From stroke of dawn
'Til setting Sun,
Be with me, Lord,
As though we're one.

Give me strength,
Stay by my side.
Oh, sacred Sun,
With me abide.

Greeting the morning Sun is an excellent thing to do with an animal familiar. Our animal allies are often more attuned to the patterns of nature than we are and can act as guides. A cat, for instance, will find a sunbeam coming through a window and bathe in the warmth and the glow. A practitioner of Natural Magick should know to do the same whenever opportunity arises.

Sunset Meditation

Sunset is a great time to take a few minutes to reflect on your day and to wish the Sun well in its journey to the East. Take your Natural Magick Journal with you outside and find a comfortable place to sit facing west. Again, try to find an uncluttered view of the sunset, if you can. Begin this reverie about 15 minutes before the Sun goes down so you still have some light.

Think over the magickal moments of your day. Jot down the ones that seem worth holding on to. Remember, our "failed" magickal attempts are sometimes as important to remember as our successes. This is also a good time to note one or two things you are especially thankful for, and one or two things Nature gave you to enjoy during the day.

Cauldron Bubble

Start a journal dedicated only to your Natural Magick endeavors. Make entries about your meditations, dreams, rituals, recipes, parties, and festivals. Make notes of your efforts that worked, as well as experiments that didn't turn out so well. Looking back over it from time to time, you will be able to see your growth in the practice.

Connecting to these moments and actually writing them down can help dispel the stress and negativity of the mundane world and reconnect you to the peace and tranquility of Nature's Spirit.

As the Sun slips below the horizon, let yourself be fully in the moment. Note the deep reds and purples in the sky. Feel the evening breeze pick up. Watch the shadows lengthen and then disappear as the stars come out. Breathe in and out slowly and deeply.

Now, even if you have to go back inside to do the dishes, you should feel relaxed and ready for mundane chores.

Food of the Sun God: Herb and Tomato Pizza

A lot of foods honor the God, but for something different, try a fresh herb-and-tomato pizza using some of the flavors sacred to the Sun. Making your own whole-grain crust ensures that it will be fresh and healthful. This recipe makes four thin-crust 8- to 10-inch pizzas.

For the pizza crust:

> ¼ ounces (2 tsp.) dry yeast
>
> 1⅓ cups lukewarm water
>
> ¼ cup whole-wheat flour
>
> 3½ cups all-purpose flour
>
> 2 tsp. salt
>
> 2 tsp. sugar
>
> 2 tsp. olive oil

Mix the dry yeast with ⅓ cup of warm water and set aside. In a large bowl, combine the whole-wheat flour, ½ cup of the all-purpose flour, salt, and sugar. Add the dissolved yeast and the remaining 1 cup water. Beat with an electric mixer on high for 2 or 3 minutes. With the mixer on low speed, gradually add in the olive oil and beat until well blended. With a large spoon, stir in enough of the remaining flour to create a soft dough that holds together and pulls away from the sides of the bowl. It will be sticky!

Cauldron Bubble

Adding 2 teaspoons of wheat germ to the dry ingredients not only pumps up the vitamins in this dough, but it is an additional homage to the Lord because all grains are sacred to him.

Turn out the dough onto a well-floured surface, and knead until smooth and elastic, adding more flour as needed. However, do not add more than the total 3½ cups called for. Too much flour creates a heavy, chewy dough rather than the crisp pizza crust you're trying to attain.

Place the dough in a large, lightly greased bowl, cover with a damp cloth, and place in a warm spot to rise. Let it rise until doubled in bulk, about two hours.

To roll out the dough, separate into four equal pieces. Cover your fingers with flour, and then place a ball on a generously floured work surface. Press down on the center of the ball with the tips of your fingers, simultaneously stretching the dough with your hands. When the dough has doubled in width, use a floured rolling pin to roll out the dough until it is very thin. The outer border should be slightly thicker than the center. Transfer the dough to your pizza pan or cookie sheet. The dough may not be perfectly round. Don't worry about it—some famous chefs agree, "Never trust a perfectly round pizza." If any holes have appeared, just pinch them closed. Repeat with the remaining balls.

To assemble the pizza:

For a lighter alternative to the usual sauce-and-cheese pizza, slice one ripe tomato into very thin slices and lay the rounds on top of the crust. Chop ⅛ cup each fresh rosemary, basil, and lemon thyme, and sprinkle them evenly over the tomatoes.

You may, of course, use dried herbs in place of fresh and substitute any combination of herbs that strikes your fancy. Sprinkle on a few sesame seeds and cracked black pepper to taste.

Bake in a 425°F oven until the crust is lightly browned—12 to 15 minutes.

If you don't want to assemble all of the pizzas, bake the crusts without toppings and freeze them for later use.

The Sun gives the vital spark of life to all living things. It is a powerful Deity that we can use to re-energize our bodies and our Spirits. Plus, a little Sun worshipping gives you a great reason to be outside enjoying Nature!

The Least You Need to Know

- The Sun God literally gives life to Earth and all of its inhabitants.

- Sun worshippers are found in nearly every culture, dating back centuries. Usually the Sun is depicted with masculine yang energy, but sometimes, as in the csase of Japanese, goddess Amaterasu, the Sun expresses the feminine.

- Natural Magicians celebrate the solar cycle of the year and the various aspects of the Lord in each season.

- Rituals at sunrise and sunset honor the daily birth and death of the Light, which mirrors the larger, seasonal birth and death of the Lord.

Full Moon Glow

In This Chapter

- The history of Moon worship
- Rituals during the Full Moon
- What is a Blue Moon?
- Crystal and stone Moon magick
- Celebrations of the Full Moon
- Sacred Moon herbs

Famous in song and poetry, the Moon has captured our imaginations since before recorded time. On the physical plane, the Moon doesn't have a strong impact on us. A Full Moon affects the tides, and some people reason that because our bodies are made up largely of water, it pulls on us, too. But it isn't life giving in the same way the Sun is. It has, however, sparked our imaginations, tickled our romantic urges, and been the subject of some of our best myths and folktales.

On the spiritual plane, it is a powerful ally to a Natural Magician. Timing your spells and rituals to coincide with the phases of the Moon creates a natural energy that enhances your own Natural Magick.

By the Light of the Silvery Moon

Worshipping the Moon has been practiced since earliest recorded time. It is mentioned in the oldest literatures of Egypt, Africa, Babylonia, India, and China, among others. Moon worship is founded on the belief that the phases of the Moon and the growth and decline of plant, animal, and human life are related. In some societies, food is laid out at night to absorb the rays of the Moon, which are thought to have power to cure disease and prolong life. In some central African tribes it is customary for a mother to bathe her newborn child by the light of the first Full Moon. The Moon is frequently equated with wisdom and justice, as in the worship of the Egyptian god Thoth and the Mesopotamian god Sin. The Moon god Sin is usually depicted as an old man with a long beard. His emblem is the crescent Moon—sometimes represented as a boat or the horns of a bull. Mount Sinai is named for him.

However, for a time, the Moon was believed to exude evil into the world. One commonly held superstition was that the Full Moon could make a person insane—hence the word *lunatic* from *luna*, the Latin word for the Moon. Nights of a Full Moon were supposed to be extremely unlucky because hellish beasts and demons such as werewolves drew their sinister powers from its dark energy. Today, however, she is back in favor, with many pagans and Wiccans honoring her and asking for her assistance in rituals.

Liguana's Grimoire
The Inuit peoples, whose homeland stretches from the northeastern tip of Russia across Alaska and northern Canada to parts of Greenland, create spiritual masks from wood depicting the woman in the Moon to use in rituals and festivals.

In some cultural traditions, the Moon is considered masculine, which may be where we get our legend of "The Man in the Moon." In an old Lithuanian legend, when the young maiden is asked about her parents, she replies, "My mother is the beauteous Sun, and my father the bright Moon." For most Natural Magicians, though, the Full Moon is the embodiment of the Goddess; she is Maiden, Mother, and Crone. She is the yin balance of the Source of All.

Full Moon Rituals

The Full Moon each month is a particularly potent magickal ally. Some of your best magick can be created under her influence and with her guidance. Although there is only one night every month on which the Moon is totally full, a Natural Magician knows that two days before and two days after the Full Moon are also good times for magickal endeavors. Use this chart to guide your spellcrafting.

Full Moon Magick

Month	Good For ...
January—Wolf Moon	Spells involving organization, ambition, career, politics; healing for the knees, bones, teeth, skin
February—Ice Moon	Spells involving science, freedom, friendship, breaking bad habits or addictions; healing for the calves, ankles, blood
March—Crow Moon	Spells involving music, art, telepathy, dreams; healing for the feet and lymph glands
April—Planter's Moon	Spells involving authority, rebirth, leadership; healing for the face and head
May—Flower Moon	Spells involving love, money, acquisition; healing for the throat and neck
June—Strawberry Moon	Spells involving communication, writing, travel; healing for the arms, hands, and lungs
July—Blood Moon	Spells involving the home and for honoring lunar gods and goddesses; healing for the chest and stomach
August—Corn Moon	Spells involving authority, courage, fertility; healing for the upper back, spine, heart
September—Harvest Moon	Spells involving employment, health, diet; healing for the intestines and nervous system
October—Hunter's Moon	Spells involving justice, unions, balance (spiritual and otherwise), artistry; healing for the lower back and kidneys

continues

Full Moon Magick (continued)

Month	Good For ...
November—Snow Moon	Spells involving power, psychic growth, sex; healing for the reproductive organs
December—Cold Moon	Spells involving travel, sports, truth, animals; healing for the liver and thighs

It is very likely that you will find different names for each month's Full Moon, depending on which source and traditions you use. It really makes no difference what you call the Full Moon; these correspondences still apply. And of course, you don't have to wait for the "correct" Full Moon. These guidelines just help add the appropriate Goddess energy to your own natural energies to meet your desires.

Drawing Down the Moon

This ritual is a common one among Wiccans and should be part of a Natural Magician's repertoire as well. It is a way of drawing Moon energy into yourself and connecting with the divine. There are as many ways to perform this ritual as there are Natural Magicians. Here is one way.

Go outside during a Full Moon and stand or sit quietly for a few minutes until you feel the Moon energy vibrating all around you. You might want to place a mirror in front of you to reflect the moonlight, but it isn't required. Welcome the Goddess into your Spirit and say something like the following:

> *Mother Moon both strong and bright*
> *Fill me up with Goddess light.*

When you feel full of the Moon's power, the ritual is complete.

Spells to Cast Once in a Blue Moon

Just what is a Blue Moon? There are two definitions for a Blue Moon. According to the more recent definition, a Blue Moon is the second Full Moon in a calendar month. For a Blue Moon to occur, the first of the Full Moons must appear at or near the beginning of the month so that the second will fall within the same month (the average span between two moons is 28 days). That second one is called a Blue Moon.

An older definition for the Blue Moon is recorded in early issues of the *Maine Farmer's Almanac*. Between 1932 and 1957, instead of the calendar year running from January 1 through December 31, the almanac relied on the tropical year, defined as extending from one winter solstice ("Yule") to the next. Most tropical years contain 12 Full Moons—3 each in winter, spring, summer, and fall—and, as in the previous chart, each is named for an activity appropriate to the time of year. But occasionally a tropical year contains 13 Full Moons so that one season has 4 Moons rather than the usual 3. That fourth Moon of the season is the Blue Moon.

Liguana's Grimoire

Liguana's daughter Shaleina was born just after a Full Moon. On the next Full Moon, her aunt, her grandmother, and her great-grandmother gathered in a circle of women to hold her up in the moonlight and speak their blessings for her and call her by name. They asked the blessings of Grandmother Moon. When Shaleina's own grandmother held her, she looked at her and said, "Hello, Sheina." The birth certificate says Shaleina, but the Moon knows her other name as well.

Many Natural Magicians regard a Blue Moon as a special gift from the Goddess and look upon it as a good time to set new goals for themselves. Write your goals on a piece of paper, fold the paper in half, and place it the light of the Full Moon. Ask the Goddess for the strength and endurance to work toward your goals successfully. In the morning, burn the paper in the flame of a candle you have anointed with an oil you especially enjoy. The smoke will help carry your goals to the ears of the Goddess. Your resolve to get started on them will amaze you.

Moon Magick Crystals and Stones

Crystal or stone magick is a very simple and inexpensive way to perform Natural Magick. Stones and their wonderful spirits are all around us. When charged with Full Moon glow, they are even more powerful. It is simple to charge a crystal with Moon glow energy: Simply clean it and place it in full moonlight overnight. You can actually begin the ritual the night before the official Full Moon and leave it until the day after the Full Moon. This three-day ritual represents the three aspects of the Goddess: Maiden, Mother, Crone.

Gem Water to Raise Psychic Abilities

Spells to strengthen divination and psychic abilities can also be cast at Full Moon time. One way to do this is by brewing up a little gem water. Any clear crystal can be used for this spell. Clear quartz and clear topaz, for example, are both good for this ritual.

> **CAUTION**
>
> **Stir Gently ...!**
>
> On the day you sip the gem water, avoid caffeine, alcohol, cigarettes—anything that disrupts your own natural energies. Pure of body, pure of mind!

First, clean and charge your crystal. Hold the crystal in your right hand and visualize the energy from your body flowing into the crystal, filling it with your essence. Next, place the crystal in a clean glass jar with a lid. Fill the jar with spring or distilled water, and place it overnight in the light of the Full Moon. This gem water can be sipped slowly throughout the day to heighten your connection to the All and its powers. Use it up within three days, though, or it loses its potency.

Healing Moonstones

Like the Full Moon illuminating an otherwise dark path, moonstones bring a sense of comfort in fearful times. They are healing stones, and their energy assists in the healing arts that work on the body's etheric self. These are stones that prefer not to change hands too often. It's best to make a lifelong connection with a moonstone, if you can. If it works well with your energies, it should stay with you. If it doesn't, pass it on and look for another moonstone to connect with.

Indian Astrology Is "By the Moon"

In Indian astrology, the Moon is the signifier of the mind. Because the Moon is the heavenly body closest to the Earth, Indians believe that the magnetic influences of all other planets reach Earth through the Moon.

Also, because the mind is ruled by the Moon, all influences on a person, whether physical, mental, psychological or supernatural, affect the human mind. The body is ruled by the Sun. Because the body may or may not respond to the mental, psychological, or supernatural influences, in India, horoscopes are based on your Moon sign, not your Sun sign, which is traditionally used in the Western Zodiac.

Moon Festivals Today

Many cultures still celebrate the Full Moon with festivals and revelry. In South Korea, for example, the first Full Moon of the Lunar New Year is called Daeboreum, and the first day of the first Full Moon (Taeborum) is celebrated. Celebrants spin fire cans at night whose fiery paths create a Full Moon circle in the darkness. Children spin Catherine Wheels, a circular firework made of wood chips and straw. The traditional belief holds that if people wish upon the Full Moon that day, their wishes will be granted.

> ### Liguana's Grimoire
>
> The name Catherine's Wheel is applied to devices from many disciplines. Fireworks, electrical apparatus, and others have Catherine's Wheels. Basically, this is a circular object that spins. A legendary Christian martyr of the fourth century, Catherine of Alexandria protested against the worship of idols. Emperor Maxentius had her tortured on a wheel and beheaded. She is often pictured with a spiked wheel and a book.

Taeborum is the time to perform rites averting disasters and bad luck. The typical dishes eaten at this festival include five-grain rice—a mixture of steamed rice, Indian millet, red beans, millet, and black beans—and sweet rice—a combination of dried vegetables such as fern braken, radish leaves, pumpkin leaves, eggplant, and mushrooms seasoned with sesame oil and various spices, and nuts. It is said that if at dawn on Taeborum you eat walnuts, chestnuts, and peanuts while praying for good health, all bad spirits will be frightened away.

Full Moon Celebrations: Sweet Rice Balls

Whether you're celebrating Taeborum or another Full Moon, you can serve this sweet treat to symbolize the Moon Goddess. These are very sweet little balls of rice, fruit, and nuts. The round shape symbolizes the Full Moon above, and the cinnamon and nuts attract wealth and prosperity. Rice is generally considered a fertility grain, which is why we still use the pagan tradition of throwing rice at newly married couples; it encourages a long and fruitful marriage. The success of this recipe depends on using only sticky or sweet rice, no substitutes, with the right amount of water.

5 cups sticky rice (also called sweet rice)

4 cups water

15 chestnuts, peeled and chopped (or substitute ¾ cup chopped hazelnuts or walnuts)

5 dates, pitted and chopped

¼ cup pine nuts

1¼ cups brown sugar

1 tsp. caramel sauce

¼ cup soy sauce

1 TB. sesame oil

½ tsp. ground cinnamon

Soak the sticky rice in the water for 4 to 6 hours. Rinse the rice, stirring it through your fingers until the water is clear, not milky.

Put the rice and the rest of the ingredients into a large, heavy pot, mixing well. Add just enough fresh, cold water to cover the top of the rice by about ¾ of an inch. An easy way to measure the water is to use the knuckle test—the water should come up to the first joint of your knuckle. The trick here is to steam the rice during the final cooking phase, not boil it as in traditional Western recipes.

Bring the water to a light boil uncovered. Turn the heat to the lowest setting, cover, and simmer until the rice is cooked through, 15 to 20 minutes. Remove from heat and let the rice sit covered for an additional 10 minutes.

Let the mixture cool slightly and then form into small balls. This recipe will make approximately three dozen rice balls, depending on how large you make them.

Other Moon Celebrations

Many Chinese-Americans still celebrate the Moon festival on the fifteenth day of the eighth month of the lunar calendar when the Moon is full. San Francisco's Chinatown, led by the Chinatown Merchants Association, holds a celebration each year. The Chinese Moon festival tradition dates back thousands of years.

In Chinese celestial cosmology, the Moon represents the female principle, or yin. During ancient autumn Moon festivals, women took center stage because the Moon is considered feminine. Only women took part in Moon festival rituals on the night of the Full Moon. Altars would be set up in households, and when the Full Moon appeared, women would make offerings of incense, candles, fruit, flowers, and Moon cakes.

Cauldron Bubble

To find Full Moon festivals near you, check with local Chambers of Commerce in cities around you. Or just throw your own backyard Moon party. Build a bonfire and serve foods that are seasoned with spices and herbs sacred to the Moon.

Connect with Moon Energy Through Scrying

Scrying is a method of opening the mind to voices and images from other realms. Full Moon scrying is best done outside in sight of the Moon. A black shiny surface is required, so a bowl or plate that has a black glaze, or a large piece of black obsidian is ideal.

Position yourself comfortably where the moonlight reflects on your dark surface. Look closely at your bowl, stone, or plate. It's okay to let your mind wander. Scrying is designed to elicit daydreams and bring forth your subconscious thoughts. Try not to intellectualize what you are doing, seeing, or thinking about. Just look into the Moon glow reflection and let the ideas and images flow. It's a good idea to keep a scrying journal, keeping track of the date and what sign the Moon was in, as well as anything you may have seen, heard, or thought during the exercise. Remember, scrying takes practice. Make it a monthly journey to other realms.

Magickal Bounty

Scrying is the name given to the ancient technique of gazing into an object such as a crystal ball for the purposes of divination. You can also achieve visions from gazing into flames, mirrors, a shallow bowl of water, a black stone, or even black ink.

Bathe Yourself in a Moonlit Rainbow

This is another way to experience Moon energy. Most of us have experienced rainbows during the day, either through sunlight shining through moisture in the air, or

Magickal Bounty

A **prism** is a triangular piece of glass or plastic. To get it to produce a mini rainbow, you allow a narrow strip of white light to fall on one face of the triangle. The light bends inside the prism and comes out on the other side as a spectrum of red, orange, yellow, green, blue, indigo, and violet.

through a multifaceted crystal or *prism*. Few people know the magick of capturing Moon rays with crystals.

First you need as large a prism as you can find. You can test your prism in a sunbeam so you know just how to hold it to create a rainbow, and you also will have that image to compare with the moonshine rainbow.

Choose a very clear, Full Moon night. Take your prism outside and place it where moonlight can shine directly on it. Now, moonlight is not nearly as strong as sunlight, of course, so you probably won't see rainbow colors right away. Hold your hand close to the prism, moving it around enough to see the rainbows reflected on your palm. Once you have a rainbow in your hand, slowly walk away from your prism, positioning your hand to keep hold of the rainbow. Keep the rainbow on your hand and move as far from the prism as you can without losing it. Now move your face into the reflection, in place of your hand, and experience the brilliance reflected onto your eyes. While you bathe in the reflected moonlight rainbow, keep your mind open for thoughts and images that may come to you. This is another good thing to practice and then journal about every clear Full Moon.

Throw a Lantern Festival

The point of a lantern festival is to let the lanterns represent Moon energy. The magickal principle here is that anything mundane that resembles a spiritual object can be used to connect with that object's energies.

You can create lanterns by wrapping tissue papier-mâché around a balloon, letting it dry, and then popping the balloon to leave the hard, round shell. Cut a hole in top of your lantern big enough to put candles in.

The tissue paper for the lanterns should be colors associated with the moon, such as white, cream, or yellow, or a combination of all three. Making the lanterns is a good project for a group, stretching out over several days.

Moon lanterns can be used to call on the energies of the Moon, especially if you are housebound or the sky is cloudy. If lanterns are reserved for just Full Moon nights, they become magickal tools for Moon meditation and focus.

After-the-Festival Food

The feast you prepare for Full Moon celebrations should include foods and herbs sacred to the Moon. Liguana's favorite choices are shown in the following table.

Sacred Moon Plant	Magickal Correspondence
Anise seed	Protection, banishing negative energy
Cabbage	Good fortune, prosperity
Cleavers*	Love and friendship
Ginger	Power, success, money
Jasmine	Love, money, sleep, dreams
Lettuce	Protection, loyalty, love
Poppy	Fertility, love, money, luck, sleep
Sesame seeds	Love, strength, abundance
Wild rose	Love, purity

Indicates the plant is inedible; not for human consumption.

> **Liguana's Grimoire**
>
> Cleavers, also called fragrant bedstraw herb, are little clinging vines that have spoke-shaped leaves and are sticky. Liguana's kids love to wear them as bracelets, crowns, and belly bands in the summer. They also have cleaver fights to see who can stick the most cleavers on their opponent.

Salads for the Goddess

A simple tossed lettuce salad or chopped cabbage slaw is a traditional dish to serve at Moon festivals. The rounded shape and overlapping leaves of the lettuce or cabbage symbolize the shape of the Goddess. Topped with a sesame oil dressing, either one is even more Goddess-appropriate.

For the sesame dressing:

¾ cup red miso (available in Oriental grocery stores and health-food stores)

3 TB. sugar

3 TB. rice wine

2 TB. hot water

2 tsp. soy sauce

¼ tsp. sesame oil

1 TB. sesame seeds, toasted

In a small bowl, combine the miso and sugar. Blend well. Add the rice wine, hot water, soy sauce, sesame oil, and sesame seeds. Whisk until well blended. Toss with salad greens or shredded cabbage. Makes approximately four servings.

The Moon Goddess is a strong, fierce, yet benevolent Deity. Like a lioness, she both cares for and defends her Natural Magician children. Because the Moon reflects the light from the Sun, the pale orb in the night sky could be said to represent a woman's reflective nature, her internal response to the world. The Full Moon's silver glow spreads a soft, protective night light across the planet. Celebrate her!

The Least You Need to Know

- The three aspects of the Goddess, represented by the Moon, are the Maiden, Mother, Crone.

- The Moon is most often considered a feminine deity, but some traditions still consider the Moon masculine.

- Full Moon festivals have been held for centuries across all cultures and are still being organized today.

- Any object that mimics the Full Moon's round shape can be used to connect with her energies.

Part 4

Natural Magick with the Faery Realm

Although Natural Magick exists on a mundane as well as a spiritual level, it sometimes needs to call on the faery realm for help. Tapping into the power of sylphs, salamanders, undines, gnomes, and tree spirits can strengthen your magickal energy.

Chapter 14

Sylphs, Salamanders, Undines, and Gnomes

In This Chapter

- The difference between the Elements and the Elemental spirits
- Seeking sylphs
- Searching out salamanders
- Expecting undines
- Knocking for gnomes

Natural Magick is *not* "high magick," and although ceremony is used, its rituals are much less prescribed and very malleable, depending on the person practicing. Natural Magick consists largely of folk practices and country spells.

Liguana, who considers herself a green witch and a kitchen witch, works with Elementals (as opposed to the Elements) from that perspective. She is also a high priestess, which is the part of her that relates to the Elemental spirits.

Who and What Are the Elemental Spirits?

We've already touched on these spiritual beings in earlier chapters (sylphs in Chapter 4, salamanders in Chapter 5, undines in Chapter 6, and gnomes in Chapter 7). Now let's explore them a little deeper.

The clouds aren't beings. The flames aren't beings. Neither are there little people under ground or on the waves ruling all that goes on there. Why, then, have we spent so much time on Elemental beings if there are no such things? There are several magickal principles to explain this.

The first one is that if you know the name of something, you have a way to connect with its energy and power. But how do you know a "salamander" is the correct guardian spirit for Fire, for instance? The beauty of this law is that you do not have to know the exact and true name. If enough people put their thoughts and energies into recognizing an Elemental force as a salamander, then that is at least one name for that particular phenomenon.

Magickal Bounty

Anthropomorphizing means seeing in another thing what we are familiar with in ourselves, thereby making a human connection. **Synergism** is from the Greek word *synergos*, meaning "coming together." It refers to the Divine and humans working in tandem.

Another magickal truism is that anything can be seen as a living, sentient being, whether or not common sense or conventional wisdom sees it that way. What's more, relating to a thing as if it were an entity is a way to connect to and work with its power. Magick is accomplished through connection and *anthropomorphizing*.

And finally, there is the magickal principle of *synergism*. Synergism makes strong magick. If enough people believe there are entities ruling the Elements, they will bring those entities into being.

So, then, sylphs, salamanders, undines, and gnomes are Elemental spirits. *Spirit*, in this case has two meanings. A spirit is a being that exists in the etheric realm and is not frequently perceived on the physical, human plane. It is also an internal spark, the quintessence of a feeling, time, or place, as in the *Spirit of '76* or "team spirit." When we work closely with the higher, self-aware Elemental beings, we evoke both of these concepts.

Though it's common for Wiccans and other Natural Magicians to call the Elements or the energies they represent when casting a circle, it is less common for the Elemental spirits to be called. Invoking the Fire Element, for example, is calling into

ourselves the qualities of passion and drive
and excitement. Evoking the salamanders is
calling for the assistance of sentient beings
made of the Element Fire and epitomizing
those characteristics we recognize as fiery. It's
a subtle distinction but a very important one.
An Elemental spirit has a mind of its own. It
might choose to aid your magick. It might not.
When dealing with Elemental spirits, a Natural
Magician's goal should be to connect with these
beings and to gain their favor.

Stir Gently ...!

In ritual, a Natural Magician calls to the Elemental beings to join her but never summons them or otherwise attempts to boss them around. Spirits do not respond well to someone who is rude or demanding.

When we cannot perceive something with our mundane senses, it is often difficult to feel a connection. Initially, this can be true with the Elemental spirits. Descriptions of these beings can be found in the folklore of many cultures. They are certainly well described in many modern fantasy role-playing games as well. We don't discount any of these images. There are commonly accepted ideas of what these beings are like. Researching is a good way to begin a quest for connection.

Immersing yourself in an Element does not necessarily lead to getting acquainted with the Elemental spirit. Calling, welcoming, and presenting gifts are great ways to catch an Elemental's attention.

In Search of Sylphs

Sylphs are useful allies to have when you want to be creative and need inspiration. They are often perceived as long, fast-moving cloud beings. Some people try to photograph sylphs as a hobby, watching the skies for a vaguely humanoid shape in the clouds. Almost everyone has looked at clouds and imagined that they see shapes of animals or Volkswagens or other earthly things. (Looking for shapes in the clouds is a wonderful way for children to connect with sylphs. Play the game with them, but remember to let their own imaginations see the shapes. There are no right answers in this game!) The sky and the wind and the clouds work together to bring out our imaginative selves. This is the energy of the sylphs as well.

Sylphs are beings that don't stay in the same place long. Calling a sylph is a little like trying to hold smoke. Expect these airy ones to come and go quickly. Catching their attention and letting them know you welcome their visits are very important first steps before calling upon them to do magick with you.

One way to attract sylphs is to use steam or smoke. The magickal principle here is that anything that resembles something else can help you spiritually connect with that something else. The easiest thing to use for this purpose is some form of incense, preferably one known to correspond with Air or thought, such as galbanum or frankincense. Woodwind instruments and bells are also helpful in attracting a sylph's attention.

Each morning for a full cycle of the Moon light your incense and spend a few minutes focusing on the smoke. Note the shapes and swirls as it dances upward in the air. Try to think only of the smoke, and let your mind accept whatever images it sends to you. Say out loud:

> *Mighty sylphs of the Air, I welcome your guidance.*
> *Great ones, I honor your wisdom.*
> *Accept this smoke, this scent, this sound,*
> *a gift from my spirit to yours.*

> **Cauldron Bubble**
>
> A quick and easy way for a Natural Magician to honor the spirits of Air is to hang wind chimes outside, where the breeze can play with them often. The higher pitched they are, the better, to catch a sylph's attention.

Then ring your bell or play your flute, or in some way make music with the wind or your breath. When you are comfortable with the sound you have offered, extinguish your incense and go on with your day, remembering to look to the sky now and again. You might never see a sylph, but they will surely notice you.

Calling Out to Salamanders

Salamanders are helpful when you need to rid yourself of negative thoughts and energies. If you have been ill or had unpleasant events occur in your life, it's easy to wallow, blame, or otherwise keep that negativity close to your spirit. Fire Elementals purify and cleanse so you can move on. They also give vitality and excitement to whatever magick you do.

Whenever you light a fire, the salamanders are aware, so attracting their attention is very easy. Honoring and welcoming salamander energy will strengthen any Fire magick you do. One way to do this is by lighting a red or orange candle each day for a full cycle of the Moon. It is best to light it at midday or early evening. Say out loud to the flame:

Welcome mighty salamander spirits.
I honor you within this rite.
Be you welcome and honored today
And at every fire I light.

Focus on the flame and your intent to communicate with salamanders. Try to see nothing but what the flame shows you. You might be given images from the realm of the salamanders. Be open to whatever comes to you. When you are satisfied with your communication, blow out the candle.

Bonfire celebrations draw salamanders, especially if there is also dancing and singing. If you are in a place where you can have a bonfire, devote some energy to calling the salamanders when you first light the fire. Use the same chant you use with your candle lighting. Burning dragon blood or olibanum incense on red coal at the edge of your fire is another way to honor and connect with these energetic spirits. Salamanders like passion and enthusiasm, so try a little salsa music at your next bonfire. Or pick some hot jazz to spice up the gathering.

> **CAUTION Stir Gently ...!**
>
> Always be cautious about building a bonfire if the weather has been unusually dry. Rather than taking chances, buy a large metal garbage can or an old oil drum, and build your bonfire in a contained space.

Playing with Undines

If your magick is based on relationships and emotional connections, you might want to call upon the undines to help you. As with the other Elemental spirits, it's best to make yourself known to them and honor them first. Undines are seldom seen with normal human vision. Those who perceive them do so with a psychic sight that sees into the etheric realms. Fortunately, visioning is just the sort of thing undines like to help with.

To look for Water spirits, take yourself to a moving body of water and sit comfortably on the shore nearby. Undines love soft singing and stringed instruments, so if you play and sing, so much the better. Make music for a while, then quietly gaze into the water. Try to focus on nothing but the water's movement. Undines are often described as having humanlike forms that shimmer and ripple with the rhythms of the moving water. Look especially where the water froths or bubbles around rocks or plants. Keep your eyes only on the water, and allow your mind to open to any images the water gives you.

Whether or not you are successful at seeing an undine, when you are done looking for one, offer up crumbs of sweet cake. (Any kind of sweet cake can be offered to undines except chocolate, which is more suitable for salamanders.) Sprinkle the crumbs on the water, saying:

> *Mighty undines, Water spirits,*
> *Accept this gift from my hand.*
> *Always will I honor you,*
> *Though I am a creature of the land.*

You can quickly attract an undine's attention and call it to your home by taking water with you from your undine-seeking excursion. Set a cup several yards from the water's edge. Then run into the water until you are up to your knees. Scoop up as much liquid as you can hold in your cupped hands and run it back to the cup, pouring in whatever you have left when you get there. Run back and forth, water to cup saying, "Undines, undines, undines!" again and again until the cup is full. You might find yourself laughing at this ridiculous operation. That's good. Undines love merriment and games. Transfer your water to a jar with a tight lid and take it home with you. Once there, add it to a birdbath or a fish pond or put it in a vase for flowers. Look at it often and remember your sense of play as you gathered it. The undines will also remember.

> **Cauldron Bubble**
>
> If you live in a place without a body of water nearby, know that undines also flourish in underground streams and unseen waterways. Use a divining rod to locate hidden underground streams (see Chapter 6).

Attracting Gnomes

Gnomes are very good helpers if you have outdoor projects to accomplish. Given that they are beings who bestow prosperity and abundance, they are especially good to have around if you have a farm or garden. It's pretty common to see funny little gnome statues being used as lawn art. Few people know that the magickal purpose of gnome statuary is to attract their attention and blessings on the garden. You don't have to go out and purchase gnome lawn ornaments to do this. There are simpler, more natural ways.

One way to attract a gnome's attention is to create a stone tower. It doesn't have to be huge: just three rocks stacked one atop the other. It does need to hold up to wind and rain, so be sure they fit snugly. Set up your tower in an out of the way corner of your yard and focus on your intent to attract gnomes while you are doing it. Walk around the stone tower three times. The first time say, "I call the gnomes of this place." The second time around say, "I welcome the Earth guardians on this land." The last time you circle your stone tower, say, "I honor the great gnomes for their work. This tower is to honor your presence." Now sprinkle an offering on the stones. Appropriate offerings are grains or flour, sugar, or crumbs of cake or cookies. Next time you cast a magickal circle and call the gnomes of the Earth Element, they will listen.

As in all things magickal, calling Elemental beings takes practice. Don't be discouraged if you fail to connect with them right away. Keep at it, and one day, they will surprise you!

The Least You Need to Know

- ◆ Attracting Elemental beings requires calling them, welcoming them, offering them gifts, and thanking them for their presence.

- ◆ Elemental beings cannot be ordered around and respond only to polite, respectful requests.

- ◆ Calling down the Elements is not the same thing as inviting the Elemental beings to your ritual.

- ◆ Elemental beings are sentient creatures who might or might not choose to help you with your Natural Magick.

Chapter 15

Expect the Unexpected

In This Chapter

- What do we mean by faeries?
- Attracting and employing faery magick
- Making your home and garden faery friendly
- Talking to plant devas
- Warm milk punch to share with the faery folk

This chapter is about faeries. The very first thing we want you to understand is what we mean when we use that word. Faeries are spirit beings similar to Elementals. A major difference is that Elementals range far and wide, whereas faeries tend to be what some magickal traditions call "spirits of place." They are often perceived as nomadic, yet they have definite, preferred territories. Nearly every human culture has recognized one form of faery or another. They are the Sidhe to the Gaelic/Celtic peoples, the Menehune to the Hawaiians. The Inuit and Athabascan people of the North tell legends of the Billikens who roam the snowy wastes. In Australia, the Bunyips are sometimes seen in the wild places. Leprechauns, sprites, brownies—as Natural Magicians, we use the term *faery* to represent all of these beings from all cultures.

There is not simply one type of faery called by different names. There are so many varieties and subspecies that we could take up the rest of this book exploring and explaining them. We aren't going to do that. We definitely recommend research, however, so you know what you are looking at when you see a being from the faery realm.

How Natural Magicians Relate to Faeries

Other than being entities of the spirit realm, what do faeries have to do with Natural Magick? Faeries are magickal beings themselves, skilled in the use of energy flows. They tend to be linked closely to the natural world, preferring wild places to cultivated and managed areas. As a practitioner of Natural Magick, you want to be in harmony with all beings around you. Most especially you want to be at peace with entities who can easily make your existence more colorful and enjoyable—or more miserable—at their whim.

> **Liguana's Grimoire**
>
> Liguana recommends a good neighbor policy with faeries. Honor them for the good that they do and make your home a welcoming place for them. If you become known as a friend of the faery realms, you will have gained powerful, magickal allies indeed.

The first thing you need to do to attract the attention of your local faeries is to immerse yourself in nature. Spend quality time meditating under a tree or in a woodsy area of your yard or a nearby park. Focus on the feel of the air around you, the sound of the trees and the grasses, the smell of the outdoors. The average person pays so little attention to the natural world; faeries will be surprised by your obvious desire to connect.

Connecting with the Fair Ones

Next, make the places in and around your home faery-friendly. The Fair People love singing and dancing, especially if done out of doors. Periodically, have dance parties at your home with others who seek to attract faeries. Wear bright colors and billowing fabrics. Play music that is upbeat and easily danced to. Even if no faeries are obvious at your parties, you'll still have a good time and be in a better frame of mind to experience the faery realm.

Decorate your home with glittering, shiny things. This could be as simple as hanging crystals in your window. Tiny, blinking holiday lights are faery-friendly decorations all year long. Shiny marbles in a glass vase are an intriguing addition to your home decor as well. No one else need know you displayed them prominently to catch a faery's eye. And by the way, keep your home reasonably neat, as faeries are put off by clutter.

Chimes outside will make faeries take notice. They will be happier if the chimes are high pitched and tinkling bells rather than metallic gongs or rattly wood, stones, or shells.

Liguana has a statue of a garden faery holding a bowl shaped from a leaf. She often puts wine or beer or milk or fresh water in the bowl, especially on festival days. That way the Fey will feel included.

Friendly Faery Magick

Making your environment faery ready is an important part of the plan to attract faeries and their magick. How do you know they are there—and what do you do with them when you have them? It's tough because, even less than Elementals, they don't take direction. The best you can do is set things up so they like you and naturally look out for you just like a good neighbor would.

How do you know the faery people have responded to your friendly overtures? The trees and flowers and shrubs will grow very quickly, looking fuller and brighter. Faery energy is like fertilizer for plants. The more visits you have by the Fey Ones, the better your garden grows.

> **CAUTION**
>
> **Stir Gently ...!**
>
> Not every faery being has good intentions. If you hear faeries telling you to do things you don't want to do, tell them you refuse to listen. You are not a puppet and you are not required to fulfill all their desires. Approach communication with the Sidhe as a powerful, magickal being who wishes to be on friendly terms. Respect faeries and require them to respect you as well.

If you hear a high-pitched ringing or buzzing, you could be close to faeries. This could be the sound of their movement through space or the chatter of their communication with each other. Be sure you are not mistaking bees or hummingbirds for faeries, though; the sound is quite similar.

Some people see faeries as bright sparkles or flashes of light, here and then gone in an instant. Sometimes there is color to the sparkle, but usually it is just white light. Catching a flash in your peripheral vision might not mean you are seeing a faery. If this happens more than once in a while, or if you see sparkles in the air whenever you are out among the green, growing things, either you need to visit the eye doctor or you have attracted the attention of the Fair Ones.

Communication with the Faeries

So you've made your home a welcome place for faeries and faery magick. Now you see and hear them all the time. What comes next? Communication. If you let these beings know you want to understand them, they will often put forth the effort to talk to you, especially if they consider you an agreeable and pleasant human. Not every attempt at communication will work, but here is a good way to break the ice and become open to voices from the faery realm.

Go to a place where you have seen or heard signs of faery magick. Make yourself comfortable in a chair or on a blanket. Take some very slow deep breaths. Try to get yourself into a meditative state—that is, perceive all around you and stop talking to yourself in your head. This is the single most important factor when listening for voices from other realms, be they dragons, Elementals, or faeries. Still your internal chatter.

Now say a greeting out loud to the faeries. You can address them as faeries, spirits of place, or Fey Ones. It doesn't matter what title you use. They will understand whom you are addressing. Tell them that you are happy they are around and that you want to hear their voices. If the chiming or buzzing starts up around you, say out loud that you cannot understand what they are saying, though you know they are speaking. What often happens at this point is that a single being is chosen to communicate with you. You probably won't hear its words with your ears. It will be more like telepathic communication. That is why it's so important to learn to still your own internal voice. The faery voice might sound different from your own or it might not. Be open and listen carefully. You will probably learn a lot more about faeries than we could teach you.

Liguana's Grimoire

Liguana once lived in a magickal place with a faery mound (a small hill that houses faeries) in the woods behind the house. People who came to visit would often leave colorful stones or other offerings for the spirits of that place. One morning as she lay in bed, she heard chimes within a few feet of her head. She had heard with her ears, not with any psychic sense, so she was sure she could see the faery who was so close by. She even called out to it, "Don't go! I want to see you!" She's sure she was, by then, quite alone in the room.

Using a large stone or piece of wood, you can create a communication device. This would serve as a place faery and human alike could go when they need to connect. That way you don't have to traipse through the woods or head out to your backyard to seek out the Fair Ones.

The wood or stone should have a smooth surface and feel good to the touch. It should be small enough to carry without difficulty and large enough to be seen across a room. A carving is fine, if you happen to have one. The shape is not as important as the feel.

Take your faery touchstone to the place you encountered the most Fey activity. Again make yourself comfortable, with the object set in front of you. Lay your fingers lightly upon it. Say out loud your intention of better communication with the Fair Folk. Tell them you offer up this piece for them to inhabit or leave their messages in. Wait for sights or sounds that tell you they heard you. Say, "I touch this object, you touch this object, that our voices may sound clearly to each other." As before, still your internal chatter and listen for the telepathic whispers of the faery people. Using a touchstone means you can call for visitations and communications wherever you are. Do this exercise often so the vibrations of your magickal energies and the objects energies will be familiar to beings from other realms. With practice, it gets easier.

Faery Folklore and Trivia

The folklore of many nations around the world includes stories of magickal little people. Although the stories are similar, each faery being has its own haunts and specialties. Most Natural Magicians won't get a chance to travel to all of these far-away places, but we thought it would be fun to share some other Natural Magicians' faeries.

Most people easily recall the leprechauns of Ireland. Very small sprites, they sometimes live in farmhouses or wine cellars but are partial to meadows and green spaces. They are known to aid Natural Magicians when asked properly and perform small labors for them. They are especially good at repairing shoes or other objects made of leather.

People who ask for a leprechaun's help should always leave a gift as a thank-you. Leprechauns are especially fond of tobacco and ale. In return, they leave small objects that bring luck and fortune. Because they live close to Nature, it might be an acorn, a pretty stone, or a handful of sweet grasses.

Menehune of Hawaii

In Hawaii, the mischievous Menehune roam the deep forests at night. Each mene-hune has a distinct personality and appearance; no two are identical. They are cun-ning creatures and, therefore should be avoided unless a special favor is absolutely needed of them. They are expert builders, and stories abound of dams and buildings being completed overnight when a Natural Magician leaves the right supplies and asks for help.

They are also extraordinary archers. To reverse the feelings in an angry person, ask the Menehune to use one of their magick arrows to pierce the heart of the person to ignite feelings of love instead. Menehune also enjoy cliff diving, so if you hear splashes in the night in Hawaii, it is possibly a Menehune diving into the ocean. If you search carefully and avoid being seen, you might catch a glimpse of the little beings.

Australian Bunyips

According to Aboriginal legend, Bunyips are creatures that lurk in swamps, bill-abongs, creeks, riverbeds, and waterholes. They emerge at night, making terrifying, blood-curdling cries. Fearsome creatures, they prefer to be left alone but will provide protection for people who have treated them well. To attract the help of a Bunyip, leave some raw meat close to the water you think they live near and state out loud what you fear may harm you. They should be approached with caution, though; they are highly unpredictable and can sometimes resort to violent solutions.

Billikins and Snowy Places

Billikins generally live in the snowy regions of Greenland, Russia, and other arctic places. They help people who become lost to find their way home and like warm furs and moccasins as a thank-you. Inuits think of them as "the beings of things as they ought to be." Sighting one of them is looked on as a hopeful sign that whatever is wrong will get better.

Plant Devas

Every flower, every tree, every wildflower—in fact, every plant—has its own "deva" or faery, and by connecting with that deva and asking its help in growing plants that we are hoping to grow, we can improve the fertility of anything that is growing in our garden or indeed anywhere.

In Hindu scriptures, the word *deva* refers to all life that is invisible. The word is derived from Sanskrit, meaning "to shine"—hence, the "shining ones" and the "resplendent ones." Hindus believe that each magickal place on Earth each has its own deva or spirit watching over it.

You can even connect with the deva of a house plant. Sit in a comfortable position facing the plant, close your eyes, and take a few deep breaths. Feel yourself let go of all thoughts and all tensions, and take several more deep, relaxing breaths.

> **Liguana's Grimoire**
>
> For a truly delightful book about plant devas, read *The Findhorn Garden* (Perennial/ HarperCollins, 1976). Wonderful plants and vegetables were grown on land that was almost purely sand, and it is thought that much of the inspiration and energy for this came from the various plant devas.

Begin to send verbal messages to the plant, either by speaking aloud or in your thoughts. Introduce yourself to the plant and its deva. Thank the plant for its beauty and energy, and for enhancing your environment. Tell the deva what it means to you to have this particular plant in your home. Say anything else that occurs to you.

Now stop talking and listen for a response. Notice if words form in your mind that seem to come from the plant, or if impressions seem to pop into your awareness, like a sudden realization that this plant is very happy. Don't judge any message that seems to be coming. Try asking questions, such as, "Do you like the place you are sitting? Would another place be better?" Wait for a response, which you will either hear intuitively or sense in some other way.

Use this same technique to connect to the plants in your garden or flower bed. You will be amazed at how lush, green, and fertile your yard and garden will look.

Keeping a little wild space in your garden is essential for working with the garden devas or faeries because they need an uncultivated place so that they can rest and play. So if you want the help of the faeries with building a beautiful garden for yourself, pay them by leaving them their own little plot, and add a few beautiful beach pebbles or shiny stones. Put a tiny earthenware dish in the wild space that will fill up with rainwater for them.

Warm Milk Faery Punch

Faeries love milk-based drinks. This warm punch is the perfect offering to leave in your garden in the early spring to wake up the devas and let them know you welcome them to your home. Put a small cup of this brew in a sheltered place once there is no more danger of frost. Share the rest with your family and friends. Then start going through your new seed catalogues.

> 4 cups spring or bottled water
>
> 8 whole cloves
>
> 1 tsp. fennel seeds
>
> 4 whole cardamom pods
>
> 1 cinnamon stick
>
> 1¼-inch thick slice fresh ginger
>
> 3 bags Darjeeling tea (or any other good black tea you like)
>
> 1 cup low-fat milk
>
> ¼ cup sugar
>
> 4 (3×½-inch) strips orange peel
>
> Additional cinnamon sticks (optional)

Combine the water, cloves, fennel seeds, cardamom, cinnamon stick, and ginger in a medium saucepan and bring to a boil. Reduce heat to low; cover and simmer 10 minutes. Remove the saucepan from the heat and add the tea bags. Cover the pan and let the mixture steep 30 minutes.

Strain the liquid into another saucepan. Add the milk, sugar, and orange peel. Bring to a simmer, stirring gently until the sugar dissolves. Garnish with the additional cinnamon sticks, if desired. Serves 4—plus the faeries.

The Least You Need to Know

♦ Faeries are "spirits of place," unlike Elementals, who exist everywhere.

♦ Natural Magicians can ask faeries for their help and guidance but must remember to thank them with a gift.

◆ The best way to attract faeries is to make your home and yard appealing to them.

◆ Most cultures in all parts of the world tell stories about small magickal creatures.

Chapter 16

Tree Spirits

In This Chapter

- Traditional tree rituals
- Tree folk and spirits
- Trees and their magickal correspondences
- Tree rituals for the Natural Magician
- Nut butters to make and share

Beautiful, solemn, and wise, trees are the largest living beings on this planet. Trees can reach the highest heavens and penetrate the deepest secrets of the Earth. They are ancient and sacred and provide the perfect focal point for meditation, enlightenment, guidance, and inspiration. Trees are the guardians of the forests and all of the sanctified places that must not be spoiled. On the physical plane, they provide us with shade, fruits and nuts, and mundane objects such as lumber and paper. We build our homes in the thick of them and mourn the empty space when one has to be cut down.

On a spiritual plane, they can offer Natural Magicians wise counsel if we learn how to listen to them. Their energy vibrates at a very low level, so it can be relaxing and stress-relieving to spend time with them. Trees are the epitome of patience, so any ritual you perform that involves a tree requires your patience as well. Trees move slowly and communicate slowly. They stay in the same place, once rooted, and watch.

Tree Traditions

Trees have been objects of worship in all parts of the world, but perhaps the most familiar to us are the European traditions. Trees prevailed widely and figured prominently in the popular festivals of European peasants. Many of their old customs have carried over to today's modern world.

Spring Rituals

In spring or early summer, or even on Midsummer Day, it was the custom to go out to the woods, cut down a tree, and bring it into the village, where it was set up amid general rejoicings. Or people cut branches in the woods and fastened them on every house. The intention of these customs was to bring home to the village, and to each house, the blessings that the tree spirit has in its power to bestow—hence, the custom in some places of planting a May tree before every house, or of carrying the village May tree from door to door so that every household could receive its share of the blessing.

> **Liguana's Grimoire**
>
> The tree that was generally regarded as sacred in Palestine was the oak, or the terebinth, which in hot countries, especially the more southerly of those about the Mediterranean, takes the place of the oak. It was called allon, which means "divine tree."

In the 1600s, on April 30 families sat a green bush before their doors strewn with yellow flowers. In areas where timber was plentiful, they erected tall, slender trees, which were left throughout the year to protect the village. In some regions, a young tree 10 or 12 feet high was planted before each house on May Day so it appeared to be growing; flowers were thrown over it and strewn about the door.

In the north of England, it was formerly the custom for young people to rise a little after midnight on the morning of the first of May and go out with music and blowing horns into the woods, where they broke branches and adorned them with nosegays and crowns of flowers. They returned about sunrise and fastened the flower-decked branches over the doors and windows of their houses. This provided protection for the inhabitants of the house.

Among ancient customs still practiced by the Cornish today is the tradition of decking their doors and porches on the first of May with green boughs of sycamore and hawthorn, and of planting trees, or, rather, stumps of trees, before their houses.

Winter Rituals

In the German-speaking countries, the Christmas tree is part of the pre-Christian tradition of the 12 Rauhnächte. The tree is put up on December 24 and taken down after New Year's or on January 6, known as "Twelfth Night." Rauhnächte literally means 12 harsh or wild nights, which later became the "Twelve Nights of Christmas." Western tradition celebrates the "Twelve Days of Christmas" with partridges in pear trees, among other things.

Winter in the northern countries was harsh. The early Germans observed the changes in Nature in autumn when plants and leaves of trees began to change color, shriveled up, and fell to the ground. This was followed by winter, with blistering ice and snow, when Nature seemed dead to them. They blamed evil spirits for the "killing." Only a few trees, the evergreens, stayed "alive," and to the Germans, they became a symbol of immortality. Good spirits and the magic power of the evergreen were believed to resist the life-threatening powers of darkness and cold. They believed in the special powers of these trees; wherever they were, evil spirits could not go, so the people brought the greenery into their homes.

Christmas trees have not always been associated with the winter holidays across the world. The basis of tree use can be traced back before the birth of Jesus Christ to early Egyptians, who brought palms indoor as symbols of eternal life. Ancient Jewish religious feasts used decorations made of tree boughs.

> **Liguana's Grimoire**
>
> The custom of lighting a Yule log, which dates back to the twelfth century, was known in most Europeans countries, notably in France and in Italy where the Yule log was called a *ceppo*. It was said that the cinders of this log could protect the house from lightning and the malevolent powers of the devil.

In the Western world, most experts consider our use of trees during the winter holidays to be derived from Rome. The Romans exchanged tree boughs with friends for luck. The Roman winter festival was celebrated by decorating the house with tree boughs and greenery. Trees were paraded around with candles and trinkets attached to the branches, much like our holiday trees today.

Use a Little Tree Power

Here are some of the most common trees in North America and how they might be used in spellcrafting and ritual. Sometimes a tree will speak to a Natural Magician in a way no one else can hear. Don't hesitate to join your energy with that tree's natural energy. Being chosen by a tree is a special gift and supersedes any lore passed down about magickal correspondences.

Tree	Magickal Correspondence
Alder	Protection, divination, persistence, endurance, overcoming obstacles
Apple	Choice, love, healing magick, wisdom, psychic journeying
Ash	Used in spells requiring focus, strength of purpose; links inner and outer worlds
Aspen	Competence, humility
Beech	Guidance from the past to gain insight; protection
Birch	Fertility, healing spells, cleansing and purification, patience, renewal
Blackthorn	Fate; outside influences that must be obeyed
Elder	Purifying; connection with Mother Earth, insight, psychic work, faery magick
Elm	Adds stability and grounding to a spell
Fir	Clear vision, divination, psychic powers
Hawthorn	Protection, love, marriage spells, strength through adversity, connection with faeries
Hazel	Knowledge, wisdom, and poetic inspiration
Holly	Spells for sleep and rest; eases the passage of death; connection with the Lord, home, protection
Larch	Wards off evil, protection, induces visions
Maple	Success and abundance
Oak	Protection, strength, success, stability, optimism, clarity of thought
Pear	Love, temptation
Pine	Releases guilt

Tree	Magickal Correspondence
Poplar	Resistance, communication, endurance, conquest
Rowan	Protection, control over enchantment, connection with the wild world, challenging old ideas
Willow	Cycles, rhythms, healing pain or illness, physical and psychic journeying, flexibility
Yew	Enhances magickal and psychic abilities; induces prophetic visions; death and rebirth, wisdom, love

Tree branches can be turned into wands and staffs to call to other Elements in Natural Magick rituals. Some trees' fruits, flowers, bark, and nuts can be added to recipes or used in an *infusion* for perfumes and oils. Experiment with tree leaves, twigs, and bark to bring some natural protection into your life.

Magickal Bounty

An **infusion** is basically a tea, although not all infusions are edible. Steep branches or bark, leaves, and flowers in warm water to make a fragrant base for perfumes and oils. Cedar is an especially pungent wood.

Tree Folk

Although Druids are sometimes identified as wizards and soothsayers, in pre-Christian Celtic society, they formed an intellectual class comprising philosophers, judges, educators, historians, doctors, seers, astronomers, and astrologers. The word *Druidae* is of Celtic origin; it stems from the Greek word *drus*, meaning "an oak," and *wid*, meaning "to know" or "to see." *Dru-wid* means "oak knowledge." The oak, together with the rowan and hazel, was an important sacred tree to the Druids. In the Celtic social system, Druid was a title given to learned men and women possessing "oak knowledge" or "oak wisdom."

The Druids emerged from the ancient Celtic tribes at a time when the people had to live close to nature to survive. By the light of the storyteller's fire and with the play of the harp, the Druids dreamed magick for their people. They gathered in the deep woods, bringing together their mysticism and philosophy, their insight and learning. Their spirits emerged from the tides of the sea, the light of the Sun and Moon, the wind in the trees, the howl of the wolf. In this way, they created an institution that inspired, frightened, and uplifted their world. Druids filled the roles of judge, doctor, diviner, mystic, and clerical scholar—they were the religious intelligentsia of their culture.

The mythologies describe Druids who were capable of many magickal powers, such as divination and prophesy, control of the weather, healing, levitation, and shapeshifting themselves into the forms of animals.

Fauns

The masculine spirits associated with trees are sometimes called fauns. Fauns are graceful woodland creatures. They know nothing of evil and ugliness. They love singing, playing music, and dancing. On warm summer days, you'll find them basking in the Sun.

Physically, they are usually depicted as half human, half goat. They live in the woods gathering food and enjoying themselves. They sleep outdoors, and feel uncomfortable entering a house or enclosed space. In winter, they either move southward to avoid too much snow and cold, or stay beneath spruce and pine trees. Some people believe they watch over hibernating animals in the winter and cuddle up with them for warmth.

Liguana's Grimoire
One day, Liguana's daughter said she had chosen her magick wand tree where she would cut a branch to be her wand when she turned 13. She took Liguana to see the tree. It was a 3-foot tall madrona, so bedecked with ribbons and jewels it was almost bending over. They talked about how long it might take for the tree to get big enough to give up a branch. Shaleina said she'd gladly wait. She had spoken to this little tree, and they had an understanding. How could Liguana argue with that?

Natural Magicians can call on fauns to help protect a wooded area or the wildlife that lives within. Take a gift to them, some cakes or small trinkets, and listen for the music of the wind in the trees to see if you've connected with them.

Wood Nymphs

The feminine spirits who preside over the groves and forests are the wood nymphs, or dryads. Each one is born with a certain tree over which she watches. A dryad lives either in a tree, in which case she is called a hamadryad, or close to it. The lives of the dryads are connected with that of the trees; if the tree perishes, the dryad dies with it. If this is caused by a mortal, the gods will punish the person for that deed.

Dryads are especially drawn to the color red and love musical chimes. On chilly spring nights as the trees are just beginning to bud, leave a small dish of warm milk out for the nymphs. Their dance of delight can help the budding trees wake up.

> **CAUTION**
>
> **Stir Gently …!**
>
> The dryads themselves will punish any thoughtless mortal who would somehow injure a tree. Before you cut down a tree, carve your initials into it, or break off its branches, think carefully. Always keep the tree's best interest at heart.

If you don't buy into fauns and nymphs—and some Natural Magicians don't—just remember that trees have a soul and a spirit, no matter how you envision them. This is why we recommend that you ask a tree's permission to pick its fruit or nuts, or to take a branch to use as a wand or in a protection spell. It's the polite thing to do.

Trees and Natural Magick

Magickal people make a connection with tree spirits for several reasons. First, it feels good to connect with a being so wise and self-assured, as most trees are. Second, we want to emulate tree beings, taking in energy from the sky and from the Earth. We want to be conduits of magickal power, just as trees naturally are.

Befriend a tree. An important thing to do while teaching yourself the ways of Natural Magick is to closely connect with at least one tree. You want to feel an affinity for the tree, and you want the tree to feel the same for you as well. (Liguana's parents planted a tree in their yard each time a grandchild was born. There are 10 trees out there in the world honoring and celebrating the life of 10 young people. Planting a tree is an excellent way to commemorate a special occasion.)

Go to a place where there are many trees. A forest, a park, and even a wooded backyard are all acceptable. Spread a blanket on the ground and sit in silence with the trees. Trees are quiet, slow-moving beings. You should be, too. Listen to the wind in the branches. Watch the leaves move, and notice what birds and other creatures the trees shelter. When you feel you and your chosen trees have become accustomed to each other, go to a tree that interests you and put both hands on its trunk.

Whisper your intent to know this tree better. Always speak very quietly around trees. They don't appreciate fast movement or noisy mammals. While touching the tree, try to still the talking in your mind. Thoughts about what you are having for dinner, for instance, are distracting and prevent you from concentrating on any feeling the tree may be sending you. Stay with the tree for as long as it takes to feel open to its magickal energy or its individual personality. When you feel you have succeeded, thank the tree and give it a gift. Some magickal practitioners give herbs or wheat or even fertilizer. Others put rings or other jewels high up in the branches or bury them at the base of the tree. Commune with your tree often. Empathy takes comfort and familiarity, and these take time to develop.

Raising Energy

An exercise commonly used for grounding and raising energy is the tree exercise. To do this, you must stand with your feet about 3 feet apart, with your knees slightly bent and your arms at your side. Close your eyes and visualize yourself as a tree. Your roots are growing down into the soil and spreading out as they go deeper and deeper into the Earth.

Feel the energy current in the soil and pull that energy up through your roots. Feel its warmth and gentle vibration as it rises into your trunk. Breathe slowly, raising your arms a little bit with each inhalation. Your arms become your branches as you reach upward. With your arms above your head, elbows slightly bent, let your branches sway slightly and feel the magickal current in the air around you. Pull that energy into yourself through your branches as you breathe out, sending the warmth into the ground.

Liguana's Grimoire

"By oak, by ash, by thorn" is an oath to lend authority to a promise or pledge. Liguana's coven members put their hands on the hilt of her sword and said, "By oak, by ash, by thorn, I do swear to honor the ancient wisdoms of the craft, to respect all creatures as aspects of the Divine, to listen to the elders, nurture and love the young ones, and support and cherish my brothers and sisters on this spiritual journey."

As a Natural Magician, you are moving and channeling the magick of Earth and Sky, taking it in and passing it on for other beings to use. This is the magick of trees. Their breathing supports all life on Earth. When you understand this in your mind and body, slowly lower your arms and take one more breath in and out, sending any extra magickal energy back into the soil.

Acquiring a Wand

Trees are experts at letting energy flow through them. For this reason, Natural Magicians use their branches for their wands and staffs. Whereas a staff is a found thing, a wand is generally gathered or harvested with the magickal properties of the donor tree in mind.

Some people have several wands, each from a different tree. A person might have an oak wand to use when doing magick to maintain control in a difficult situation. The same person may have a willow wand for healing magick and an applewood wand for relationship magick.

> **Cauldron Bubble**
>
> Once you've found a tree that speaks to you, ask it if you can harvest one of its branches as a wand. Use a sharp object to cut it cleanly and neatly. Thank the tree for its gift to you.

Liguana's own wand was found. It was the first Full Moon after her year and a day initiation. Walking with some friends on a city sidewalk, completely surrounded by a concrete landscape, she was chatting away about how she needed to get to a forest to find a wand for herself. As she was saying this, she stumbled on a small branch, though there was no tree in sight. To amuse her friends, she picked it up and waved it around as if she was painting a mural with her magickal energy. It felt good in her hand, and her friends were gaping in surprise and wonder at the directed energy they could almost see and feel coming from the end of the wand as she waved it. To this day, she is uncertain what type of tree gave her the wand. When she uses it, she feels powerful and playful and lighthearted all at the same time.

Magickal Tree Recipe: Nut Butter

Nut butters you make yourself provide an excellent source of protein and minerals without the chemicals of processed spreads. The basic recipe is the same for all nuts, but you may have to adjust the amount of oil you need, depending on the nut you've chosen. Be creative! In addition to peanuts, try using almonds, cashews, macadamias, hazelnuts, pecans, walnuts, or even Brazil nuts.

2 cups raw, unsalted nuts

2–4 tsp. vegetable oil

Salt to taste

In a food processor or blender, grind the nuts into a fine powder. Slowly blend in the vegetable oil 1 teaspoon at a time until you have the consistency you want. Too much oil will make your butter greasy—too little will make it impossible to spread. Just as you have to get to know a tree, you have to get to know your varieties of nuts. Each one requires a slightly different amount of oil, depending on how soft and oily they are naturally. Once blended, stir in a little salt. This recipe yields ¾ to 1 cup of nut butter.

Most nuts take on the spirit of the tree from which they came. Nut butters are not only nutritious, but they are the perfect way to join your own spirit with a tree's protective spirit. Enjoy!

Natural Magicians need to commune with trees on a regular basis. Their energy is solid and grounding. It might take you a whole growing season to connect to your tree, but it is well worth the time and effort.

The Least You Need to Know

- Many cultures through the ages have brought trees into their homes to protect the family within.

- Working with trees takes a lot of patience and quiet time. They communicate slowly.

- Natural Magicians must always ask a tree's permission before cutting a branch or picking its fruit.

- Nut butters are a good way to take a tree's spirit into a Natural Magician's own spirit.

Part 5

Harvest to Seed to Harvest: Nature's Cycle

Growing and preparing food is a vital part of a Natural Magician's bag of tricks. This part gives you recipes, both vegetarian and meat dishes, for every season. Inviting your family and friends to your table automatically brings Natural Magick into your house. *Bon appétit!*

Chapter 17

Witches' New Year: Autumn Harvest

In This Chapter

◆ A Samhain menu

◆ Pork for the New Year

◆ Stuffing for new beginnings

◆ An updated pumpkin pie

◆ Shortbread for the soul (cakes)

A Samhain feast on October 31 commonly includes pork, apples and pomegranates, various root vegetables, rice, cranberries in all forms, shortbread or some type of dried fruit bread as soul cakes or offerings to the ancestors, and sweet potato or pumpkin pie for dessert. It is also common to serve dark foods, nuts and berries, and squash.

While notes about organic foods and free-range meats are sometimes included with individual recipes, the recipes in all of the chapters in Part 5 assume the use of fresh organic products whenever possible, including free-range meats humanely killed and wild-caught fish responsibly harvested. These products cost more but will make everything taste better and improve the positive energy in your food.

All of the recipes in Part 5 are designed to serve eight people, more or less, occasionally with some leftovers.

Appetizers to Whet the Appetite

Because Samhain festivals often begin outdoors with a bonfire before moving indoors, appetizers are often finger foods and dips that can be served at room temperature. Begin with chips of all kinds. Don't overlook those made from root vegetables such as beets, carrots, and turnips in addition to the standard corn and potato chips. An assortment of crackers is also a nice addition.

Raw vegetables are good as appetizers, too, especially radishes, carrots, turnips, kohlrabi, parsnips, and cabbage wedges.

Serve a dip of hummus or try the following roasted vegetable dip.

Roasted Eggplant Red Pepper Spread

In this recipe, roasting the vegetables beforehand brings out their flavor. This is an "Earthy" dish that is good for stability in the face of new endeavors and for protection. Serve it alongside Greek olives, feta cheese, and pita wedges for a Mediterranean flair.

1 medium eggplant, peeled and chopped into 1-inch cubes

2 red bell peppers, seeded and chopped into 1-inch cubes

1 red onion, peeled and chopped into 1-inch cubes

2 cloves garlic, minced

3 TB. olive oil

1½ tsp. salt

½ tsp. black pepper

1 TB. tomato paste

Preheat the oven to 400°F. Place eggplant, peppers, and onions in a large bowl and toss them with garlic, olive oil, salt, and pepper. Spread mixture onto a cookie sheet. Roast for 45 minutes or until vegetables are lightly brown and soft. Stir occasionally so they roast evenly.

Place the mixture in a food processor or blender. Add tomato paste and process into a chunky blend.

Queen's Crown Roast of Pork with Pomegranate Glaze

This crown roast evokes the Goddess's crown and makes a dramatic presentation for a Samhain feast. Liguana believes that pork is traditional at Samhain celebrations, due to the mundane practice of butchering hogs right before winter. Hams were cured and pork was salted down to preserve the meat during the months when feeding livestock was difficult. But a fresh cut of pork was a Samhain treat.

The spices in this recipe support honorable deeds and courage for the New Year (thyme), passion for up-coming endeavors (cumin and allspice), and love and friendship (pomegranates). These are the perfect blessings to bestow on family and friends as you begin the New Year and face winter's blustery onslaught.

Ask your butcher to prepare a crown roast, or just substitute a rack of pork ribs or even a boneless pork roast of about 5 pounds. Any of these will work fine, but try to find free-range pork raised on organic feed. It will taste fresher and have more positive energy. This is the brief time of year when pomegranates are available, and they make a tangy-sweet glaze supercharged with antioxidants.

1 TB. cooking oil (such as canola or corn oil)

12-rib crown pork roast (about 6 or 7 pounds), rack of pork ribs, or boneless pork roast

Wild Rice-Cranberry Stuffing (recipe follows)

1 tsp. kosher salt

1 tsp. cumin

½ tsp. dried thyme

Dash of allspice

Dash of black pepper

1 cup pomegranate juice

¼ cup packed brown sugar

1 TB. red wine or red-wine vinegar

1 clove garlic, minced

Pomegranate seeds and fresh mint leaves for garnish

Line a large roasting pan with foil and brush with cooking oil. Place crown roast (or ribs or pork roast) on the foil. Mound stuffing in center of roast. (See below for alternate cooking methods for the stuffing.)

Preheat the oven to 450°F. In a small bowl, combine salt, cumin, thyme, allspice, and black pepper. Rub over roast. Cut a piece of foil in a circle about the size of the inside of the crown roast. Brush with more cooking oil and place the circle, oil side down, over rice stuffing.

Put stuffed pork in the oven and roast for 20 minutes. Reduce oven heat to 325°F and roast for about 2 more hours, or until a meat thermometer registers 160°F. After the first hour, remove foil from top of rice.

When roast is cooked, carefully remove to a platter and cover loosely with foil. Set aside. Put roasting pan on the stove over one or two burners set on medium-high heat.

In a small bowl, combine pomegranate juice, brown sugar, red wine or vinegar, and minced garlic. Add about ½ cup of pomegranate mixture to the roasting pan to deglaze it. Scrape off the roast bits while stirring the juice with a wooden spoon. Add the remaining pomegranate mixture and boil until juice has thickened and reduced by half, stirring constantly. Remove from heat and brush or drizzle over pork roast.

Garnish with mint leaves and pomegranate seeds, and serve with a green salad.

Wild Rice-Cranberry Stuffing

Rice is a grain that relates to fertility, not only in the physical sense but also as it pertains to creativity in mental endeavors. Cranberries are a light fruit that corresponds to the Element of Air and its properties of new beginnings, the intellect, and creative imagination. What could be more appropriate for a New Year's celebration?

Roast some of this stuffed in the crown roast, or cook it all separately in a roasting pan or a crock pot.

1 cup wild rice, uncooked

2 cups water

1 cup dried cranberries, unsweetened

½ cup dried currants, unsweetened

1 organic orange

1 TB. canola or corn oil

3 leeks, white and pale green parts only, minced

2 cloves garlic, minced

½ to 1 tsp. kosher salt

Black pepper to taste

Combine rice, water, cranberries, and currants in a medium saucepan. Cook over medium heat for about 1 hour or until tender.

Juice orange and cut off *zest*. Set juice aside. Finely chop zest.

In a separate sautée pan, heat oil over medium-high heat. Sautée leeks and garlic until soft but not browned. Remove from heat. Stir in zest, salt, and black pepper.

When rice is tender, put it in a large bowl. Toss in leek mixture and combine. Drizzle orange juice over and combine. Stuff pork roast, and bake remaining stuffing in a baking pan in the oven with pork (if you have room) during the last hour of cooking. Or cook in a crock pot on high for 2 hours or until heated through.

Magickal Bounty

Zest, sometimes known as peel or rind, is the colored outer layer of oranges, lemons, and limes. A small amount of zest gives a strong characteristic flavor of the fruit, enhancing its magickal power. You can grate zest with the fine edge of a standard grater, but avoid the white part beneath the peel; it will leave a bitter taste.

Heaven and Earth

This recipe, an apple and potato side dish, is based on a traditional German recipe that combines apples, which swing in the heavens and attract love, with potatoes, which grow in the earth and promote stability. It sounds like an unusual taste combination to many non-Germans, but it is a satisfying and balancing meal or side dish.

8 medium to large red or Yukon gold potatoes, peeled (optional) and diced

6 medium to large tart apples, such as Granny Smith, peeled, cored, and thinly sliced

1 TB. apple cider vinegar

1 TB. brown sugar

6 slices bacon

1 medium yellow onion, peeled and sliced into rings

1 TB. butter for the baking pan

2 TB. chopped chives or green onions

Sour cream for garnish (optional)

Put two large saucepans or Dutch ovens filled with salted water on the stove and heat on high.

Boil potatoes in one pot and apples in the other pot, cooking both until tender, about 20 minutes for potatoes, 10 minutes for apples. Drain potatoes and toss with vinegar. Drain apples and toss with brown sugar.

Heat a skillet over medium-high heat. Add bacon and cook until crisp. Remove bacon and drain on paper towels. Add onions to bacon fat and cook until crispy and golden. Remove and drain on paper towels.

Cauldron Bubble

If you would like to substitute turkey bacon for traditional pork bacon, you can do so, but you will have to add 3 or 4 tablespoons of cooking oil to the pan to sautée the onion.

Preheat the oven to 400°F. Assemble the casserole: Butter a 9×9-inch square baking pan (preferably glass or ceramic) or oval cassoulet. Add half potatoes, spread apples over potatoes, cover apples with remaining potatoes, and then arrange onions and bacon over the top. Bake for 30 minutes or until heated through. Remove and garnish with chopped chives or green onions and dollops of sour cream.

Frost-on-the-Pumpkin Pie

Pumpkins are, of course, a traditional fall treat, whether you're celebrating Samhain or Halloween. Their shape invokes the Goddess as she prepares to lose her Lord to the underworld during the winter months. Evoking the Earth Element, which heralds stability and abundance, pumpkins can be used in a sweet dish, which is most common, or in a savory dish with pungent spices. Fresh pumpkin can replace squash in almost any recipe.

> ### Liguana's Grimoire
>
> The first jack-o'-lanterns were not pumpkins. Originally, the Irish hollowed out turnips, rutabagas, gourds, potatoes, and beets. They placed a light in them to ward off evil spirits. In the 1800s, a couple waves of Irish immigrants came to America. The Irish immigrants quickly discovered that pumpkins were bigger and easier to carve out. From then on, pumpkins were used for jack-o'-lanterns.

This updated version of a classic pumpkin pie adds crunchy nuts and a streusel topping. This version uses a press-in-the-pan crumb crust made from shortbread cookies. You can use the cookies in the following recipe for this, or your favorite purchased shortbread. The lower-fat milk substitutions will make a difference in texture, but the pie will still be tasty.

2 cups shortbread cookies plus ½ cup for topping, finely crushed

1 cup (2 sticks) unsalted butter, melted

2 cups pumpkin purée (organic canned pumpkin works well, or bake a pumpkin yourself and scoop out the flesh)

3 eggs, lightly beaten

½ cup honey

1 cup packed brown sugar, divided in half

½ tsp. salt

1½ tsp. ground cinnamon

½ tsp. ground ginger

¼ tsp. ground nutmeg

1 cup whole milk (you can substitute low-fat milk)

½ cup heavy cream (you can substitute low-fat evaporated milk)

½ cup chopped walnuts

½ cup powdered sugar

2 TB. cream

Preheat oven to 425°F. In a large bowl, combine 2 cups cookie crumbs with ½ cup melted butter. Toss to coat. Press into the bottom and partway up the sides of a 9-inch pie plate, preferably glass or ceramic.

In the same bowl, combine pumpkin purée, beaten eggs, honey, half the brown sugar, salt, cinnamon, ginger, nutmeg, milk, and heavy cream. Stir gently with a wire whisk or a fork until uniform. Pour into the pie crust.

Bake for 15 minutes. While baking, in a small bowl, combine remaining ½ cup cookies, ½ cup butter, ½ cup brown sugar, and walnuts. Toss to combine.

Remove pie from the oven and lower oven temperature to 350°F. Sprinkle topping over pie. Bake at 350°F for an additional 45 minutes or until a sharp knife inserted into the center of the pie comes out clean. Remove from the oven and cool to room temperature.

In a small bowl, combine powdered sugar and cream, whisking with a whisk or fork until smooth. Drizzle over the pie. Serve at room temperature or chilled.

Shortbread Soul Cakes with Saffron and Currants

Classic soul cakes are often puffy buns made with a yeast dough. This version is crunchier, richer, and easier, but it retains the classic currants (or make it without them) and saffron for just a hint of yellow tint and flavor. Saffron attracts wealth, and currants are useful in maintaining friendships.

> 1 cup (2 sticks) butter, softened to room temperature
>
> ½ cup plus 2 TB. superfine sugar (sometimes called caster sugar or bar sugar)
>
> ¼ cup confectioner's sugar (powdered sugar)
>
> Pinch saffron threads or pinch turmeric powder (about ⅛ tsp.) (optional)
>
> 2 cups unbleached white flour
>
> ½ cup currants (optional)
>
> 2 TB. brandy or orange juice (optional, use only if using the currants)
>
> ½ tsp. almond extract

Preheat oven to 375°F. Put butter in a large bowl and beat with an electric mixer or stand mixer until light and fluffy. Add ½ cup superfine sugar, confectioner's sugar, saffron or turmeric powder, and flour. Beat on low until combined, then on high for 2 minutes.

Soak currants in brandy or orange juice for about 5 minutes, then add currants to the dough, discarding leftover brandy or juice. Add almond extract and beat on low just to combine.

Spoon out dough onto an ungreased baking sheet, preferably an "airbake" sheet or a ceramic sheet (such as a pizza stone). Form into a large, flat circle, about ½ inch thick. Flatten with a rolling pin to make it smooth.

Score into 16 wedges with a sharp knife, cutting about halfway through the dough. Prick each piece all over with a fork.

Stir Gently ...!

Saffron is the world's most expensive spice. There are only three saffron threads per flower, and it has to be hand harvested. The most important rule for saffron is to not use too much. A very little bit goes a long way and, if overused, becomes overpowering and leaves a "medicinal" flavor.

Bake for 15–20 minutes or until just barely pale golden around the edges. Do not overcook! Shortbread should be mostly uniformly pale in color. Remove from the oven and sprinkle with remaining 2 tablespoons sugar. Let cool 5 minutes. Cut through dough to separate wedges. Cool an additional 10 or 15 minutes. Carefully remove shortbread to a plate or cooling rack using a thin metal spatula (shortbread is crumbly!). Serve warm or at room temperature. Store in a covered container.

Samhain festivals are joyous celebrations not in honor of death, but to remember and commune with the Spirits of the loved ones who've gone before. Put a little of the shortbread out as an offering to those Spirits. Remember, this menu is just a suggestion. If your family has favorite dishes, by all means serve them instead. The most important part of any celebration is to enjoy each other's company.

The Least You Need to Know

- Pork is a traditional meat to serve at a Samhain festival.

- When you're planning your holiday menu, be sure to consider root vegetables you might not have thought of previously.

- Although Halloween jack-o'-lanterns were not originally made of pumpkins, they have become traditional holiday fare.

- Samhain is a time to remember and honor your ancestors and friends who have passed before.

Chapter 18

Preparing the Earth: A Winter Pantry

In This Chapter

- ◆ Cooking from your larder
- ◆ A stew to warm your heart
- ◆ Beef in beer or apple cider
- ◆ Good-luck spice cake
- ◆ Chocolate and spices for a frothy blend

Preparing meals during the winter months generally means utilizing what's in the larder—making the sumptuous feast or two for holidays, yes, but also serving dishes made of beans and legumes and dishes from grains.

Warm, spicy drinks and dried fruits are regular additions for people living seasonally. Milk is still plentiful during these months, so any dairy-based dishes are good. Few eggs should be used, as generally the chickens have slowed down with the darker season. Soups and stews and chili are good in winter, especially with fresh bread. Chocolate in any form warms the body and is good for the Spirit.

Winter Stew

This stew is flexible and can be a great way to use whatever you have—leftover vegetables or the produce you have stored in your pantry or freezer. This can be a meat-free first course to the beef roast in old ale that follows this recipe, or add beef, pork, chicken, turkey, or fish to make this a main dish. You can also make this the day after you make the beef roast recipe following, adding leftover beef roast to this stew. In other words, feel free to adapt this according to what you have. Natural Magicians sometimes cook by instinct.

Magickally speaking, this stew heightens psychic ability (cinnamon), protection for loved ones (cumin and oregano), stability, and common sense (mushrooms and root vegetables), and strengthens protection (garlic). This stew soothes both body and Spirit, which we can always use during long winter months.

½ cup dried wild mushrooms, sliced (such as crimini, porcini, shiitake, chanterelles, oyster mushrooms, or a combination)

½ cup boiling water

1 TB. cooking oil

1 TB. unsalted butter

1 medium yellow onion, chopped

3 cloves garlic, minced

2 tsp. dried cumin powder

2 stalks celery, diced

1 cup diced beef, pork, chicken, turkey, or fish (optional, and can be cooked or uncooked)

1 tsp. dried oregano

1 quart water or organic vegetable or chicken broth (you will use this a little at a time)

1 medium turnip or white potato, peeled and diced

1 medium winter squash (butternut or acorn) or large sweet potato or yam, peeled and diced

¼ tsp. cinnamon

> **Liguana's Grimoire**
>
> When Liguana's oldest son was living at home, they had one lean winter when money was pretty tight. They ate from the larder, lots of beans and rice and lentils. One day he said, "Mom, I've noticed we've been having a lot of ... health food lately. How long can we expect this trend to continue?" She assured him things would change by summer, and, of course, they did.

1 cup kale, chopped (or ½ cup frozen spinach, thawed)

½ cup Madeira wine or apple cider

1 tsp. salt, or to taste

Freshly ground black pepper, to taste

Put dried mushrooms in a small bowl and cover with boiling water. Set aside.

In a soup pot or Dutch oven, heat oil and butter over medium-high heat until you can smell butter and it is just starting to sizzle but not yet brown. Add onions, garlic, and cumin powder. Stir to coat and continue stirring until onion is soft and garlic is golden, about 10 minutes.

Add celery, meat or fish if you are using it, oregano, and ½ cup of water or broth. Continue stirring and cook until celery is soft and liquid is reduced by about half, about 10 minutes.

Add turnip or potato, squash or sweet potato, and cinnamon, and another ½ cup water or broth. Stir and cook for 10 more minutes.

Drain mushrooms and add to the soup pot along with kale or spinach and Madeira or apple cider. Add remaining water or broth. Heat until the soup comes almost to a boil, then lower the heat to medium-low, cover, and simmer for 1 hour. Add more water or broth, if necessary, but the stew should be thick.

Uncover and cook for an additional 30 minutes, stirring occasionally. Season with salt and pepper to taste, and serve with a loaf of crusty bread.

> **Cauldron Bubble**
>
> This stew is easy to make, but for an even easier version, soak mushrooms in boiling water, drain, and then combine all ingredients in a crock pot and cook on low for 8 hours.

Beef Roast in Old Ale

This delicious dish will fill the whole house with its succulent aroma. Using beer or apple cider helps to tenderize the beef as it roasts. If you can't find old ale, you can substitute stout or porter. The alcohol cooks off, but if you prefer not to use beer, you can substitute beef broth or a beef broth/apple cider mixture. Using beef broth alone will work, but the end result might not be as tender as you had hoped, especially if you begin with a cheaper cut of beef.

Because this recipe requires an extended baking time, it utilizes Earth and Fire energies. Charge your ingredients to enhance stability and passion. (See Chapter 21 for directions on charging ingredients.)

This recipe uses thyme, which attracts love and friendship; pepper, for passion; and beef, which attracts the god energies. It is a filling, comfort dish that packs a punch both nutritionally and magickally. Instead of a traditional holiday goose or turkey, substitute this savory main dish.

> 4- to 5-pound rib-eye roast (or any lean, boneless beef roast, preferably organic)
>
> 1 TB. dried thyme
>
> Salt and black pepper to taste
>
> 1 (12-ounce) bottle old ale (try Theakston Old Peculiar, or your favorite old ale)
>
> ½ cup apple cider
>
> 1 TB. unsalted butter
>
> 1 TB. brown sugar

Preheat the oven to 450°F. Rub thyme, salt, and pepper all over roast. Put roast in a roasting pan with the fat side facing up.

Pour out ½ cup of old ale and set aside. Pour remaining ale over the roast and put in the oven.

Roast for 15 minutes. Reduce heat to 400°F and roast an additional hour or slightly longer, until an instant-read meat thermometer reads 125–130°F (this is for medium-rare to medium).

Take the roasting pan out, put the roast on a platter, and cover with foil. Set aside.

Put the roasting pan over one or two burners on the stove. Turn the burner(s) to medium-high. Deglaze the pan with apple cider, scraping with a wooden spoon or wire whisk to remove the browned bits in the bottom of the pan. Add butter, brown sugar, and remaining old ale. Continue stirring until the sauce thickens and turns glossy.

Slice roast and serve with sauce.

Leftovers of this recipe make delicious roast beef sandwiches. Serve them on crusty French bread with some beef bouillon as a dipping sauce.

Parsnip Purée with Garlic Cream

Sweeter and creamier than mashed potatoes, this recipe makes use of a lesser known winter vegetable. Parsnips enhance yang or masculine energies, and garlic provides protection. Boiling the parsnips introduces the Water Element, which encourages intuition and feminine Goddess energies.

> 4 medium to large parsnips, peeled with ends and tips cut off, sliced into 2-inch lengths
>
> 8 cloves garlic, peeled
>
> ¼ cup unsalted butter
>
> ¼ cup cream or whole milk, or a little more
>
> ½ tsp. salt
>
> Pinch of white pepper

Put a large pot of water over high heat. Add parsnips and garlic cloves. Bring to a boil. Cook until parsnips and garlic cloves are tender and easily pierced with a fork, about 20 minutes.

Drain parsnips and garlic cloves in a colander and put in a large bowl. Add butter, cream or milk, salt, and pepper. Mash with a fork or process through a potato ricer. When parsnips and garlic cloves are slightly mashed, beat with a mixer on low speed (parsnips don't get gummy like mashed potatoes, so you can use a mixer). Or stir vigorously with a fork or wire whisk until smooth and creamy. Add more milk or cream if parsnips seem too dry.

Serve as a side dish. This recipe is delicious with the Beef Roast in Old Ale.

> **Cauldron Bubble**
>
> Try other white winter vegetables in place of the parsnips—cauliflower, turnips, rutabaga, or kohlrabi, for example. Add a few onion slices to taste.

Spice Cake with Dried Fruit

This variation of a classic spice cake is like a cornucopia of stored winter produce: root vegetables, apples, and dried fruits laced with cinnamon for psychic awareness, and nutmeg and ginger for wealth and prosperity. This is an especially good cake to serve around the beginning of the New Year. Drop a well-washed silver coin into the batter. The person who finds the coin will have good luck in the coming year. (Be sure to warn everyone about the coin beforehand so no one chips a tooth!)

3 cups unbleached all-purpose flour

½ cup oat flour (put old-fashioned oats in a blender and pulse until ground)

1 TB. baking powder

1 tsp. baking soda

¼ tsp. salt

1 TB. cinnamon

1 tsp. ground ginger

½ tsp. nutmeg

1 cup light brown sugar

2 eggs

1 cup unsweetened applesauce

½ cup mandarin oranges, drained

2 large carrots, grated

½ cup raisins

6 dried apricots, snipped into small bits

3 prunes, snipped into small bits

¼ cup buttermilk or plain yogurt

Zest from one organic orange

1 tsp. vanilla extract

Powdered sugar and whole dried apricots for garnish

Preheat oven to 350°F. Lightly grease and flour a 9×13-inch cake pan.

Combine all ingredients except garnishes, in order, in a large bowl, mixing after each addition. Pour into pan, scraping with a rubber scraper to get all the batter.

Bake for 30 minutes or until a toothpick inserted in the center comes out clean. Sprinkle with powdered sugar, top each slice with a dried apricot, and serve warm or at room temperature.

This cake is excellent the next morning for breakfast, too. Thin slices can be toasted and slathered with butter for a special treat.

Steaming Spiced Chocolate

This is a warming drink when first coming in from the cold, or a sweet after-dinner alternative to coffee. This drink can serve as dessert, but it also makes a fine last course along with or following a small slice of the Spice Cake with Dried Fruit.

This recipe enhances psychic awareness (cinnamon), attracts wealth (nutmeg and cloves), and can be shared in small amounts with the faery realm as an offering or a thank-you (see Chapter 15). Faery folk are especially fond of milk-based drinks. Set a small cup or saucer of this hot chocolate in your backyard to thank them and welcome them to your garden. Any small cup will do, but doll tea sets are just the right size.

> 4 cups whole or low-fat milk
>
> 2 cinnamon sticks
>
> 2 whole cloves
>
> 1 TB. honey
>
> 8 oz. bittersweet or semisweet chocolate, chopped into small pieces
>
> Whipped cream (sweetened or unsweetened, depending on your preference) and ground nutmeg for garnish

In a large saucepan over medium heat, combine milk, cinnamon sticks, and cloves. Heat just until tiny bubbles form around the edges, but do not allow milk to boil. Reduce heat to medium-low.

Using a fork, remove the cinnamon sticks and cloves. Add honey and chocolate. Stir constantly until chocolate is completely melted. Pour into mugs.

Serve hot, topped with a spoonful of whipped cream sprinkled with nutmeg.

CAUTION

Stir Gently ...!

Don't substitute powdered cinnamon for cinnamon sticks in this recipe. You'll wind up with gritty sludge in the bottom of the cup.

Liguana's Grimoire

At one time Liguana lived in a ground-floor apartment in Seattle. The winter always meant short rations, and soup and stew were commonly on her table. She took to inviting friends and neighbors over to share. People would often tap on her window and wave a loaf of French bread, asking what else was for dinner. Showing hospitality and feeding those around her not only helped build a strong community, but increased her sense of being a powerful magickal person, sharing her larder and receiving back threefold.

Several holidays can be celebrated during the winter months—Winter Solstice, Yule, Christmas, Kwanza, Hanukah, New Year's, and Candlemas, to name a few. All of them celebrate the rebirth of the light in some way. But there are also lots of long, dreary, dark days when Natural Magicians have to dig deep into their psychic selves to work a little magick. Winter food should be warm and robust and should nurture the Spirit as well as the body. Use spices liberally, and choose cooking methods that are long and slow, to fill the house with delicious aromas. Just as Earth's energies slow down during winter, so should you.

The Least You Need to Know

- Dig into your pantry for dried beans, grains, and fruits during the winter months.

- Charge even everyday family meals with protection, health, and peace to get through the dark days of winter.

- Slow-cooking methods such as baking and crock pot cookery are especially good calming energies to add to a winter menu.

- Sharing your winter pantry with others enhances your Natural Magick by sending goodness back to you threefold.

The Seed Grows: Flavors of Spring

In This Chapter

◆ Eating off the land

◆ Steaming vegetables for a creative salad

◆ Frittata extraordinaire

◆ Going a-mothering cake

◆ Preserving edible flowers as decoration

Recipes for the spring and early summer can use lots of fresh stir-fried baby vegetables, fresh salads, and sweets decorated with candied flowers. Everything during this time of year is tender and young—and so yummy after a season of not eating fresh but relying on stored instead.

Dairy is limited during the spring, but eggs are everywhere! Spinach and chard and radishes are up, as are young dandelion greens and calendula flowers. Asparagus is available this time of year, rhubarb begins to ripen, peas are incredibly sweet, and the first tiny red strawberries start appearing.

This is the time to eat off the land. Preserving and canning come later, at the end of summer, when luscious surplus needs to be saved for leaner times. Now is the season to revel in freshly picked produce.

Spring Salad

This salad contains all the elements of spring: tender baby vegetables, lightly steamed hard-boiled eggs, and a fresh-herb-infused dressing. It is both beautiful and tasty, a meal in itself if served with fresh bread.

This recipe includes basil to attract wealth, dill weed and garlic to banish negative energy, and eggs to honor the Lady. Steaming the vegetables adds the Elements of Air and Water, which encourages creative imagination and intuition. This is the time for Natural Magicians to release anything holding them back and begin with a fresh start, just like Nature is doing.

1 cup thin green beans, cut into 1-inch lengths

1 cup pencil-thin asparagus, cut into 1 inch lengths

½ cup spring peas, shelled

6 baby carrots, cut into long, thin strips

1 TB. cooking oil, if sautéeing

2 cups fresh baby greens

1 cup fresh baby spinach leaves

8 new potatoes, boiled and cut in half

1 cup plain yogurt

½ cup sour cream

Zest and juice from one lemon

¼ cup extra virgin olive oil

1 TB. fresh dill weed

1 TB. fresh basil, chopped

1 clove garlic, minced

4 hard-boiled eggs, peeled and sliced

Put green beans, asparagus, peas, and carrots in a steamer and steam for about 10 minutes or until bright green (and, in the case of carrots, orange). Or sautée very briefly over medium-high heat in 1 tablespoon cooking oil.

Toss baby greens and spinach leaves in a large salad bowl. Add beans, asparagus, peas, carrots, and boiled potatoes.

In a medium bowl, combine yogurt, sour cream, lemon zest and juice, olive oil, dill weed, basil, and garlic. Whisk until smooth. Pour over the salad and toss to coat. Arrange sliced eggs over the top and serve.

Fiddlehead Frittata with Ham and Hollandaise Sauce

A spring delicacy, fiddleheads are the young fronds of certain types of ferns. Although the word *fiddlehead* could refer to any fern shoots, only one variety, the ostrich fern, is considered edible. These tightly curled green shoots are picked before their leaves unfurl; gathered from the wild, they are rare and expensive.

These curled, snail-like fern shoots taste like a combination of asparagus and artichokes. If you can't find them, substitute pencil-thin asparagus or artichoke hearts for this recipe. It might not be quite as exotic, but we guarantee it will be just as tasty. If you'd rather make this a vegetarian dish, simply omit the ham. There are plenty of flavors in this recipe, even without the meat. If you use the ham, be sure to offer a special blessing to the animal that provided its flesh to you.

> **Stir Gently …!**
>
> As always, when you gather food from the wild, if you aren't absolutely certain it's edible, don't pick it. Most edible ferns come from Maine. Those growing in your area could be toxic. You can order fiddlehead ferns online for a brief time in the spring, usually between the end of April and late May.

A perfect Ostara brunch dish, this recipe promises wealth and prosperity, protection and the banishing of negative energy, and heightened psychic awareness. Using the fresh fiddlehead ferns (or asparagus) reminds us of new beginnings.

    1 cup fiddlehead ferns, tail ends cut off, rinsed well, and patted dry

    1 TB. olive oil

    2 TB. unsalted butter

    2 medium leeks, most of green part and roots cut off, thinly sliced

2 cloves garlic, peeled and minced

1 cup diced ham

6 eggs

1 TB. fresh tarragon, chopped

1 TB. fresh basil, chopped

Zest from one lemon (use juice for the Hollandaise Sauce, recipe follows)

¼ cup freshly grated Parmesan cheese (optional)

Hollandaise Sauce

Preheat oven to 450°F. Put fiddlehead ferns in a roasting pan in a single layer and drizzle with olive oil. Roast for 10 minutes. Remove from the oven and set the oven to broil.

In a large oven-proof skillet, melt the butter over medium-high heat. Sautée leeks, garlic, and ham until leeks are tender but not browned, about 10 minutes.

Meanwhile, in a separate bowl, beat eggs with a fork until combined. Add herbs and zest.

Pour egg-herb mixture over leeks, garlic, and ham. Lower heat to medium. Arrange fiddlehead ferns over the top and sprinkle with Parmesan cheese (if using it). Cook until bottom is set, about 4 minutes. The top should still look runny.

Remove the skillet from the heat and put under the broiler. Broil until the top is set but not browned, no more than 1 minute. Remove the skillet from the oven and slide the frittata on a plate. Cut in wedges and serve with Hollandaise Sauce.

Liguana's Grimoire

Liguana has had up to 24 chickens free-ranging all around her yard. One of her favorite things about spring is hunting eggs. With several herds of chickens wandering through the woods and in and out of bushes, it's easy to see where the tradition of Easter egg hunting came from. She gets a sense of spontaneous joy when she finds beautiful brown or green or white eggs the chickens have hidden for her.

Hollandaise Sauce

This version uses the blender or food processor and is so easy that you'll want to make this bright, creamy-tart sauce all the time. The paprika adds a little passion and excitement to this dish, so serve it to your friends as well as to your partner.

½ cup (1 stick) unsalted butter

4 egg yolks

Juice from 1 lemon

Paprika

½ tsp. salt

Clarify butter: Put butter in a small saucepan and heat over medium until the foamy milk solids rise to the top. Skim them off and reduce heat to low.

In a blender or food processor, combine egg yolks, lemon juice, paprika, and salt. Blend or process on high for 1 full minute. Through the top of the blender or the food processor feed tube, pour warm butter in a slow stream. Blend for an additional 15 seconds. Serve immediately.

Makes about 1¼ cups.

May Basket Cake

This recipe is a variation on an old English Lenten tradition of "going a-mothering," in which children would bake cakes and deliver them to mothers. While this tradition may have come to represent gifting the Mother Church, it was originally a celebration of Mother Earth's renewal of animal and plant life each spring. The lavender evokes a feeling of peace and calm, while the strawberries attract love and luck.

Liguana's children follow a May Day tradition of gifting elderly ladies who have no children of their own. They make paper or cloth baskets, decorate them with ribbons, and fill them with fresh flowers. The tradition is to leave the basket hanging on the doorknob, knock, and run away. The children have come to believe it's good luck if the neighbor lady never finds out who gifted her.

¾ cup (1½ sticks) unsalted butter, softened

1¾ cup sugar

4 eggs

2 cups unbleached white flour

1 tsp. salt

1 cup currants

½ cup fresh strawberries, chopped

Zest from one organic lemon

Zest from one organic orange

Zest from one organic lime

1 TB. fresh organic lavender petals

2½ cups Almond Paste (recipe follows)

Almond Butter Cream (recipe follows)

Crystallized pansies, violas, and violets (recipe follows)

Small, fresh, whole strawberries with their tops for garnish

Preheat oven to 350°F. Butter and flour an 8-inch *springform pan*.

In a large bowl, combine butter and sugar. Beat with an electric mixer until light and fluffy. Add eggs one at a time, beating well after each addition.

Sift flour and salt together, then add a little at a time, beating well after each addition.

Using a spatula or large wooden spoon, fold in currants, chopped strawberries, citrus zests, and lavender petals. Pour one third of batter into the pan. Spread half of almond paste in a thin layer over batter. It doesn't have to be even, and if almond paste is too stiff to spread, just form disks with your hands and place over the batter. Pour next third of batter over almond paste. Cover with remaining almond paste. Pour in rest of batter.

Bake for 1 hour or until the cake is golden and springs back lightly when gently pressed with your finger. Remove and cool on a wire rack.

Magickal Bounty

Springform pans are made with a removable base and a buckle-joined vertical rim. Buckle the side with the base in place, and you're ready to bake. Unbuckle when done, the rim springs open, and removal of really moist cakes is a breeze. All springform pans leak a little. Use aluminum foil on the outside of the pan to prevent this.

When cool, frost with almond butter cream, piping a shell border around the edge and, if desired, a basket-weave design on the sides (use a flat icing tip and pipe sections at a time, first making a couple of vertical lines, then making the horizontal lines over and tucked under to look like a basket). Top the cake ("filling" the basket) with crystallized flowers and small fresh strawberries.

Almond Paste

Almonds are generally thought to bring money and wisdom to those who eat them. You can make this almond paste ahead of time and store, wrapped in plastic, for up to a week at room temperature or up to a month, refrigerated. If you refrigerate, bring the almond paste to room temperature and then knead it, adding some water, if necessary, before using.

If you want to use the almond paste to make candy or to stuff dates or other dried fruits and you don't plan to cook it, and you are concerned about using raw egg whites, you can eliminate the egg whites and increase the light corn syrup to ¼ cup. If you are using this in the May Basket Cake, you will be cooking it, so you needn't worry about the egg whites.

> 1½ cups blanched whole almonds
>
> ½ cup powdered sugar
>
> ½ cup granulated sugar
>
> 2 egg whites
>
> 1 TB. light corn syrup
>
> ¼ tsp. almond extract

In a food processor or blender, combine almonds and both sugars. Process or blend until almonds are finely ground and combined with sugar. Add egg whites, corn syrup, and almond extract. Process or blend until thoroughly combined. Turn out onto a pastry board or other hard clean surface dusted with powdered sugar. Knead with your hands to combine. If the paste seems too crumbly, add water a teaspoon at a time until smooth.

Makes about 2½ cups.

Almond Butter Cream

This frosting is good on many different kinds of cakes. If you are using it for the May Basket Cake, use the yolks from the two egg whites in the previous recipe for almond paste. Waste not, want not!

½ cup (1 stick) unsalted butter, softened

4 cups powdered sugar

Dash of salt

2 egg yolks

1 TB. amaretto liqueur (or 1 tsp. almond extract)

1 TB. cream, or a little more

Put butter into a large bowl and beat with an electric mixer on medium speed until light and fluffy. Add 2 cups of sugar, salt, and egg yolks.

Beat on low until thick and smooth. Add amaretto or almond extract and cream, then add remaining sugar, ½ cup at a time, until good spreading consistency (you might not need all the sugar). If the butter cream seems too stiff, add a little more cream or milk.

Crystallized Flowers

These pretty edible flowers are beautiful when painted with egg whites and dusted with superfine granulated sugar.

Stir Gently …!

We can't say this often enough: if you are not certain a flower is edible, we suggest not using it. Be sure the plants have not been sprayed with chemicals, and wash them well before using to remove any dust or dirt on the petals.

Use a clean small artist's paintbrush for this recipe, but be sure it has never been used with paint. Reserve it for food use only. Use crystallized flowers as a garnish on desserts, from cakes to custards. If you don't want to use egg whites, use method #2.

Harvest edible flowers from your yard, but only if you don't use lawn or garden chemicals, and your neighbors don't, either. Pick them in the morning, just after the dew has dried, for the freshest, plumpest flowers. Some edible flowers are violets, violas, pansies, borage, hollyhocks, lilacs, roses, geraniums, marigolds, and impatiens.

Ingredients for method #1:

> 1 cup of well-rinsed flowers, stems cut off
>
> 1 egg white at room temperature, lightly beaten with a fork or whisk
>
> ½ cup superfine sugar

Carefully paint each flower petal with the egg white, then sprinkle with superfine sugar. Set the flowers on wax paper to dry. Or let them dry in an oven set to 150°F for several hours, for a crunchier result.

Ingredients for method #2:

> 1 cup violets, violas, and/or pansy flowers, stems cut off
>
> 1 cup superfine sugar
>
> ¼ cup water
>
> Dash cream of tartar

Combine sugar, water, and cream of tartar in a small saucepan and heat over medium-high, stirring constantly, until sugar is completely dissolved. Remove from heat. Using a small tongs or tweezers, dip each flower in the sugar water, then set on wax paper to dry.

Natural Magicians utilize this time of year not only to harvest the first, tender shoots and vegetables but also to prepare the soil to plant the fruits and vegetables that will become ripe in late summer and early fall. It is a time to reacquaint ourselves with the feel of earth between our fingers, the warmth of the sun on our shoulders, and the taste of green in our mouths.

The Least You Need to Know

- Spring is a time of renewal both for the Earth and for our Spirits.
- Spring provides a Natural Magician with a bounty of fresh produce which can make for very powerful magick.
- Never eat food you've gathered wildcrafting unless you're absolutely certain it's edible and pesticide free.
- Plan spring menus around the freshest herbs and vegetables available. They disappear all too soon.

Chapter 20

Bring in the Bounty: Summer's Produce

In This Chapter

◆ Using summer's bounty

◆ A light pasta salad with magickal overtones

◆ A summer stew from your garden

◆ A fruity dessert right off the tree

◆ We all scream for ice cream

From mid- to late summer into early fall, most fruits and vegetables ripen. Peaches, plums, pears, apples, grapes, sweet corn, tomatoes, zucchini—they all mean summer bounty. If you're a garden witch, the excess can almost be overwhelming. This is the time of year that Natural Magicians make the most of the surplus, not only in their menus, but also in canning and freezing for the winter days coming up.

Meat of all types is more plentiful, so meals are often more based around meat during this time. Poultry dishes abound as people eating seasonally (at least, those raising chickens) cull the flocks of those not producing well. Of course, dairy is back—yogurt, cheese, custards. Eggs are still plentiful, too.

Spring Chicken Pasta Salad with Cucumber-Yogurt Sauce

This refreshing, light pasta salad dressed in cool cucumber-yogurt sauce is perfect for hot days, especially when served with a cup of gazpacho and fresh fruit for dessert. This recipe starts with chicken on the bone with skin because the meat is more flavorful this way. The actual recipe doesn't use the skin. You can also make an even lighter all-veggie side dish of this pasta salad by simply leaving out the chicken; it will still taste good. Just cook the onion with the spices in the olive oil and add to the pasta without the chicken, to retain that Middle Eastern flavor.

The combination of cinnamon, walnuts, and caraway seeds enhances awareness, adds stability, and encourages generosity. Cumin helps build self-reliance, and adding the jalapeño strengthens the spell and adds a little passion to the mix.

2 cups stubby pasta (such as cavatelli, fusilli, conchiglie, farfalle, or gemelli)

2 whole chicken breasts on the bone with the skin (sometimes these come in halves, in which case, get four halves)

1 cup chicken broth

1 cup water

1 TB. olive oil

1 tsp. cumin

½ tsp. cinnamon

¼ tsp. caraway seeds

½ cup red onion, finely chopped

2 stalks celery, trimmed and sliced

1 carrot, shredded

1 green pepper, cored, seeded, and chopped

1 large tomato, cored and chopped

1 small jalapeño pepper, cored, seeded, and minced (optional)

½ cup golden raisins

1 cup chopped walnuts

Cucumber-Yogurt Sauce (recipe follows)

Watercress for garnish

Cook pasta according to package directions, rinse, drain, and put into a large bowl.

Put chicken in a large skillet, breast side down. Add broth and water. Poach over medium-high heat until cooked all the way through, about 20 minutes (you can cut open the meat to check for doneness—you'll be chopping it up anyway). Add more water or broth during cooking, if necessary.

Cauldron Bubble

Tired of tears when you're cutting onions? Try lighting a candle and placing it next to where you're chopping. The flame affects the potency of the compound that causes the tears. And while you're lighting it, say a blessing for the meal.

Remove chicken from broth and allow to cool until you can handle it. Peel off the skin and separate as much meat as you can from the bones. Cut meat into bite-size chunks. Discard bones, skin, and cooking water. (If you live with animal companions, you can give the discarded chicken skin to the dogs and cats—but never the cooked bones! Chicken bones splinter easily and can become lodged in an animal's throat or abdomen. You don't want your furry friends to have to take an emergency trip to the vet.)

In the same skillet, add olive oil. Heat on medium-high until the olive oil releases its aroma, about 3 minutes. Add cumin, cinnamon, caraway seeds, and onion. Stir to combine and cook for 5 minutes. Add chunks of chicken and toss to coat, then put chicken and juices and spices into pasta. Add celery, carrot, green pepper, tomato, jalapeño pepper, raisins, and walnuts to the pasta. Mix together.

Pour Cucumber-Yogurt Sauce over the salad and mix until everything is coated in the sauce. Garnish with watercress. Serve cold or at room temperature.

Cucumber-Yogurt Sauce

Mint attracts material gain and is sometimes used to protect travelers who are on a journey. Mint and garlic together are a powerful blend to banish negativity.

2 cups plain yogurt

1 large cucumber, peeled and chopped

1 TB. red onion, minced

1 clove garlic, peeled and minced

3 fresh mint leaves, minced (or ½ tsp. dried)

> **Magickal Bounty**
>
> A classic Middle Eastern dish, **falafel** is a vegetarian treat made of ground chick peas and spices. Traditional recipes deep-fry the patties. They are often served in pita bread with lettuce, tomatoes, and yogurt dressing.

1 TB. freshly squeezed lemon juice

1 tsp. salt

Dash of cayenne pepper (optional)

Freshly ground black pepper to taste

Combine all ingredients and stir until smooth. Pour onto pasta salad or serve as a condiment to Middle Eastern dishes such as *falafel* or gyros.

Makes about 2½ cups.

Peasant Stew

Stew might seem like winter food, but this recipe is rich with the produce that peaks in midsummer. Based on the classic thick vegetable soup from Tuscany served over chunks of bread and drizzled with olive oil, this summer stew is even better (and more authentic) the next day, so if you have the time, make it a day ahead and store it in the refrigerator. Then just warm it up, adding just enough water to prevent scorching. This stew should be thick.

This might seem like a lot of stew, especially if you're only cooking for one or two. But if your garden or the farmer's market is overflowing with veggies, make up a batch to freeze or can. You'll appreciate the taste of fresh summer vegetables when there's snow on the ground.

You'll notice that there are no spices in this recipe except salt and pepper. This not only allows the flavor of the fresh vegetables to come through, but it also makes a purifying, cleansing meal.

¼ cup extra-virgin olive oil

1 small white onion, peeled and chopped

4 cloves garlic, minced

4 stalks celery, trimmed and sliced

2 carrots, scrubbed, trimmed, and sliced

1 cup packed spinach leaves, washed and chopped

1 large zucchini, chopped

2 small or 1 large yellow summer squash, trimmed and chopped

1 cup fresh green beans, trimmed and cut or snapped into 1-inch lengths

1 green pepper, cored, seeded, and chopped

1 red pepper, cored, seeded, and chopped

1 small green cabbage, cored and cut into slivers

2 quarts organic beef, chicken, or vegetable broth

2 (12-ounce) cans cannelloni (white beans), drained and rinsed

Salt and pepper to taste

1 large loaf Italian bread, preferably day-old

½ cup fresh Italian parsley, chopped

½ cup grated Parmesan cheese

Extra-virgin olive oil for garnish

In a large soup pot or Dutch oven, heat the olive oil over medium-high until it releases an aroma, about 5 minutes. Add onion and garlic. Cook, stirring constantly, until onion is soft but not brown, about 5 minutes.

Add celery, carrots, spinach, zucchini, summer squash, green beans, green pepper, and red pepper. Stir and cook until ingredients soften, about 10 minutes.

Add cabbage and 1 cup of the broth. Stir and cook until cabbage wilts and releases its juices, about 10 more minutes.

Add remaining broth, and reduce heat to medium. Simmer, stirring occasionally, for about 1 hour, adding liquid only if the stew becomes dry. Stir in the beans and cook for an additional 15 minutes. Season with salt and pepper to taste.

Fill each person's bowl with chunks of Italian bread. Ladle stew over bread, then garnish with Italian parsley and Parmesan cheese. Finish each bowl by drizzling a few teaspoons of olive oil over the top.

Juicy Fruit Crumble

Summer is the time for big, bright orchard fruit burgeoning with juice and bright juicy berries. Use fresh peaches, nectarines, plums, apricots, strawberries, blueberries, raspberries, cherries, or whatever combination of fruit looks freshest and best in this sweet fruit crisp. Serve this crumble with homemade or good-quality ice cream (see following recipe) or frozen yogurt.

Ginger is a good spice to use if you want to heighten your creativity or banish a worrisome mood. Cinnamon and nutmeg attract romance, and the use of orange flavoring (alcohol or nonalcoholic) encourages sensitivity and compassion.

> 4 cups of fresh summer fruit, cut into chunks (except for berries, but cut larger strawberries into bite-size pieces)
>
> ¼ cup white sugar
>
> 1 TB. orange-flavored liqueur, such as Grand Marnier or Kirsch, or orange juice
>
> ½ cup unbleached white flour
>
> ¾ cup rolled oats
>
> ¼ cup shredded coconut (optional)
>
> ¾ cup packed light brown sugar
>
> ½ tsp. salt
>
> ½ tsp. ground cinnamon
>
> ¼ tsp. ground ginger
>
> ¼ tsp. ground nutmeg
>
> ½ cup (1 stick) unsalted butter, chilled and cut into pieces

Preheat oven to 350°F. In a large bowl, combine fruit, white sugar, and orange flavoring you've chosen to use. Toss to coat and set aside.

In the bowl of a food processor or in another large bowl, combine flour, oats, coconut (if using), brown sugar, salt, cinnamon, ginger, nutmeg, and butter. Process by pulsing several times or cut with a pastry blender until the mixture resembles coarse crumbs.

Pour the fruit into a deep-dish pie plate or 9-inch square baking pan. Sprinkle topping evenly over the fruit. Bake for 1 hour or until topping is golden brown and fruit is bubbling. Serve warm, at room temperature, or cold.

Cauldron Bubble _____

You can adjust the amount of sugar you use in the filling, depending on how sweet the fruit is that you are using. Add a little at a time and then taste. You can always add more.

Midsummer Night's Cream

This recipe is a great excuse to pull out that ice cream maker you hardly ever use. You need to chill the cream, so start this the day before you want the ice cream. Super-simple to make, this ice cream is made extra special with heavy cream. This ice cream is also a great base for adding flavorings. Try a little cinnamon, instant coffee, a handful of chocolate chips, chopped nuts, or fresh berries. For a special treat, add liqueur such as Kalhua, Frangelico, or Armagnac, but don't add these until the very end, when the ice cream is already frozen. Alcohol can keep ice cream from freezing effectively.

Vanilla enhances memory and is also a real attraction for the faery realm. Refer to Appendix C for additional ingredients to add, depending on your magickal desires.

> 4 cups heavy cream
>
> 1 vanilla bean or 1 tsp. vanilla extract
>
> 1 cup superfine sugar

Put cream in a large, heavy saucepan. Split the vanilla bean and scrape seeds into cream (if using vanilla extract, you will add it later). Heat cream over medium heat just until bubbles appear around the edges. Do not allow cream to boil. Remove from heat.

Add sugar and stir until it is completely dissolved. Add vanilla extract, if you didn't use the vanilla bean. Pour ice cream mixture into a container and cover. Refrigerate overnight.

Cauldron Bubble _____

Remember that the magickal correspondences we suggest throughout this book are just that—suggestions. You'll notice, in fact, that we don't always use an herb or a spice for the same magickal reason. Always follow your own instincts.

Freeze in your ice cream machine, using the directions for that machine. At the end, add any optional flavorings or additions, such as chocolate chips or fruit. This ice cream doesn't get very hard; it is more the consistency of soft serve. After freezing it in the ice cream maker, you can freeze it for a few hours to make it firmer.

Summer and early fall days are the perfect time to host a party or just gather your family together for a special meal made with summer's freshest ingredients. Outdoor rituals are especially appealing while the nights are balmy or just slightly crisp. Build a bonfire and end the ritual with cakes and ale (see Chapter 23) or toasted marshmallows for the young at heart.

The Least You Need to Know

- Summer magick uses fresh ingredients right out of your garden or from your local farmer's market or grocery store.

- Pick fruits and vegetables at their peak of freshness and can or freeze the surplus to enjoy in the winter months.

- Meat-based meals are often featured at this time of the year, but the abundance of fresh produce means lots of vegetarian meals as well.

- Always listen to your inner magician when choosing herbs to use for a specific Natural Magickal purpose. There are no "wrong" ones to use.

Part 6

Organic Craft of Natural Magick

Adding a little deliberate Natural Magick to your cooking is as simple as paying attention to the flavors you're serving, saying a few magick words over the soup pot, and approaching your meal with reverence and appreciation to the Earth that provided it for you. Ethical eating is the hallmark of a Natural Magician. Plus, a bonus "gem" of a chapter helps you connect your magick with Nature.

Chapter 21

Charging Nature's Bounty with Magickal Intent

In This Chapter

- ◆ Charging food for magickal purposes
- ◆ Creating sacred space in the kitchen
- ◆ Cooking consciously
- ◆ Cooking methods to enhance intent
- ◆ Charging plants

Although Natural Magicians use magick in all kinds of ways, charging food and other organic material can easily fit into a daily routine. After all, we eat every day. By charging a few ingredients, you can turn any meal into a magickal event. For example, charging the rosemary sprinkled into your family's food with prosperity energies encourages not only monetary gains, but also job opportunities and success in school. The little pinch of salt added at the table or while cooking can be charged with cleansing energies. Passion can be stirred into a soup by charging the cracked black pepper or chili spices.

These rituals can be simple or more complex and formal, depending on the occasion. Charging something magickally requires creative visualization. The ability to clearly envision your desired end result takes a little practice. Visualizing is simply a matter of using your imagination. If you can close your eyes and "picture" your desired outcome, you're visualizing.

Natural Magick in the Kitchen

Kitchens and dining rooms are rooms filled with the scents and sounds of family, friendship, special occasions, and laughter. They are sacred spaces where we find nourishment, not only for our bodies, but also for our Spirits.

The kitchen reflects our connection to the physical realm and the Earth. When we are connected to the Elements and to the God and Goddess, Natural Magick becomes part of everyday experiences and expressions. What could be more sacred than nourishing our bodies with healthful food? After all, it is the body that houses the Spirit. There are so many occasions for bringing the sacred into the kitchen.

> **Cauldron Bubble**
>
> Stay tuned in to what special energies your immediate family might need to have added to an everyday meal to give them a boost through the day. A big exam, an audition for the orchestra, a request for a raise, meeting a deadline—all of these can be magickally encouraged.

Feasts at the end of ceremonies, welcoming a baby, blessing a new marriage, enjoying a simple luncheon with close friends, or having a romantic picnic with a partner—all are reasons to work a little magick.

Charging food with magickal intents helps to internalize the magick and increase the power of spells. Meals need not be elaborate to be powerful. Even a simple tossed salad, when prepared with awareness and intent, can carry a powerful charge that will merge with the loved ones who will be enjoying the homemade cooking.

Charging an Ingredient

So how does a Natural Magician charge an ingredient? Here's the simplest way. Hold the ingredient in your hands and concentrate on what you want it to do. Visualize the object performing its purpose. Picture the energies of what you want flowing from your heart and mind, down your arms, through your hands, and flooding into the object with your power of intent. (If you want to charge an ingredient that isn't possible to hold, such as flour or milk, pour it into a large bowl and just lay your fingertips lightly on top of it. Remember to wash your hands first!)

Charging herbs and other ingredients before using them in spellcrafting aligns the vibrations of the items involved with your magickal need. It is a process designed to increase the effectiveness of your spell, ritual, or magickal work.

You shouldn't charge an ingredient until you are ready to use it. However, a preliminary enchantment can be performed if the herb or plant is collected from the wild or a garden. While actually cutting an herb for a specific spell, the need should be stressed, as should the plant's role in fulfilling that need—for example:

> *I gather you, basil,*
> *Herb of the Sun,*
> *To increase my wealth and prosperity.*

A Simple Charging Ritual for Several Ingredients

Perhaps you want to magickally charge an entire recipe at once. Pour the ingredients into a bowl, casserole dish, or pot, depending on what the recipe requires. Sit or stand calmly and gaze into the bowl. Sense the vibrations waiting within the flour, herbs, or vegetables; see them emerging from the ingredients or lying in wait. Lean toward the bowl and place your power hand (usually the one you write with) within it, lightly touching the food. Leave it motionless for a few seconds. Visualize your need strongly.

Run your fingers over the surface of the mixture. Still strongly visualizing your need, send it into the food. Feel your fingertips charging it with energy. If you have trouble holding the image in your mind, chant simple words that match your need, such as, "May this dish bring all who partake of this meal safety and health."

When the ingredients are tingling with power or when you sense that the charge is complete, remove your hand and finish the recipe.

Cauldron Bubble

Not fond of cooking? "Fast" meals can also be magickally charged. Precooked, frozen dinners, instant soups, even preseasoned frozen vegetables can be infused with your good intentions. Just visualize your intent and speak your goal out loud.

It is especially easy to charge herbs and spices using this simple ritual. As you visualize your desired outcome, picture the plant itself. See the energy flowing from each leaf, flower, and root. Breathe deeply of the herb's or spice's special aroma. Then send your Will to join with its natural energies.

Creating a Sacred Kitchen

Creating sacred space in the kitchen is a very important first step in performing any Natural Magick. First, clear all unnecessary clutter from the area in which you will be working. Wipe down all surfaces and sweep the floor east to west (to mimic the direction the sun takes), if possible.

Weather permitting, open the windows and put some fresh flowers in the space. Add some magickal symbols to the area that appeal to you. Perhaps some dried red roses for love, lavender for relaxation and peace of mind, a peacock feather for inner vision and magickal clarity, a pine cone to bring in the good energy of vitality, a pentacle made from dried flower stems to symbolize the five Elements.

Finally, invite a Hearth Goddess, such as Hestia (the Greek goddess of the hearth fire who presides over domestic life), to bless your meal. Call on your Hearth Goddess or any God or Goddess that corresponds to your intent for that meal. Turn on some inspiring music to put yourself into a joyful mood. Start cooking!

Conscious Cooking

As you cook, pay attention to your intuition. Feel confident in straying from the written recipe. Out of fettuccine? Substitute any pasta shape you have on hand. In your favorite spice cake, leave out the raisins and walnuts and use dried cranberries and pecans instead. Don't care for cilantro? Toss in a handful of oregano. If you allow a sense of playfulness to come into your kitchen, you might discover ways of cooking things that you would never have thought of before. Cooking should be a relaxing, uplifting experience for a Natural Magician.

> **CAUTION**
>
> **Stir Gently ...!**
>
> Don't tackle a difficult recipe or a six-course meal on days you feel rushed or overly stressed. Without meaning to, you could be infusing the dishes with all of that negative energy and passing it along to your family. On hectic days, keep your meals simple.

When making a magickal meal, choose a day when you are not rushed and are free to take a bit of extra time. Remember to choose foods that are in season, when you can (see the recipes in Part 5). During the Waxing Moon and early spring, try dishes for creativity and inspiration. During a Waning Moon and the cold winter, serve up some comfort foods for rest and relaxation. The extra time taken to charge or bless the food becomes part of the mystical cooking process.

While you work, your attitude toward the work and the meal changes its function from simply filling hunger to internalizing vibrant magick. Try some humming, singing, or chanting as you cook. Either speak your intent aloud or say it quietly to yourself. Really get in the mood. Have fun. The joyful energy you are feeling during the cooking process will be felt energetically when the food is consumed.

Cooking Methods and the Elements

If you have a specific magickal intent in mind, you might want to plan recipes that use a cooking method that enhances your desired outcome. Steaming or poaching, for example, uses the Elements of Water, which enhances intuition and psychic power, and Air, for healing and intellectual endeavors. Baking uses the Elements of Earth, for renewal and regeneration, and Fire, which adds passion and zeal. Other cooking methods can be connected to the elements using a little common sense. Flambé, fondue, and grilling are also Fire, of course. Digging a pit on the beach for a clam bake is Earth. Boiling enhances the Water Element. As always in Natural Magick, use your own intuition.

Liguana finds that many Natural Magick cooking "rules" are often based in superstition, without a lot of sound reasoning behind them. For example, there's a notion that a pot should always be stirred *deosil*, never *widdershins*. She believes this is to keep the magick and nutrition in rather than banishing it. She prefers to stir with a wooden spoon when making soups and stews in a big pot; it just seems right to her. If you have old pots and pans that have been passed down through generations, these often contain special magickal energy. Sometimes cooking utensils will speak to you. Listen to their vibrations and use them lovingly.

Magickal Bounty

Deosil means clockwise and **widdershins** means counterclockwise. Although these are often thought of as Wiccan terms, other traditions such as ayurveda also stir food in specific directions to enhance its positive energy.

We know that kitchen magicians are busy and sometimes need to take shortcuts to match their hectic schedules. But we feel obligated to say something about microwaving. The most delectable flavors come from slow cooking with a lot of love added in. You might need to microwave to reheat leftovers or to thaw something frozen, but actually cooking a meal? This process really doesn't relate to one of the Elements, so use it sparingly as a cooking method. It's better to cook extra portions when you have the time and freeze them to thaw out another day.

A Magickal Offering

As magickal people, we also have an opportunity to keep higher ideals in mind when we shop, when we prepare and serve food, as well as when we eat it. When you cast a magick circle, you are creating sacred space suitable for the gods to enter. Your kitchen area and the table where you serve your food should be managed the same way. The wiser you become in the ways of magick and channeling magickal energies through your body, the more you will understand that each meal is an offering to your magickal self as well as all beings around you.

Pappardelle Pasta with Mushrooms, Olives, and Thyme

This recipe uses all of the Elements, so its energies can enhance many magickal intents. The mushrooms reflect Earth energies; boiling the pasta and adding parsley enhance Water energies; the light, flat noodles are both Air and Earth; and the red pepper flakes call to Fire.

> 4 oz. dried mushrooms (such as porcini or chanterelle)
>
> 4 cups boiling water
>
> 8 oz. pappardelle, egg noodles, or other long, flat pasta
>
> 16 kalmata olives, pitted
>
> ½ cup fresh parsley leaves
>
> 2 TB. olive oil
>
> 1 tsp. thyme
>
> ¼ tsp. crushed black peppercorns or coarsely ground black pepper
>
> Salt to taste

Place dried mushrooms in a bowl and pour 4 cups of boiling water over them. Let sit 30 minutes to allow the flavors to infuse. Drain the mushrooms, reserving 1 cup of the stock.

Cook pasta according to the package directions. While pasta is cooking, combine the olives, parsley, olive oil, thyme, black pepper, and soaked mushrooms in a food processor or blender. Blend until a chunky purée forms. Transfer to a warm serving bowl large enough to accommodate cooked pasta.

Drain pasta, then add it to the bowl and toss to combine. Add ¼ cup of the mushroom water and toss again. Taste and add salt, if needed. Add more water, if necessary. Pappardelle has a tendency to absorb liquid quickly, so more water might be needed. The sauce should cling to the ribbons of pasta but should not be dry. Serve immediately. Serves 2 as a meal, or 4 to 6 as an appetizer.

Simple Blessings

When the meal is ready to be served, put some candles on the table. Maybe create a seasonal centerpiece. Make it a special occasion, even if it's just another seemingly ordinary night. Have a date with the God and Goddess, and with yourself and your friends and family. Before beginning the meal, have everyone at the table hold hands and say a blessing. You can make up your own, or use something like this:

> *Thanks to the Lord for the food we eat.*
> *Thanks to the Lady for her gifts so sweet.*
> *Thanks to the farmer who labored long.*
> *Thanks to the animals for their bodies strong.*
> *Thanks to the hands that prepared this meal.*
> *Thanks to all who turn the wheel.*

Another good blessing to use is this one:

> *Back of the loaf is the snowy flour*
> *And back of the flour the mill,*
> *And back of the mill is the wheat, the shower,*
> *The Sun and Nature's Will.*

Other Food Traditions

Hindus worship a group of deities in their pantheon. This might include, for example, Shiva, Vishnu, Ganesh, and many others. They often prepare food to lay out in front of a statue of one of their gods. The meal is blessed as it is prepared, and blessed again by the Divine as it enjoys the food in spirit.

Likewise, the Krishnas get up very early in the morning to prepare lots of yummy food that they lay out in front of a statue of Sri Krishna and his consort, Radha Rhani. The entire time the food is being prepared, the cooks are chanting praises to the Divine in its many incarnations. They offer the food first as spiritual food for

Cauldron Bubble

Think about making your table's centerpiece a God, Goddess, or Elemental's symbol. Use a cornucopia, a bowl of seashells, a candelabra, or a bowl of fresh flowers. The dishes can be blessed by the Spirit as your guests arrange themselves to partake of the blessed food.

spirit beings. It has to smell wonderful and look delectable. So the Divine enjoys the food in spirit and, in turn, blesses it. Then the devotees can enjoy the blessed food.

Natural Magicians can use this tradition, too. As you prepare a meal, think about the Lord and Lady, the Elements, the Elemental beings, and your magickal intent for the meal. Reach out to whatever deity speaks to you. Place the dish in front of a symbolic figure of that deity while you call your guests to the table. As the food is blessed in Spirit, it adds an earthly blessing to the family and friends who sit around your table.

Charging Inedible Plants

Ferns are grown on the front porches of thousands of homes, but most people are not familiar with the tradition behind it. Ferns were originally planted by the front door to protect the home from wayward and errant magickal energies. The fern on your front porch should be charged with protection energies.

Planted beside the mailbox and charged properly, heather ensures that good news always finds its way to your home. A bed of basil in your garden attracts prosperity. Planting a rose garden attracts romance, and a daisy patch will bring good friends your way. To help create a peaceful home, plant a gardenia bush or lavender or violets.

Concentrate on your purpose while you are purchasing your plants. When you get them home, spend some time connecting with the energies of these plants. It's good to speak your intentions out loud to them. You might say something like, "I brought you here to your new home so we may all live in peace and harmony together. Thank you for your gifts." Plant them in the Waxing Moon phase so they are infused with the most Earth energy. Touch them and smell them often. Plants recognize affection and naturally respond to it, growing stronger, blooming more, and spreading their magickal energies over a wider area. (See Chapter 10 for more magickal flower and herb correspondences.)

Charging living plants with magickal energy is basically the same process you use for charging ingredients for cooking. Visualize what you want the plant to do, focus on joining your magickal will with the plant's energy, lightly rake your fingers through the blooms and leaves, and say:

> *Living [name of plant]*
> *Join your energy with mine*
> *Bring [magickal intent] to this home*
> *And all who enter here.*

Offer the plant a little water or fertilizer as a thank-you.

Many green Natural Magicians are astounding gardeners. Their tomatoes are the biggest and juiciest, their potato hills yield up more than anyone's, their strawberry patches are lush and full. Charging plants as you put them into the ground helps to magnify your harvest.

Again, the ritual is to visualize the outcome, speak your intent out loud, place the plant into the ground, and give the plant a little water. The vegetables, herbs, and fruit you plant don't have to be focused on only one magickal correspondence. In other words, tell them you'll get back to them about what their magickal purpose might be in the future.

To grow the healthiest garden you can, hoe and weed while the Moon is in a Fire sign—even better if it's in a waning phase. Smooth, rake, and otherwise prepare the ground when the Moon passes through an Earth sign. Plant when the Moon is dark or waxing and passing through a Water or Earth sign.

There is a tradition in Wicca of having young children jump over the rows of new plants in the Spring, sometimes carrying wands and bells to attract and honor the God aspect of the Divine, said to fertilize and energize all growing things. The energies of children are naturally magickal. Letting children help with all aspects of gardening will give vitality to anything you grow.

The Least You Need to Know

- ◆ Charging food is the simple task of combing the natural energy of plants and animals with your own magickal will.

- ◆ Even simple family meals can be charged with a magickal intent. You do not have to be a gourmet cook to put love and magick into your meals.

- ◆ The basic steps in charging organic material are to visualize, say your intentions out loud, and push your energy to join with theirs.

- ◆ Don't forget to magickally charge the plants growing in and around your house.

Chapter 22

Ayurvedic Eating in a Nutshell

In This Chapter

- Starting with astringent to stimulate the appetite
- Salty to energize your life
- Sour to clear the palette
- Spicy to warm the Spirit
- Bitter to balance your emotions
- Ending with a sweet

Although we don't pretend to be able to give you all the ins and outs of ayurvedic eating in one chapter, we are going to try to give you some of the basics. In ayurveda there are six tastes or rasas: sweet, sour, salty, bitter, pungent, and astringent. Generally, people who follow this diet believe all meals should include at least a small amount of each taste, which is more satisfying and has a balancing, harmonizing effect on your body and Spirit.

You can, of course, make any of these recipes on their own, but as they are written here, they are designed to be consumed in one meal in order of appearance: astringent, salty, sour, pungent, bitter, and sweet.

Astringent: Pink Pucker Aperitif

An astringent *aperitif* stimulates the appetite and prepares the body for food. One of the best ways we know to add astringency to a meal is with a good, puckery red wine. Serve a wine high in tannins (ask your wine merchant), for high astringency. The older the wine, the lower the tannins and the lower the astringency, so look for young, fresh, new full-bodied reds. The most tannic tend to be from California rather than Europe. Try Cabernet Sauvignon, Pinot Noir, or Syrah (called Shiraz in Australia).

> **Magickal Bounty**
>
> The custom of having an **aperitif** originated in France. It is a drink, usually alcoholic, or a glass of wine sipped before a meal to stimulate the appetite. This combination of fruit juices serves the same purpose.

You can serve red wine as a before-dinner drink. Even if you serve wine with the meal, consider beginning with the following astringent nonalcoholic juice cocktail.

Juices are also good for clearing your Spirit psychically. This drink prepares both your body and your Spirit to be nourished.

You can increase or decrease the amount of this recipe easily. Increase and put it in a punch bowl with ice for a party, or use ¼ cup of each kind of juice, shake with ice, and make a single cocktail for yourself.

1 cup grapefruit juice

1 cup pineapple juice

1 cup pomegranate juice (or substitute orange, white grape, or cherry juice)

1 cup cranberry juice (not the sweetened kind, but the 100 percent cranberry kind)

8 spears fresh papaya

1 organic lime, cut into 8 wedges

Combine juices in a pitcher and chill for at least 2 hours. When ready to serve, fill eight old-fashioned glasses with ice. One or two cups at a time, pour juice mixture into a shaker filled with ice and shake vigorously, then pour into glasses. Or, in two batches, put juice with an equal amount of crushed ice in the blender and blend until smooth. Serve over ice (unless blended with ice) and garnish with a spear of papaya and a wedge of lime. Serves 8.

Variations: Just before serving, pour 1 cup ginger ale into the pitcher of juice or into a punch bowl with the juice. Serve over ice. (Don't add ginger ale if you are going to shake the juice in a shaker.) Or, if you're hosting adults, you can turn this into a "real" cocktail by adding a shot of vodka to each glass. (This is an after-ritual treat only! Alcohol can affect your natural energy and, therefore, the effectiveness of your magick.)

Salty: Smoked Fish Pâté

Make the smoked fish yourself for this recipe, or buy freshly smoked fish from your local fresh food market. This works with any white fish, or oily fish such as salmon, tuna, or mackerel. Use what looks fresh and good, as well as a fish that is wild-caught and responsibly fished.

This recipe combines salty smoky fish and sea salt with the sour flavors of crème fraîche and lemon for a bright clear flavor. In ayurveda, salt is calming and relieves anxiety, while sour is clarifying and sharpens the senses.

To smoke your own fish, pack in kosher salt for 12 hours, rinse off, then smoke in your home smoker for about 6 hours, according to your smoker's directions.

Serving fish attracts the Water Element, which heightens intuition. Perhaps that's why we talk about fish as brain food.

>   1 pound smoked fish, cut into chunks
>
>   ½ cup sake (or substitute a dry white wine)
>
>   ¼ cup (½ stick) unsalted butter, softened
>
>   ¼ cup crème fraîche or sour cream
>
>   1 TB. sesame oil
>
>   Zest and juice from 1 organic lemon
>
>   1 tsp. sea salt

Put the fish pieces in a small bowl. Cover with the sake. Let sit for 30 minutes, or up to 2 hours.

In the bowl of a food processor or blender, combine butter, crème fraîche or sour cream, and sesame oil.

Cauldron Bubble

You can make your own crème fraîche by stirring together 1 cup of buttermilk and 3 cups heavy cream. Cover loosely with plastic wrap and let it sit at room temperature for 60–72 hours or until it resembles sour cream. It will keep for up to 2 weeks in the refrigerator. Use in place of sour cream.

Process until smooth and creamy. Add fish and sake. Process until smooth and whipped. Stir in lemon zest, juice, and sea salt. Mound on a platter or in a bowl and serve with salty, crisp crackers. Garnish with sprigs of dill and umeboshi plums (pickled plums), which add a dimension of sour and astringent properties, further accentuating the Asian flavors of this pâté. Makes about 2½ cups.

Sour: Yogurt Parfait with Apricots and Cherries

This colorful sour course cleanses the palate and re-energizes the appetite. Yogurt heals the stomach and enhances digestion, while the sour aspects of apricots and cherries awaken the senses and induces creativity. Use plain yogurt rather than sweetened for this recipe. Whole-milk yogurt has a delicious creamy texture, but nonfat plain yogurt is also delicious and, obviously, lower in fat and calories. You can halve or double this recipe easily.

2 cups sour cherries, pitted, fresh, or frozen thawed

32 oz. plain yogurt

2 cups fresh or dried apricots, coarsely chopped

¼ cup pistachios, chopped

8 thin curls of lemon zest

In each of eight tall, narrow parfait glasses or champagne flutes, layer ¼ cup cherries, ¼ cup yogurt, ¼ cup apricots, ¼ cup yogurt; then garnish with a sprinkle of pistachios and a thin curl of lemon zest. Makes 8 parfaits.

> **Cauldron Bubble**
>
> The tastes in a meal need to balance each other. For example, if you have a sweet rice, have a sour chutney, such as tomato. If you have a sour rice, serve a sweet chutney, such as mango. In the ayurvedic tradition, the main meal at lunch and dinner is always just soup.

Pungent/Hot: Chicken Molé

This Mexican classic is often made with chicken or turkey, and either will work in this recipe. There are many varieties of molé—black, red, green, yellow. This reddish-black version is spicy, rich, dark, and redolent with ground chilies, nuts, tortilla, spices, and chocolate. Traditionally, this recipe is also served with whole chicken pieces, but it is easier to eat and you can get every drop of the sauce if you debone and shred the chicken pieces. You can use breasts only, or a combination of pieces for white and dark meat. This dish tastes exotic and very special. It is both warming and invigorating, and its pungent, hot character awakens the senses and expands consciousness and passion.

Chilies grow in gardens all over the country, not just in the southwest. Use them fresh, or preserve them by drying, smoking, or freezing to add spice to a dish even when they are no longer in season. Depending on who you ask, you might hear very strong opinions about which chilies you should use in molé. Our take is that you should use the ones you can get fresh or dried locally, or at least regionally. Even better, use the hot chilies you can grow in your own garden. Some of the chili choices you might use include jalapeño, serrano, poblano, New Mexican, Anaheim, chipotle (smoked jalapeño), mulato (dried, similar to ancho), pasilla (dried chilaca), ancho (dried poblano), and habanero (super hot, use with caution!). Pasillas are traditional chilies to use in molé, if you can find them.

CAUTION   Stir Gently ...!

Be very careful working with hot chilies. Always use rubber gloves when chopping, or risk getting chili oil in your eyes (especially if you wear contacts) or on your face. This hurts! Even if you scrub your hands with soap, they can still retain chili oil, even into the next day. Also open the windows and turn on the exhaust fan over your stove when roasting, frying, and blending chilies, or you will feel it in your eyes and in your throat.

If you want this dish to be extra spicy, use the seeds from the chilies. If you want a milder dish, discard the seeds and just use the pepper flesh.

Although we generally associate chocolate with sweet treats, it isn't actually sweet by itself. In this dish, the bittersweet chocolate lends a rich taste that combines perfectly with the spices. Guests won't be able to put their fingers on the ingredient giving the chicken its exotic flavor.

This recipe might look intimidating because it has so many ingredients, but it really isn't difficult at all. It just takes a long time. You prepare the separate parts, you blend them separately, and then you cook them, a little at a time, until you have a lovely thick, dark sauce. Add the chicken, simmer, and, voilà, you have a pungent, spicy feast, and you can be very proud of yourself. Molé tastes even better the next day, so you might want to cook this on a day when you have a lot of time, and then warm it up and serve it the next day.

20 small to medium chilies of varying hotness, depending on your tolerance (try 10 mulato or ancho, 5 chipotle or jalapeño, 3 pasilla, 2 serrano, or any other combination you can find and want to try)

¾ cup corn oil

2 cups boiling water

2 corn tortillas

2 slices pumpernickel or other dark bread

1 small white onion, chopped

4 garlic cloves, peeled and minced

1 cup raw mixed nuts and seeds (almonds, sesame seeds, sunflower seeds, pumpkin seeds, walnuts, pecans—whatever you can find that looks fresh and good, but try to include about half nuts and half seeds)

3 quarts (12 cups) chicken broth

1 large or 2 medium firm tomatoes (they can be unripe, even green), cored and chopped

½ cup raisins

2 TB. tequila (optional, for soaking the raisins)

¼ cup natural peanut butter

1 small avocado, peeled, pitted, and mashed

1 tsp. cinnamon

½ tsp. black pepper

1 tsp. chopped fresh oregano

½ tsp. dried thyme

Pinch of ground cloves

4 oz. bittersweet chocolate, shaved or chopped into small pieces

1 TB. sea salt

½ cup packed brown sugar

4 lb. chicken pieces, on the bone with skin (about 2 whole chickens cut up, 4 whole breasts, or 8 half-breasts)

Additional ¼ cup sesame seeds for garnish

Preheat oven to 375°F. Take the stems off all the chilies (wear rubber gloves and don't touch your face). For a milder molé, shake out and discard the seeds. Or just shake out some of them, leaving some for extra flavor and heat.

In a large skillet, heat ½ cup of the corn oil over medium-high until you can smell the oil. Open the windows and turn on the exhaust fan; then carefully add chilies and fry, stirring gently, for 10 minutes, until they start to turn crisp and darken in color. Take chilies out of the oil and put them into a large bowl. Cover chilies with boiling water and set aside.

Tear tortilla and dark bread into pieces and add to the oil. Add onion and garlic. Stir and fry until the bread is crispy and onion and garlic turn golden brown. If some onion or garlic begins to look burnt, that's fine; it just adds a nice deep color to the molé. This should take about 15 minutes. Remove skillet from the heat and set aside.

In a large baking pan with sides (so they don't slide off), spread out nuts and seeds. Roast nuts and seeds until they turn dark brown, stirring occasionally. The smaller nuts and seeds will roast faster and turn darker. That's fine. This should take about 15 minutes. Remove and cool.

Now you will make a series of purées using the blender or food processor. Don't wash out the blender or food processor between steps. First, add the tortilla, bread, and onion/garlic mixture to the food processor or blender. Add 1 cup chicken broth. Process until smooth, then pour into a small bowl. Next, add the nuts and seeds and 1 cup chicken broth. Process until smooth, then add to another small bowl.

Next, drain the chilies and add half of them to the blender or food processor. Add 1 cup chicken broth. Process until smooth, then pour into another small bowl. Repeat with the rest of the chilies. Put these all together in one small bowl. Next, add tomatoes, raisins (with the soaking tequila, if using it), peanut butter, avocado, cinnamon, pepper, oregano, thyme, and cloves. Add 1 cup chicken broth. Process until smooth, then pour into a small bowl.

Heat a large soup pot or Dutch oven over medium-high. Add remaining ¼ cup corn oil. When oil is hot and you can smell it, work in reverse order. First, add tomato/raisin purée to the pot. Cook, stirring constantly, until the mixture gets dark and thick, about 15 minutes.

Add chilies and cook, stirring constantly, until the mixture gets dark and thick again, about 15 more minutes. Add nut and seed mixture and cook, stirring occasionally, for another 15 minutes. Add onion/garlic mixture and cook, stirring occasionally, for another 15 minutes. Stir in chocolate, salt, sugar, and remaining chicken broth. Stir until chocolate melts, about 5 minutes, then allow to simmer, stirring occasionally, for about 1 hour.

While the molé is cooking, poach the chicken in water until cooked through. Remove, cool, peel off the skin, pull the meat from the bone, and shred. Set aside. (As a more traditional option, you can roast the chicken pieces and serve whole in the sauce.)

Remove the molé from the heat and allow to cool a little bit. In small batches, purée in a food processor and put through a strainer so you have a smooth sauce. At this point, you can put the molé in a covered container and store in the refrigerator or freezer until you are ready to use it.

To serve, return the sauce to the Dutch oven and combine with the shredded chicken. Stir and cook over medium heat until heated through and bubbly, about 30 minutes. Or combine chicken and sauce in a crock pot and cook on high for 2 hours or low for 4–6 hours. Serve in bowls, over hot cooked rice or on its own, and garnish with additional sesame seeds. Serves 8.

Bitter: Asparagus Salad with Greens and Bitter Ale Dressing

This bitter salad incorporates asparagus with bitter greens and the classic bitter flavors of orange peel, ginger, turmeric, and sesame oil, spiked with India Pale Ale, the most bitter of the beer styles. (You can substitute orange juice and a dash of Angostura bitters for a nonalcoholic version.)

Ayurveda considers sesame oil the most balancing and *sattvic* of the oils, and its bitter properties clear and cleanse the senses and balance the emotions. Serve after or with the chicken molé to balance the spice and reorient the palate. This salad is best in the spring, when asparagus is young and tender.

2 lb. fresh asparagus, woody ends trimmed, cut into 1-inch pieces

2 cups curly endive, torn into small pieces

2 cups watercress, torn into small pieces

Zest and juice from 1 organic orange

1 TB. apple cider vinegar

½-inch length fresh ginger, peeled and minced

2 cloves garlic, peeled and minced

½ tsp. turmeric

½ cup India Pale Ale (IPA) or regular Pale Ale (or use ½ cup orange juice with a dash of Angostura bitters)

¼ cup sesame oil

¼ cup canola oil

½ tsp. sea salt

Freshly ground black pepper

2 TB. raw sesame seeds, for garnish

Steam asparagus over simmering water until tender, about 10–12 minutes. Or boil in a small amount of water until tender, about 15 minutes. Rinse in cold water.

Rinse endive and watercress in cold water and pat dry. Arrange on a platter. Top with asparagus pieces.

In a medium bowl, combine orange zest and juice, vinegar, ginger, garlic, and turmeric. Whisk until thoroughly combined. Add ale or additional orange juice, sesame oil, and canola oil. Whisk to combine. Season with salt and pepper. Whisk again. Taste, and add more salt or pepper, if necessary. Pour over the asparagus and toss to coat. Sprinkle with sesame seeds. Serves 8.

Cauldron Bubble

Spices should always be run through the hands before adding them to the recipe, to gather consciousness. Whole spices go in before ground spices. Always stir clockwise because it brings **satva,** meaning the pure quality of Nature.

Sweet: Amaretti

After this rich and filling feast, a big dessert would be too much, taxing the body rather than nourishing and restoring it. Try these crispy-chewy almond cookies, an Italian invention, served with fresh berries and a pitcher of cream, for a sweet and simple end to a spectacular meal. You can also serve this with herbal tea containing sweet herbs such as cardamom, vanilla, and cinnamon.

> 2 cups blanched almonds
>
> ½ cup sugar
>
> ¼ tsp. salt
>
> 4 egg whites
>
> ⅛ tsp. cream of tartar
>
> 1 TB. amaretto liqueur or ½ teaspoon almond extract

Preheat oven to 400°F. In a food processor or blender, combine almonds, sugar, and salt. Process or blend until finely ground.

In a large bowl, beat egg whites and cream of tartar until soft peaks form. Fold in almond-sugar mixture and amaretto or almond extract.

Line a cookie sheet with parchment paper. Spoon dough into a pastry bag with a large, plain tip, and pipe small, round mounds 2 inches apart. Dip a pastry brush in water and smooth the tops.

Bake until golden and puffy but not brown, about 15 minutes. Cool for 5 minutes, then remove cookies with a metal spatula and cool on a wire rack. Serve warm or at room temperature. Makes about 40 cookies.

Cauldron Bubble

For a light, sweet dessert, crumble leftover almond cookies into small pieces and spoon into the hollowed-out core of peach or apple halves. Sprinkle 1 teaspoon of sugar on top and bake in a 350°F oven for about 30 minutes.

Take the Bitter with the Sweet

It occurs to Liguana that a contrast can be made between the bitterness of life and the sweetness of life using food or drink symbolically. She likes hot water or milk and cocoa powder for a bitter drink, though bitter herbs can be used.

Plan a simple ritual that recognizes some aspect of life as being difficult or bitter right now. Write the aspect on a piece of paper and spend some time thinking about it. Consider how it started, what might be done to make it better, and how it's affecting the people around you.

After tasting the bitter, clean your palette with water and bread. Then a magickal person might say something like, "I have known bitter. I am now open to all the sweetness I can experience." This should be followed with the taste of sweetness. Honey is always good for this, but any sweet that appeals to you is fine.

In some ritual circles, natural practitioners pass yam chips with honey dip and say to one another, "May you know the sweetness of life and always cherish it." In this way they share the good feelings and bless each other to feel the joy.

The Least You Need to Know

- Eating some of each flavor at every meal provides balance and harmony for both body and Spirit.

- Beginning a meal with an astringent food stimulates the appetite and readies you for the flavors to come.

- Ending with a small sweet signifies the end of the meal and aids in digestion.

- In ayurvedic eating, it is desirable to encourage satva, the pure quality of Nature.

Chapter 23

Cakes and Wine

In This Chapter

◆ Magickally sharing cakes and wine

◆ Full Moon seasonal traditions ground your ritual

◆ "Cake" recipes with magickal intent

◆ Seasonal drinks to enjoy

For magickal people, sharing food and drink after raising energy does three things: It grounds the excess energy people might have built up, it allows us to commemorate the Divine so that what we take into ourselves we know is enriching us, and it allows a greater sense of intimacy and sharing among all who participated in magickal ceremony or ritual.

Food and drink are very good for grounding excess energy. It brings us back in tune with our bodies and the physical world. Some groups have a custom of passing the plate of cakes and saying, "May you never hunger," then passing the cup with, "May you never thirst." Rather than a blessing from the Divine, it is a way we bless each other.

An Age-Old Tradition

The tradition of sharing food after spiritual rituals is common in many cultures. In the Judeo-Christian religions, the coffee hour after service is a version of cakes and wine. Many Wiccan folk do cup and athame blessings of the food and drink before sharing, thus calling God and Goddess to join and bless the feast. Sharing a meal after a wedding, a christening, or a funeral is a more elaborate version of this same idea. In all situations, it is common for people to take turns bringing the goodies, which, in turn, enhances the feeling of community.

Cakes can be sweet, such as shortbread (see the recipe in Chapter 17), cupcakes, or doughnuts; or they can be savory, such as cheese and dill scones, garlic sticks, or crescent rolls. Homemade crackers and dips made from seeds are also acceptable "cakes" at winter and fall Full Moons. Any small cakes are good, as long as they're not too crumbly. Stick to white or light foods for Full Moons, and feel free to go heavy on the butter in cookies and cakes.

Liguana's Grimoire

Liguana often refers to cakes and wine rituals as cakes and ale time. In an eclectic group of magickal people, either expression might be used. One evening the discussion topic was "cakes and wine" vs. "cakes and ale." People pondered the question based on numerology and magickal sound of each phrase. They did tarot readings and pulled rune stones for inspiration. Finally, a man stood up and said, "If you whine, you don't get any cake. No one should whine in circle." Everyone laughed and the matter was settled. Liguana has said "cakes and ale" ever since.

Honey drinks are perfect for summer Full Moons, as are fruit drinks, especially with mint. Fermented drinks are usually served in the fall. If the drink is milky, it should be offered only in the winter months. For magickal living, milk drinks are not for spring—at least, not early spring. The first milk goes to babies, not farmers.

Bûche de Noël

Celebrate the warmth of friendship and communion with this cake, which is especially good served with warming Mulled Wine or Spiced Cider (recipe follows). The orange extract and cinnamon pick up the fruity notes in the wine or cider and attract love and prosperity. We like this cake unfrosted, simply dusted with powdered sugar to resemble a light, frosty dusting of snow, but you can also frost it with your favorite chocolate butter cream or icing and "rake" a barklike texture with a fork.

Originally a celebration of the Norse Midwinter celebration, Yule might come from the word *hweol*, the Saxon word for "wheel." The yule log represents an actual wheel and also symbolizes the planetary circle that makes a year. Burning the yule log also brought light and warmth to the cold winter months.

For the cake:

> ⅓ cup packed brown sugar
>
> 6 eggs at room temperature, separated
>
> 4 oz. bittersweet or semisweet chocolate, melted
>
> ½ tsp. cinnamon
>
> ½ tsp. orange extract (optional)
>
> ⅓ cup flour
>
> ½ tsp. cream of tartar
>
> 1 TB. white sugar
>
> 1 TB. cocoa powder
>
> ½ cup powdered sugar for garnish (optional)
>
> Slices of orange or whole kumquats for garnish (optional)

For the filling:

> 1 cup heavy whipping cream
>
> 1 TB. Grand Marnier or Cointreau (or 1 tsp. orange extract)
>
> 2 TB. white sugar

Preheat oven to 400°F. Line a 17×12-inch or 16×11-inch jellyroll pan with nonstick liner, parchment paper, wax paper, or foil; butter it and sprinkle lightly with flour. Shake to cover the surface with a light coating of flour and tap off extra.

Put brown sugar and egg yolks into a large mixing bowl and beat on high until light and fluffy, about 5 minutes.

CAUTION

Stir Gently ...!

Be sure to wash the beaters thoroughly so no oil remains on them, and make sure the bowl is squeaky clean. Any oil or fat will keep the egg whites from expanding effectively.

Stir cinnamon and orange extract into chocolate; then add it, a little at a time, to the brown sugar/yolk mixture, beating constantly until completely combined. Gently stir in the flour until combined.

In a separate, clean large bowl, beat the egg whites, cream of tartar, and 1 tablespoon sugar until stiff peaks form.

Gently fold the egg whites into the batter, a little at a time. Use a light touch to keep air in the batter. Pour the batter into the pan and spread it lightly and evenly over the entire surface. Bake for 15 minutes or when the cake springs back if you press it lightly with your finger. Remove from the oven and tip it carefully out of the pan.

Dampen a clean tea towel, but make sure it is not dripping—just slightly moist. While the cake is still hot, sprinkle the surface with the cocoa powder, then carefully place the tea towel over the cake. Very gently roll up the cake and allow to cool completely.

Meanwhile, whip cream, Grand Marnier, Cointreau, or orange flavoring, and sugar until light and fluffy. Then carefully remove the cake to a large surface such as a platter or cutting board. Unroll carefully and remove the tea towel. Spread whipped cream on the surface, then carefully roll the cake again, peeling off the parchment, waxed paper, or foil from the bottom side as you go. Put on a plate with the seam side down and sift powdered sugar over the top. Garnish with slices of orange or whole kumquats.

Chill for 30 minutes to 1 hour before serving. Serves 8 to 12.

Mulled Wine or Spiced Cider

Cloves and cinnamon tend to invite health, prosperity, leadership, and joy. Whether you make this out of wine or apple cider, this warm spiced drink makes a perfect beverage to chase away a winter chill.

3 cinnamon sticks, each about 3 or 4 inches long

6 whole cloves

1 vanilla bean, split in half

Zest from 1 organic orange

Zest from 1 organic lemon

10 cranberries, cut in half

2 (750-mL) bottles red wine (try a
French burgundy or a light merlot) *or*
2 quarts apple cider

Wrap all spices and the cranberries in a large
square of cheesecloth and tie with a string. Put
wine or apple cider in a large soup pot, Dutch
oven, or crock pot. Float the spice bag in the
wine or cider. Heat on medium-low until hot,
or heat in crock pot on high for 1 hour or until
hot. Serve in heat-proof mugs. Serves 8.

CAUTION   **Stir Gently ...!**

Keep the beverage at a
very low temperature, but do not
bring it to a boil, especially if
you want to keep a "kick" in the
red wine. Boiling apple cider
will change the consistency and
affect the flavor, too. You're just
warming, not cooking.

Hot Cross Buns

This traditional spring treat isn't actually very sweet—more like a yeasty roll marked
with an *X*. Served with a Spring Mint Julep (recipe follows), it's the perfect treat to
celebrate the transformation of the seasons and the rebirth of spring. This recipe is
traditionally made with currants, but you can substitute chopped dried apricots,
raisins, or even chocolate.

Cinnamon and nutmeg attract romance and can help eliminate jealousy or bad feelings. The yeast attracts the Air Element, which heightens creativity, and if you use
dried fruit, you introduce the Earth Element's stability and common sense.

1½ cup milk

2 packets or 2 TB. dried yeast

½ cup sugar

½ cup (1 stick) unsalted butter, melted and cooled

4 eggs, lightly beaten, plus 1 egg yolk

1 tsp. cinnamon

½ tsp. nutmeg

1 tsp. salt

6 cups flour

1 cup currants, raisins, chopped dried apricots, chocolate chips, grated chocolate, or a combination of any of these

1 cup powdered sugar

1 TB. milk or cream

1 tsp. vanilla extract

Warm milk over medium heat until small bubbles appear around the edges. Do not boil! Remove from heat and pour into a large mixing bowl. Sprinkle the yeast over the top of the milk and set aside for 5–10 minutes. Do not stir the mixture during this time.

To the large mixing bowl, add sugar, butter, four eggs, cinnamon, nutmeg, and salt. Beat on medium until combined, with a regular beater or with a dough-hook attachment, if you have one. Add flour, 1 cup at a time, until all flour is incorporated. If using a hand mixer, when it gets to the point at which dough is too stiff for the mixer, turn out on a floured surface and knead in the rest of flour, then knead for 10 minutes. If using a dough hook, after adding all flour, allow the machine to knead the dough for 10 minutes. Shape the dough into a ball and put in a clean buttered bowl. Turn once to coat all sides with butter. Cover with plastic or a tea towel and put in a warm place. Allow to rise until double in bulk, about 1½ to 2 hours (depending on the warmth of your kitchen).

Punch down the dough, or return to the mixer with the dough hook, and knead for 5 minutes. Add dried fruit and/or chocolate and knead until fully incorporated. Shape into 24 round buns and place on two buttered cookie sheets, about 2 inches apart. Cut an *X* in the top of each bun with a sharp knife.

Beat remaining egg yolk with 1 teaspoon of water and brush over the tops of the buns. Cover with plastic or a tea towel, and allow to rise again until doubled, about 30 minutes to 1 hour.

Preheat oven to 375°F. Bake until light golden brown, about 25 minutes.

While the buns are baking, whisk together powdered sugar, milk or cream, and vanilla extract. When they are done, remove the buns from the oven and immediately fill each *X* with icing. Serve warm. Makes 24 buns.

Spring Mint Julep

This refreshing spring drink is best with mint you grow yourself or buy from a farmer's market or nearby herb farm. (Don't substitute dried mint for the fresh in this recipe. Not only will the dried mint form a sludge at the bottom of your glass, but it won't provide the fresh, minty taste you want. Fresh mint makes the drink clear and springy looking.) Both the ginger ale and the bourbon versions are delicious, depending on your preference (and your age!).

Mint tends to attract prosperity and can provide protection for travelers beginning a journey.

> 16 fresh mint sprigs
>
> ½ cup white sugar
>
> ½ cup water
>
> 32 oz. ginger ale or 16 oz. Kentucky Bourbon

Put 8 mint sprigs into a bowl and press on them with the back of a spoon to bruise them. This will cause them to release a mint aroma and some of their natural oils.

Combine sugar and water in a small saucepan. Heat over medium-high until small bubbles form. Simmer until sugar is completely dissolved. Remove from heat. Cool slightly.

Put the bruised mint sprigs in a glass jar. Pour the sugar water over them. Refrigerate for at least 2 hours, preferably overnight.

Fill eight glasses or tumblers with crushed or shaved ice. Put about 1 tablespoon of syrup into each glass. Divide any remaining syrup between the glasses. Add 4 ounces ginger ale or 2 ounces bourbon to each class, then stir vigorously with a long-handled teaspoon until the outside of the glass turns frosty. Garnish each glass with a mint sprig. Serves 8.

Cauldron Bubble

As an alternative, make a bourbon highball with ginger ale, then add the mint syrup, which combines both versions of this recipe.

Strawberry Muffins

The fruits of summer blend into a delicious combination of sweet pink muffins, wonderful served with goblets of Sangria or Berry Iced Green Tea (recipe follows). This duo is as tasty as it is beautiful, like a summer sunset.

The applesauce and the strawberries in this recipe are good at attracting romance and cementing new relationships. Serve these during a spring Full Moon, and everyone's fancy will turn to thoughts of love!

> 2 cups sugar
>
> ¼ cup cooking oil
>
> 2 eggs
>
> ½ cup applesauce
>
> ½ cup plain yogurt or sour cream
>
> ½ cup milk
>
> 2 cups unbleached flour
>
> 1 TB. baking powder
>
> 1 tsp. baking soda
>
> Zest and juice from 1 organic lemon
>
> 1 tsp. vanilla extract
>
> 2 cups fresh strawberries, cored and coarsely chopped (or use frozen, but thaw them first)

Preheat oven to 350°F. Lightly grease three six-cup muffin tins (or equivalent) with cooking oil, or line with paper muffin cups.

Combine sugar, cooking oil, eggs, applesauce, yogurt or sour cream, and milk in a large bowl, and whisk or beat thoroughly until the mixture lightens in color.

In a separate bowl, sift together flour, baking powder, and baking soda. Add to wet ingredients and stir just until combined. Stir in lemon zest and juice, vanilla, and chopped strawberries.

Fill muffin cups and bake until light golden or until a toothpick inserted into the center of a muffin comes out clean, about 25 minutes. Cool for 5 minutes, remove from tins, and cool on a wire rack. Serve warm or at room temperature. Makes 18 muffins.

Sangria or Berry Iced Green Tea

Green tea is said to have many health benefits, including lowering your cholesterol, boosting your immune system, and helping to prevent cavities and tooth decay. Magickally it focuses your mind and helps raise your energy, so it's a good brew to sip before a ritual.

If you choose to use wine, this sweet, fruity combination is good for honoring both the God and Goddess deities after a ritual to which they've been invited.

> 2 (750-mL) bottles light red wine (try a wine labeled for sangria, or a rosé) *or* 2 quarts brewed green or white tea
>
> 4 cups fresh berries: strawberries, raspberries, blackberries, blueberries, or a combination (if the strawberries are large, cut them in halves or quarters)
>
> ½ cup sugar

> **Liguana's Grimoire**
>
> There are four types of tea: black, oolong, white, and green. The difference between the green and white teas and the others is that green and white teas are not fermented, thus keeping in the powerful antioxidants lost in the fermenting process.

Combine wine or tea, berries, and sugar in a pitcher. Stir until sugar dissolves, then chill for up to 8 hours. Serve in wine glasses with a spoonful of berries floating in each glass, or pour the whole thing into a punch bowl. Serves 8.

Bannocks

The Druids made this traditional British pancake, always beating the batter in a clockwise direction to mimic the path of the Sun and to keep positive energy in. Traditionally, bannocks are made with oats and buttermilk. This recipe adds rye flour to the mix, but you can also use whole wheat or all white, depending on what you have on hand. Serve these with soft butter and honey or real maple syrup, and a glass of creamy, silky-smooth oatmeal stout, preferably in a dimpled glass mug, the way they like to drink it in Britain.

The rye in this recipe corresponds to marriage fidelity and loyalty, and also attracts love, making it an excellent treat to share in honor of an upcoming wedding.

2 cups whole oats

1 cup unbleached white flour

1 cup rye flour

1 TB. baking soda

1 tsp. salt

1 tsp. cream of tartar

4 eggs

¼ cup light corn syrup

2 cups buttermilk

Grease a large skillet or griddle with corn oil. Heat on medium-high.

In a large bowl, combine oats, flours, baking soda, salt, and cream of tartar.

In a medium bowl, beat eggs lightly. Add corn syrup and half the buttermilk. Beat to combine. Add to dry ingredients and stir gently, adding the remaining buttermilk a little at a time, beating after each addition.

Pour batter on the griddle to form small cakes, about 2 or 3 inches in diameter. Cook until bubbles form around the edges, about 3 minutes. Flip one time and cook the other side, about 1 minute.

Serve with soft butter and locally produced honey or maple syrup, if available, and mugs of oatmeal stout. (Samuel Smith's Oatmeal Stout is a good choice. Imported from England, it is widely available.)

The Least You Need to Know

- Sharing food and drink helps ground excess energy after a ritual.

- Creating a cake and wine time helps build a sense of community and acts as a reminder to share with others.

- If you're serving a sweet drink, make the cake less sweet, and vice versa to balance flavors.

- Use a cake and wine time to bless other participants and to wish them well.

Chapter 24

Crafting Your Own Natural Magick

In This Chapter

- ◆ Embracing all of Nature
- ◆ Activities for the mundane world
- ◆ Tapping into the magickal realm
- ◆ Why focus on food?
- ◆ Caramels for your sweetie

In Chapter 1, we said tapping into the patterns of Nature begins with how you choose to live on Earth. We told you Natural Magick is powerful and satisfying because it requires an understanding of and commitment to something larger than ourselves.

Nature is the essence of the Earth's magickal flows. To be true Natural Magicians, we need not only respect and revere the natural world, but we also need to champion and protect it. We must strive to be a positive force of Nature. If our actions sustain, protect, and honor Earth, our ability to cause positive change through magick is tremendous.

Learn to Love All of Nature

An ethically responsible lifestyle is important. Equally important is a true love of Mother Nature. If you can't stand to be out in the woods because there are gnats and dirt and critters, you will inadvertently send that negativity out into the atmosphere around you. The air will vibrate with your distaste, and the power you try to raise will be filtered through that negative feeling. Yes, you can do magick in your living room, your backyard, or wherever you may be, but the truly powerful Natural Magician knows that the Earth is more than where you stand. You pull up energy while in your home, but that same energy is touching and enriching jungles in South America, deserts in Africa, and barren, icy wastes in Antarctica.

Cauldron Bubble

Spiders make you jumpy? Snakes give you the willies? Scared to death of mice? It's because you see them as unimportant and creepy. If you study them, learn how they benefit Earth, and understand their worlds, you will begin to embrace their unique qualities.

What if there is a country or climate or terrain that bothers you whenever you think about it? Let's take Antarctica, for example. Few of us would want to go out and practice our magick there. It seems like nothing but a barren, icy wasteland. If it seems like a block to your ability to love the Earth, study it. Become an expert. Learn what animals live there and whether plants exist. This advice goes for all aspects of Nature, all parts of Earth, and all things living on Earth. Magick happens through connection. Prejudice prevents connection, but knowledge and understanding promote connection.

Look to the Sunny Side

Magick requires mindfulness and a sincere effort to make things better. Remember, if you put out positive flows, positive flows will return to you. If you put out negative flows—duck!

It is not always easy to know the right path to follow or the right actions to enhance your magickal practice. In the end, you must decide for yourself what is right and why it is right. We encourage you to look over the following list of things you can do to physically cause a positive impact in your life and the world around you. Remember, what is done in the physical world has an impact in the magickal realms as well. Be a powerful force for positive change in all worlds.

- Compost.
- Recycle.

- Plant a garden.

- Volunteer in your community.

- Write poetry.

- Tell stories about good deeds and the heroes who accomplished them.

- Dance and sing often.

- Teach a class.

- Eat at least one vegetarian meal a week.

- Thank the spirits of the plants and animals who gave of themselves for your meal.

- Research other cultures.

- Find a pen pal and write often.

- Listen to music.

- Send someone flowers.

- Give a gift for no reason.

- Speak up for justice whenever you can.

- Share.

- Listen to other people's stories.

- Compliment someone every day.

- Feed the birds.

- Grow flowers.

- Enjoy a sunrise or sunset.

- Pick up litter.

- Listen to children.

- Smile.

Positive Magick, *Naturally!*

Now here is a list of things you can do to put forth positive magickal flows. Remember that the mundane and the magickal mirror each other. Being positive on the magickal plane means your everyday life is likely to be happier and more productive. Many of these we covered in depth in earlier chapters. This list is to serve as a reminder and to encourage you in your magickal life.

- Keep a Natural Magick Journal.
- Make a dream pillow stuffed with mugwort and lavender.
- Record your dreams in your journal.
- Spend time quieting your mind every day.
- Light a candle every evening.
- Burn incense.
- Seek out faeries.
- Talk to dragons.
- Seek out a special place to go to ground, center, and replenish yourself.
- Feel the warmth surrounding your body and recognize your own energy flows.
- Research various magickal practices.
- Meet with other Natural Magicians and listen for their wisdom.
- Believe in yourself.
- Do what is right.
- Be aware, live aware.
- Practice encouraging plants to grow with energy flowing from your hands.
- Share a magickal meal with friends.
- Talk to the Elements and the Elementals.
- Thank the Spirit realm for their presence in your life.

Reaching Out in the Mundane and the Magickal Realms

So we've been emphasizing that what happens in the mundane world of your everyday life is reflected in your magickal world. What does that mean? It begins with your immediate family or roommates. You should try every day to figure out how you can make their lives happier, healthier, and more productive. You can tamp down your temper, assume they're doing their best, and love them despite their "faults."

One of the most important nonmagickal rules to remember is that the only person's behavior you can change is your own. Trying to shout down or bully someone into behaving in a different way sends out negative energy—something a Natural Magician doesn't want to do.

Once you've found a harmonious way to live with your family, extend that energy to your friends. Listen to their problems with an open mind. You don't necessarily have to solve them—just be supportive. Then reach out to your neighbors. Can you help shovel the snow from their walks, mow their lawns, share your garden produce, babysit their children? Every good deed puts your magickal realm closer to you.

> **Cauldron Bubble**
>
> Your local Chamber of Commerce can suggest organizations in your neighborhood that are looking for volunteers. You should also feel free to start your own volunteer movement—involving your children in cleaning up the park or a local cemetery is a good beginning.

Next, reach out into the community. Volunteer at the homeless shelter, the women's crisis center, or the animal rescue shelter. Donate food or money when you can. Run for the local school board or a political office that appeals to you. And finally, figure out how to help your country. Join a national environmental organization, read the newspaper and know who your local decision makers are, become a foster parent. The point is to do whatever good you can in your corner of the world.

As you spread positive energy, your magickal world will become easier to access and will respond to your Will more readily. Try it! You'll feel the energy flowing through you and out into the universe with less effort. The Elements, the faeries, the dragons, the deities—they all watch the way you move through the world, and they respond to your positive energies on the physical plane by attending to your magickal desires.

Food and the Natural Magician

You've no doubt noticed we've spent a good share of this book on recipes. There's a simple explanation. What you take into your body empowers what you put out. It's not just about eating well, but also about using herbs and spices that you have charged with magickal intent. Vitamin C is just as important for your body's health as using an herb for prosperity or protection is important for your Spiritual health.

When you have developed a true love of Nature, you will instinctively know what produce is in season in your area. You will begin to have a feeling about what cooking method to use, what ingredients to choose, and how to combine them to create your own original recipes.

If you enjoy cooking, read a lot of cookbooks—and then put them away and use your intuition to create a magickal meal. Try substituting ingredients based on your family's preferences and the spellcrafting you're trying to achieve. If you're not fond of cooking, pick out a basic cookbook and follow the recipes, but add into the directions charging the ingredients (see Chapter 21) to support your magickal purposes.

How to Experiment

We've been encouraging you to experiment by altering recipes or by making up your own, but what do we mean by that? When you're cooking—for example, baking meat, stirring up a stew, or whipping up a casserole—you can alter ingredients. Add different vegetables, experiment with herbs, eliminate the meat, or use a different shape of pasta.

Magickal Bounty

Leavening is an ingredient added to a batter that will create fermentation and cause the dough to rise—for example, yeast, cream of tartar, baking soda, or baking powder.

But there is a chemistry involved with baking that even Natural Magicians have to honor. The right combination of flour, sugar, eggs, butter, and *leavening* can dramatically change the final outcome. Certainly, you can eliminate the raisins or use different nuts, but the basic recipe can't be altered.

Here's an example. The caramel color of caramels comes from a reaction between the sugar and the protein in cream, which is called the Maillard reaction. Put simply, the Maillard reaction occurs when part of the sugar molecule reacts with the nitrogen part of the protein molecule. The resulting series of reactions is not well understood even by food scientists, but it leads to the brown color. It's the same chemical process that happens when you toast nuts, barbecue meats, or put on self-tanning lotion. Why is this important to a Natural Magician?

Liguana has been emphasizing throughout this book that knowledge is power and power creates magick. The more you know about both the magickal and mundane worlds, the closer you are to utilizing Nature's energy to create your own spiritual, magickal moments. Use the charts in Appendix C to determine ingredients to use for your magickal purposes, but study cooking techniques to make sure you aren't producing inedible dishes. That would be a shameful waste.

One Last Recipe for Natural Magick: Caramels

Because we just mentioned caramels, we assume some readers now have a taste for them. Here is a particularly decadent caramel recipe. Vanilla and chocolate attract love, and adding nuts grounds the spell with stability and common sense.

1½ cups coarsely chopped nuts (try walnuts, pecans, or almonds)

1 cup chocolate chips or chopped dark chocolate

2 cups sugar

1 cup (2 sticks) butter

1 cup light corn syrup

¼ cup water

1 (5 oz.) can sweetened condensed milk (not evaporated milk)

2 tsp. vanilla

Line an 8½×11-inch cake pan with foil; butter lightly. Sprinkle the nuts and chocolate evenly over the foil.

In a heavy saucepan with steep sides, combine sugar, butter, corn syrup, and water. Bring the mixture to a boil. Add sweetened condensed milk and cook to the firm-ball stage (248° F.) Remove from the heat and stir in vanilla. Carefully pour over chips and nuts. Allow to cool. Cut into squares. Wrap individual pieces in waxed paper.

> **CAUTION**
>
> **Stir Gently …!**
>
> The syrup of sugar, syrup, and water gets very hot. Be careful as you pour it out to cool not to spill any on your skin because it can cause severe burns. This is not a recipe for children to try alone.

Honoring the All

Establishing a reverent relationship with the All is a central and profound way to walk a magickal path. You don't need to memorize incantations or spells or follow some ritual you've read in a book. You just need to listen to your inner Spirit. Creating your own rituals is empowering, and even if they change from time to time, they represent your genuine self at that moment.

Connecting to Nature and joining your energies together makes powerful magick. Pay attention to Earth's natural patterns, and watch your own magickal powers grow and expand. Live honestly in the world, and the universe will reward you with generosity and kindness. It's the best possible way to live your magickal life as a practicing Natural Magician.

The Least You Need to Know

♦ A true Natural Magician respects Earth and all the plants and animals that live on it.

♦ Learn to love all of nature, every climate, and to live ethically.

♦ Whatever you do in the mundane world is reflected in the magickal realm.

♦ Commit yourself to something larger than yourself, but take care of your family and neighbors.

Chapter 25

A Little Bonus Gem for Natural Magicians

In This Chapter

- ◆ Magick from the mineral kingdom
- ◆ Magickical correspondences of color
- ◆ The connection between magick and jewelry
- ◆ Unblocking your chakras with crystals
- ◆ Crystal divination
- ◆ Adorning Nature with crystals

So you thought you were all finished reading? Here's a little bonus for sending so much positive energy out into the universe. We *told* you that good things would come back to you threefold if you used good forces in your everyday life! Consider this your first positive blessing—a "free" chapter just for practicing Natural Magick.

In this last chapter, we are expanding our discussion of one of the oldest (and cheapest) tools to use in your spellcrafting and meditations—crystals and stones. They are obviously as old as Earth itself and they vibrate with natural energy and ancient wisdom. They remind us that we are intimately connected to all Nature. With very little effort, you can deepen that connection. When you admire the beauty in something as common as rocks, you are affirming that Nature is powerful in all of its guises.

A Look at Gems, Crystals, and Stones

We could go into a lengthy, scientific description of the differences between gems, crystals, and stones. For our purposes here, let's agree on this simple distinction: When we use the word *gem*, we are referring to the precious and semiprecious stones you find at a jewelry store—diamonds, rubies, sapphires, topaz—you get the idea.

Minerals are naturally occurring elements that are part of the Earth's crust. At last count there were over 3,500 of these individual unique elements. Minerals fall into two categories—crystals and stones. A *crystal* is a mineral whose basic atomic structure has arranged itself into one of seven crystal systems. These seven systems are cubic, tetragonal, hexagonal, trigonal, orthorhombic, monoclinic, and triclinic. Only a small percentage of any mineral will form itself into a crystal. Crystals are generally a type of quartz (there are many) and vibrate with an energy that can add power to your spell. They are often semitranslucent.

Stones or *rocks* are simply an aggregate of minerals that have fused together. They provide a stabilizing influence during spellcrafting. Stones can be found polished in gem shops, but are also found "in the wild" during wildcrafting (see Chapter 10). And then there are those minerals we think of as rocks. They aren't necessarily pretty; they are often used for mundane purposes like paving a driveway or a gravel road; they are misshapen and dirty. But rocks can be just as powerful as an expensive gem. You just need to listen.

For convenience, we will often use the terms "crystal" and "stone" interchangeably in this chapter.

Choosing Your Mineral

Any Natural Magician will tell you that the first step in enlisting a crystal or a stone to help you in your magick is to select one that speaks to you, one that just "feels right." So how does that work? It's simple, really. When you hold the crystal or stone in your hand it seems like it belongs there, or it really catches your eye.

If you buy a stone or a crystal, keep an open mind. You might think you need pink quartz, but find that a polished cat's eye stone is beckoning to you instead. There is probably an underlying reason you are attracted to a stone you didn't expect to buy. The Spirits will guide you to what you need even if it isn't what you thought you needed (or what this book suggested to you). Trust the Universe first.

Also, don't think that just because a book says that in order to achieve your goal you need to find a yellow sapphire, it means you *have* to get one. Substitution is not settling for less; it is knowledge that the Universe provides many solutions for many problems. Don't think that buying the most expensive gem will make it work better. Don't think that you even have to *buy* the crystal. Sometimes the best stone or rock is the one you come across during a hike.

What Is Your Spellcrafting Goal?

Both crystals and stones strengthen the energy of the Natural Magician's inner self, but each does it in a slightly different way. A stone gives off a very specific but subtle energy vibration, and it is the stone itself that is the source of this vibration. Stones are useful in spells that require you to be grounded and stabilized; for example, health or financial issues. Stones can also help you to focus during meditation.

Quartz crystals are sometimes called the "master stone" because they operate in a way that amplifies subtle energy vibrations. This happens because crystals, unlike stones, are not the actual source of the energy, but instead they amplify and then reflect the vibrations that exist in their immediate environment and in the Natural Magician using them. Crystals are good when a spell requires an energizing spirit like love and protection spells. They are also good for meditation.

Gems are a wearable form of crystals. Because they can be with you no matter where you are, they can be used when you want a spell to provide lasting power. Spells that enhance good health, business success, and lasting romance can all be strengthened by wearing the right gemstone. (We'll tell you more about wearing gems a little later in this chapter.)

Cauldron Bubble _____

As a Natural Magician, you should listen to your own instincts when it comes to selecting a gem, crystal, stone, or rock to use in spellcrafting or meditation. There is no "right" one other than the one that attracts you. Hold it in your hand and see if you can feel its energy connecting to yours.

Cleansing Your Stone or Crystal

Before using a stone or crystal in a ritual, you will want to cleanse it of negative energy. There are several ways to do this, and all of them are effective.

One of the most common ways is to purify your crystal in the smoke from burning sage (see Chapter 4 for more on smudging) or incense. Or use the smoke of any fragrant herb that appeals to you. Hold the stone in the smoke while you concentrate on its energy. Picture in your mind's eye the stone filling up with positive energy.

Another way to purify your crystal is to rinse it off in salt water. Use sea salt if possible and distilled or spring water and dry your crystal with a soft cloth afterwards. Some traditions suggest soaking the crystal overnight, but rinsing it thoroughly works just as well.

Placing a stone or crystal in the moonlight is another common way to purify it (see Chapter 13). It isn't necessary to wait for a Full Moon, although the brighter the moonlight, the more cleansed your crystal will be. You might say a few words to the Moon as you leave the crystal in her care:

> *Mother Moon, bless this stone*
>
> *Fill it with power like your own.*

And finally, passing your stone through the flame of a candle three times banishes negative energy. Be cautious, though. Soft stones can easily be singed by fire, which will limit their effectiveness.

When Your Crystal "Wears Out"

This may sound a bit odd, because a crystal can literally last forever, but be fore-warned that it may not be with you that long. Sometimes people "outgrow" their crystals or suddenly feel compelled to give them to someone else. This is perfectly normal and you should listen to your intuition. When a crystal or stone has fulfilled its purpose, it may send a signal that it needs to be released. Sometimes this is not voluntary. You may be going through a normal day's routine and realize that your pendant is no longer with you or come home to find the crystal by your bed has somehow vanished. Don't spend the rest of

Cauldron Bubble

If you think your crystal is "wearing down," try cleansing it and sleeping with it under your pillow or beside your bed before giving up on it. It may just need to have its "battery" recharged.

your life searching for it. If it needs to come back, it will; if not, it was no longer needed.

Color Magick Counts

One of the ways crystals and stones generate energy is through their colors. A multi-colored stone can serve several purposes, although the dominate color in the stone is usually the strongest.

Mineral Magick Through Color

Crystal or Stone Color	Magickal Correspondences
Red	Courage, perseverance, strength of will
Orange	Optimism, hope, antidote for fear or depression
Yellow or gold	Problem solving, inventiveness, joy, confidence
Green	Resolution of conflict, compassion, gratitude, monetary gain
Blue	Idealism, devotion, perspective, calm
Violet	Unity with the All, truth, devotion, responsibility, antidote for feeling disconnected or alone
Pink	Delight, compassion, playfulness, self-acceptance
White or clear	Purity, hope, spirituality, health in mind and body, clear thinking
Brown or black	Stability, common sense, practical solutions, honesty

A mixture of different-colored stones and crystals may be used when you want to achieve a variety of changes all at once. For example, a piece of pink quartz along with a piece of smoky quartz could be blessed and given to young people just starting out on their own to fill them with self-acceptance and playfulness tempered by common sense and practicality.

Liguana's Grimoire

Hanging from the rearview mirror in Liguana's car is a small, crocheted bag containing a quartz crystal, a piece of hematite, and a piece of green calcite. These are for clear thinking and open-mindedness, emotional stability, and joy in all its forms. The bag sways when she turns a corner. She reaches up to steady it and reminds herself of these blessings every time she drives.

Wearing Gems

Often we can recognize magickal people by their jewelry. They don't all wear pentacles, but it's common to see Natural Magicians with necklaces or earrings made with quartz or tourmaline points. Look in most magickal supply stores and see athame hilts and wands and all manner of spellcasters' paraphernalia studded with gems. Besides the obvious, what is the attraction people of magick have for gemstones? What is the connection between magick and jewels?

Those people fortunate enough to see magickal energy in motion often perceive it as a sparkling mist. This sparkling image of magick is frequently used in cartoons and movies. It is probably an archetypical image, an idea of what magickal energy looks like that is embedded in the subconscious mind of all people. If it glitters, sparkles, or shines, it is a mundane world reflection of a magickal flow. As we have said before, the microcosm reflects the macrocosm and the mundane can reflect the magickal. Wearing glitter and gems lets Natural Magicians decorate themselves in a way that calls magick into their lives. Add to that the magickal properties of the various gems, and you can easily see why most Natural Magicians have at least one crystal or gemstone piece of jewelry.

People of magick wear gems not just for their beauty, but also for their effect. To do this, a person must understand a gem's magickal properties and the power points of the body. Putting the right crystal in the right place can make all the difference for a person trying to make a positive change. Anklets and toe rings can be worn to affect one's sense of security and stability or to guide to the best path when on a journey. Stones or crystals worn on a belt or attached to clothing between the hip and thigh can influence the energy of creativity, sexuality, and overall vitality. Gems worn over the solar plexus can affect a person's sense of personal power and determination. Necklaces are probably the most common way people wear gems. A longer necklace may put the jewel in the vicinity of the heart or solar plexus. A shorter necklace or choker would place the gem near the throat, which is the power center for communication. Bracelets and rings assist in sending and receiving magickal energy.

Think twice before you wear your jewels in a crown or on a hat. The area between and just above your eyes is the power center for thought processes and psychic awareness. The crown of your head and just above your head is the power center for receiving and interpreting divine energy. If you aren't very well grounded and comfortable in all your other power areas, jewels on your head and especially near your forehead can disorient or mislead you. That is why in days of old only royalty or members of a priest class wore jewels on their heads. These people were either trained to correctly interpret divine messages they might receive or were considered closer to the Divine by circumstance of birth and therefore able to better receive and pass on gifts and messages from the gods.

Cleansing Your Chakras

Chakras are the openings for life energy to flow into and out of our aura. They vitalize the physical body and bring about the development of your self-consciousness. In Indian philosophy, any of the seven major chakras can become blocked, and through the power of stones or crystals and meditation, you can make the energy flow freely again.

While we don't pretend that the following ritual is an "official" one, we encourage Natural Magicians to find their own way. Here is a suggestion for a chakra meditation that should make you feel more "in harmony" with the world.

First, find seven stones or crystals that represent the seven chakras. These might be based on their color, or it might be that they just "feel" right:

- Find a red stone such as garnet or spinel for your root chakra, which is found at the base of your spine.

- Your sacral chakra is your navel and requires an orange stone such as fire agate, which is usually a brown stone with orange-red tints, or a sunstone, which is orange-brown with a metallic glitter.

- A yellow stone such as topaz or pyrite is associated with the solar plexus chakra.

- Green is the color of the heart chakra and can be found in stones such as malachite or tourmaline.

- For the throat chakra, a blue stone such as turquoise or lapis lazuli is perfect.

◆ Your third-eye chakra found at your forehead is associated with indigo, which can be found in sodalite.

◆ Your crown chakra is a violet stone such as sugilite or amethyst.

If you would rather use found stones or those already in your possession, try associating them with your chakras by holding each stone tightly in your hand and listening to which chakra responds to it. You might feel a tingling or a sort of a buzz when the stone and the chakra connect with one another.

Once you have your seven stones or crystals, sit in a comfortable position with the stones laid out in order in front of you. Pick them up one at a time and concentrate on your corresponding chakra. As you move through the stones, say the following affirmations out loud or write your own:

> *With this red stone [or "with this stone" if it isn't red] I move forward in my life with confidence and the courage to face my hardships and to be myself.*

> *With this orange stone I embrace hope and optimism and walk forward through my life with faith.*

> *With this yellow stone I embrace joy and mental clarity and bring optimism to all that I do.*

> *With this green stone I approach my life with gratitude and harmony and realize my needs will be met as required.*

Cauldron Bubble

Keep your stones in a bag made of natural fiber. Silk is a good choice, but cotton, linen, or wool works well, too. Just make sure the fabric is not a synthetic blend, because this can interfere with a stone's natural vibrations. If you prefer, you can store your stones in a box lined with a natural fabric.

> *With this blue stone I am steady, calm, and at peace with the world and everyone in it.*

> *With this indigo stone my responsibility to all life on this Earth becomes clearer.*

> *With this violet stone I become part of the All that is and renew my spiritual journey.*

Sit calmly for a few minutes, concentrating on how each chakra feels. Then thank the stones for their energy and put them into a bag until you're ready to use them again.

Divining with Crystals

There are many ways to use crystals to glimpse into the future. Some are simple, others require a little more effort. All of them involve approaching the crystals or stones with respect and reverence. Remember that fortune-telling is not a game and shouldn't be used as party entertainment.

As we've said, select crystals, stones, or gems that speak to you in some meaningful way. They might be stones you collected while on vacation or during a walk in the woods. Or they might be stones you purchase over a period of time in gem shops. However you acquire your crystals, stones, or gems, be sure to cleanse them of all negative energy before you use them.

A Simple Yes-No Pendant

One of the simplest ways to use a crystal in divination is to create a pendulum. Tie a string that is at least 12 inches long around your crystal. Any crystal or stone will work, but pick one you trust—one that you have an affinity with.

Light a candle and meditate for a few minutes on the crystal as you hold it in your hand. You and the crystal must come to an agreement before you ask the yes or no question. Decide which signal will mean "yes" and which signal will mean "no." For example, if the pendant swings left to right, that might mean yes to your question. Or the pendant might swing in a circle to mean "no." You might even want to decide on a "maybe."

State your question out loud, making sure it can be answered with a yes or no. Hold the pendant in front of you and watch how it sways.

> **CAUTION**
>
> **Stir Gently …!**
>
> Don't keep asking the question until you get the answer you want. Crystals aren't something to be toyed with, and if you don't listen to them, they'll stop working for you. Also, don't try to influence how they move— no Spirit likes cheating!

Casting Crystals

One of the more in-depth ways to read crystals is based on an old Gypsy tradition. Draw a circle with an 18-inch circumference on the ground. Take 12 stones, crystals, or gems plus 1 rough pebble, which is called a significator stone and represents the questioner. Ask the questioner to throw the stones to the ground within the circle. Then study how the stones have fallen before you read them.

If the significator stone falls out of the circle, the questioner must throw again. If it falls out a second time, the reading must wait until the next day; the crystals are not ready to answer. To read the stones you must look at what stones lie closest to the significator. The closer they are to the pebble, the more likely their influence will be felt by the questioner. The closer to the center of the circle a stone is positioned, the more immediately it is believed that the event will occur. Here are some stones or crystals you might use and their correspondences.

Divination Using Stones and Crystals

Stone or Crystal	Significance in Divination
Agate	Indicates a pleasant surprise for the questioner
Amethyst	Indicates something of value may be lost
Aquamarine	Indicates logic, a clear mind, and common sense
Beryl	Indicates an increase in intuition and psychic powers
Bloodstone	Indicates physical aches and pains; warning to slow down; an unpleasant surprise
Clear quartz	Indicates the return of good health, vitality, and strength; positive sign for the future
Diamond	Indicates a business promotion; monetary fortune
Emerald	Indicates a secret admirer; an unexpected love interest
Garnet	Foreshadows unexpected news; the imminent arrival of a letter
Green jasper	Indicates that the questioner has negative feelings about his or her position in life
Iron pyrite	Indicates the questioner is gullible and should exercise caution in believing others

Stone or Crystal	Significance in Divination
Jasper	Indicates someone older is going to affect the questioner's life; foretells an unexpected gift or legacy
Jet	Reveals unfaithfulness, either of the questioner or someone close
Labradorite	May foretell foreign travel for business or pleasure or the beginning of a relationship with someone from another state or county
Opal	Indicates an ending of some kind
Red jasper	Indicates love, deep emotions, passionate feelings
Rose quartz	Indicates that the questioner has healing abilities or knows someone who needs healing
Ruby	Indicates the questioner is too much of a perfectionist; the influence of a stranger
Sapphire	Indicates good fortune; peace and harmony in the questioner's life
Sardonyx	Indicates harmony in marriage; a potential wedding, although not necessarily the questioner's
Tektite	Signals a period of depression or withdrawal on the part of the questioner or someone close to him or her
Tiger's eye	Signals independence; the questioner is at a turning point, but the change will be for the better
Topaz	Advises questioner to exercise extreme caution
Turquoise	Indicates contentment and often shows an alternative answer to the question asked

Remind the questioner that the future is not set in stone (no pun intended!). You are merely reading what the future might bring, but the questioner has the power to make his or her own decisions. Avoid giving someone a reading that indicates something horrible is about to happen. For example, never predict death or imminent disaster; this can cause the questioner to dwell on the negative and actually bring about the very situation you were warning against. The future has not yet been written, so don't pretend you have all the answers.

Adorning Trees and Bushes

Natural Magicians often use crystals to decorate trees or bushes they pass by regularly. Tie a string around a crystal that is the right color for your spellcrafting needs. You can use them to protect your house, attract a lover, bless your family with monetary wealth … the possibilities are endless. Be sure to ask the tree or bush for permission to hang the crystal on its branch and thank both the tree and the crystal for their assistance.

Not only can you use crystals to bring good things to yourself, but you can use them to honor and call positive energies to the trees and bushes that share your home. They can hang free and increase the magickal vibrations around your plant friends every time the sunlight shines through them. You may also embed stones or crystals in the bark of a tree or place them in the crook of its branches. Don't cut into the bark to place your stones. Instead, push them into natural crevices. As the tree grows, it will grip them tightly until your crystals become part of the tree itself. Yellow, green, brown, orange, and blue are colors trees can easily relate to. These are the best colors to use when gifting plants with stones.

Go out into Nature and ask for a blessing with a special crystal as you begin in earnest—or re-dedicate yourself to—a lifelong practice of Natural Magick!

The Least You Need to Know

- ◆ Gems, stones, crystals, and rocks may be used interchangeably in magick.

- ◆ Choose a mineral that feels right or "speaks" to you.

- ◆ Different colors of gems or crystals have different magickal correspondences.

- ◆ Choose a gem or crystal to wear not just for its beauty, but for its magickal effect.

- Use a chakra meditation with crystals to unblock your energy flow.

- Crystals can be used to foretell the future but should not be used to predict disaster.

Glossary

Air   The Element associated with the East, corresponding to creative endeavors.

akasha   A word of undetermined origin meaning "Spirit."

Akashic Records   A series of tablets or books that theoretically exist to record everything that has happened in the world and everything that has yet to happen.

ama   Broadly interpreted to mean phlegm or mucus in ayurveda; an excess of mucus dampens pitta.

anthropomorphizing   To see in another thing what we are familiar with in ourselves, thereby making a connection.

Apollo   The Greek Sun god.

asana   The yoga principle of proper exercise.

athame (pronounced *a-tha-may*)   A two-edged knife, usually with a wooden or silver handle, that cuts on a spiritual plane, not on a physical one.

ayurveda   Literally means "science of life," or, more precisely, "the knowledge of life span." Its diet calls for lactovegetarianism and eating specific types of food based on what body humor might be out of balance.

Beltane   May Eve festival. One of the ancient Celtic Fire festivals. *Bel*, meaning the god Baal, and *tane*, meaning fire, literally translates to Baal's Fire.

Candlemas   Festival held on February 1 that commemorates the successful passing of winter and the beginning of the agricultural year and spring.

Catherine's Wheel   Any circular device that spins. Fireworks, electrical apparatus, and other disciplines have Catherine's Wheels.

chi   One of the oldest natural forces; it exists everywhere and in everything.

chia seeds   A vegetarian alternative to gelatin; when boiled in water, they become the consistency of gelatin.

cirrus   Wispy, feathery-looking clouds.

cleavers   Also called fragrant bedstraw herb, cleavers are little ground-hugging vines that have star-shape leaves and are sticky.

composting   Using a mixture of organic material such as leaves and manure as fertilizer.

cumulus   Large, fluffy, cotton-ball clouds.

deosil   Clockwise.

deva   In Hindu scriptures, word that refers to all life that is invisible. Many Natural Magicians believe that every growing plants has its own deva or spirit.

dhyana   The yoga principle of healthful meditation.

divining rod   A forked stick or bent wire used by Natural Magicians to find underground water.

dosha   Body humor in the ayurvedic tradition that governs the type of food you should be eating.

dragons   Powerful beings that should be called to help only in desperate cases because they are unpredictable and difficult to control.

Druids   An order of religious intellectuals who serve as prophets and sorcerers.

dryad   A female spirit usually associated with forests and trees; a wood nymph.

Earth   The Element associated with the North, corresponding to stability and common sense.

Elemental spirits   Spirits attached to one of the four Elements—Earth, Water, Air, and Fire—who can be called upon to help create Natural Magick.

equinox   Either of the two times of year when the length of the day and night are equal.

evoking   To call a spirit to you, to join alongside you in your magickal workings.

faeries   Often referred to by the Gaelic word, Sidhe, faeries exist in many forms and can bring their energy to your magick when asked politely.

falafel   Vegetarian dish made of ground garbanzo beans and spices.

familiars   Animals, real or on an astral plane, sent to help Natural Magicians with their magickal endeavors.

faun   A masculine spirit usually associated with forests and trees, who is generally depicted as half-man, half-goat.

Feng Shui   Literally, "the way of wind and water," or, symbolically, "the natural forces of the universe."

Fire   The Element associated with the South, corresponding to passion and enthusiasm.

Full Moon   The Moon in its most powerful (and visible) phase.

garam marsala   A special spice blend often used in South Asian and Indian cooking.

geomancy   European version of Feng Shui, or living harmoniously with Nature.

ghee   Clarified butter used in ayurvedic and Middle Eastern cooking.

gnomes   The Elementals associated with Earth.

God, Goddess   They represent the masculine and feminine energies that exist in everything as well as the Divine.

Green Magick   Magick that uses growing plants and organic material in spell-crafting.

Guardians   Spirits that guard the watchtowers of the north, south, east, and west.

Hestia   The goddess of the hearth; the gentlest of the Olympians.

homa   An ancient fire ritual.

infusion   A tea made by steeping flowers, leaves, or bark in warm water.

invoking   To call into you, literally into your spiritual body.

kapha   The dosha that governs the essence of Water and Earth and taste and smell.

karma   In Buddhist and Hindu teaching, the sum and the consequences of a person's actions, which determines his or her destiny.

Lammas   The first of the three harvest festivals; it is held on August 1.

ley lines   Alignments of ancient sites or holy places, such as stone circles, standing stones, cairns, and churches.

Mabon   Celebrated at the Fall Equinox, this is the second harvest festival and marks the beginning of winter preparations.

magick   Spelling *magick* with a *k* differentiates the rituals and spellcrafting Natural Magicians perform from the stage magic and sleight-of-hand tricks performed for entertainment called magic.

medicine wheel   An ancient place of prayer sacred to Native Americans, symbolizing the totality of existence.

mermaid   A mythical creature, half-woman and half-fish, that lives in the Water Element.

Natural Magician   A person who uses the Earth's natural energies and the mundane activities of everyday life to invoke powerful magick.

Natural Magick   Working with nature to effect positive changes in your life.

New Moon   The phase when the Moon is invisible in the night sky.

nymph   A faery being often associated with a particular place or terrain, such as a water nymph or wood nymph.

Ostara   Celebrated at the Spring Equinox, this festival marks the first genuine day of spring.

pagan   A person of the country or a peasant; someone who lives on and off the land.

paranayama   The yoga principle of proper breathing.

pitta   The dosha that governs the essence of Fire and Water and sight and taste.

prism   A triangular piece of glass or plastic that bends light to create a rainbow.

Ra   The Egyptian Sun god.

rasas   The six tastes in ayurvedic eating—sweet, sour, bitter, astringent, pungent, and salty.

Rauhnachte   A German word that literally means 12 harsh or wild nights; in the Western world, it became the 12 days of Christmas.

saffron   An exotic yellow spice used in Middle Eastern dishes.

salamanders   The Elementals associated with Fire.

Samhain   The festival of remembrance for the dead and the third and final harvest festival, held on October 31.

satva   The pure quality of Nature.

savasana   The yoga principle of proper relaxation.

scrying   The name given to the ancient technique of gazing into an object such as a crystal ball for the purposes of divination.

seitan   A protein made from wheat that is used as a replacement for meat in vegetarian diets.

skyclad   Naked; literally, "wearing the sky."

smoking point   The temperature at which oil begins to smoke when heated.

smudging   Cleansing a space of negative energy (or an object or a person) by fanning herbal smoke over it.

spelunking   Exploring caves; in Natural Magick, it is symbolically going back inside the Mother.

Spirit   The fifth Element that exists in all living things.

springform pan   A round pan with a removable edge used to bake extra-moist cakes such as cheesecakes.

staples   The pantry items you keep on hand to use often in everyday cooking, such as flour, sugar, baking powder, dried beans, and grains.

sthapatya veda   India's traditional science of architecture.

stratus   Layered clouds that stretch out across the sky horizontally like a blanket.

sylphs   The Elementals associated with Air; the word *sylph* comes from the Greek word *sylpha*, which means "butterfly."

synergism   The idea that regeneration comes about through a combination of human will and divine grace.

tussy mussy   In Victorian times, a cone-shaped holder often made of silver designed to hold a small bouquet for ladies to carry.

undines   The Elementals associated with Water.

vastu   A Sanskrit word that means Nature, a surrounding or environment.

vastu shastra   An ancient art and science of constructing buildings that ensures a harmonious balance between man and Nature.

vata   The dosha that governs the essence of air and touch.

vedanta   The yoga principle of positive thinking.

vegetarian   The yoga principle of proper diet.

Waning Moon   As the Moon gets smaller and heads toward a New Moon stage, it is called a Waning Moon.

Water   The Element associated with the West, corresponding to intuition and psychic powers.

Waxing Moon   As the Moon gets larger and heads toward a Full Moon stage, it is called a Waxing Moon.

Wiccan Law of Three   The idea that whatever energy Natural Magicians send out into the world, positive or negative, comes back to them threefold.

Wiccan Rede   The tenant that Wiccans follow, "And ye harm none, do what ye will."

widdershins   Counterclockwise.

wildcrafting   The practice of harvesting and using wild materials from their natural habitat for food, decoration, rituals, construction, and craft.

yin yang   In Chinese philosophy, the opposing cosmic forces that represent feminine (yin) and masculine (yang) aspects.

yoga   A Hindu discipline aimed at training the consciousness for a state of perfect spiritual insight and tranquility.

Yule   Celebrated at the Winter Solstice, this festival celebrates the rebirth of the Sun god.

zest   In cooking, the colored part of the peel of oranges, lemons, and limes, usually grated.

Appendix B

Further Reading

Amber, K. *True Magick: A Beginner's Guide (Llewellyn's New Age Series)*. St. Paul, MN: Llewellyn Publications, 1990.

Aswynn, Freya. *Northern Mysteries & Magick: Runes, Gods, and Feminine Powers*. St. Paul, MN: Llewellyn Publications, 1990.

Beyeral, D.D., Rev. Paul V. *The Master Book of Herbalism*. Washington: Phoenix Publishing, Inc., 1984.

Chase, Pamela Louise, and Jonathan Pawlik. *The Newcastle Guide to Healing with Gemstones*. North Hollywood, CA: Newcastle Publishing Co., Inc, 1989.

Christopher, Tom, and Marty Asher. *The 20-Minute Gardener*. New York: Random House, Inc., 1997.

Conway, D. J. *Magickal Mermaids and Water Creatures*. New Jersey: The Career Press, Inc., 2005.

———. *Moon Magick*. St. Paul: Llewellyn Publications, 1998.

Cuhulain, Kerr. *Full Contact Magick: A Book of Shadows for the Wiccan Warrior*. St. Paul, MN: Llewellyn Publications, 2002.

Cunningham, Scott. *Earth Power: Techniques of Natural Magic (Llewellyn's Practical Magick)*. St. Paul, MN: Llewellyn Publications, 1983.

———. *Encyclopedia of Magical Herbs*. St. Paul, MN: Llewellyn Publications, 1990.

Dubats, Sally. *Natural Magick: Inside the Well-Stocked Witch's Cupboard*. New York: Kensington Publishing Co., 1999.

Dugan, Ellen. *Cottage Witchery: Natural Magick for Hearth and Home*. St. Paul, MN: Llewellyn Publications, 2005.

Eason, Cassandra. *A Complete Guide to Magic and Ritual: How to Use Natural Energies to Heal Your Life*. St. Paul, MN: Llewellyn Publications, 2000.

Feldman, Gail Carr, and Eve Adamson. *Releasing the Mother Goddess*. Indianapolis, IN: Alpha Books, 2003.

Ferguson, Diana. *The Magickal Year*. New York: Atrium Publishers Group, 1996.

Greenbough, Aurora, and Cathy Jewell. *The Complete Idiot's Guide to Spells and Spellcraft*. Indianapolis, IN: Alpha Books, 2004.

Greer, John Michael. *Natural Magic: Potions and Powers from the Magical Garden*. St. Paul, MN: Llewellyn Publications, 2000.

Just, Shari, and Carolyn Flynn. *The Complete Idiot's Guide to Creative Visualization*. Indianapolis, IN: Alpha Books, 2005.

Liguana, Miria, and Nina Metzner. *The Complete Idiot's Guide to Wicca Craft*. Indianapolis, IN: Alpha Books, 2004.

Penczak, Christopher. *City Magick*. York Beach, Maine: Weiser Books, 2001.

———. *Magick Of Reiki: Focused Energy for Healing, Ritual, & Spiritual Development*. St. Paul, MN: Llewellyn Publications, 2004.

RavenWolf, Silver. *To Light a Sacred Flame: Practical Witchcraft for the Millennium*. St. Paul, MN: Llewellyn Publications, 1999.

————. *To Ride a Silver Broomstick: New Generation Witchcraft*. St. Paul, MN: Llewellyn Publications, 1999.

Simms, Maria Kay. *The Witch's Circle: Ritual and Craft of the Cosmic Muse*. St. Paul, MN: Llewellyn Publications, 1994.

Sjoo, Monica, and Barbara Mor. *The Great Cosmic Mother: Rediscovering the Religion of the Earth*. New York: HarperCollins Publishers, 1987.

Starhawk. *The Spiral Dance*. New York: Harper & Row, 1979.

Tognetti, Arlene, and Carolyn Flynn. *The Intuitive Arts on Health*. Indianapolis, IN: Alpha Books, 2003.

Walker, Barbara G. *The Crone: Woman of Age, Wisdom, and Power*. New York: HarperCollins Publishers, Inc., 1985.

————. *The Woman's Encyclopedia of Myths and Secrets*. New York: HarperCollins Publishers, Inc., 1983.

————. *The Women's Dictionary of Symbols & Sacred Objects*. New York: HarperCollins Publishers Ltd., 1988.

————. *Women's Rituals*. New York: Harper & Row, 1990.

Wilson, Jim. *Landscaping with Herbs*. New York: Houghton Mifflin Company, 1994.

Zimmermann, Denise, and Katherine A. Gleason. *The Complete Idiot's Guide to Wicca and Witchcraft, Second Edition*. Indianapolis, IN: Alpha Books, 2003.

Appendix C

Natural Correspondences at a Glance

Natural Magicians see relationships between things. These relationships are called correspondences. Although magickal correspondences are not literally equal to one another, you can think of them that way (such as "silver equals Moon").

In this way, one thing or symbol from the mundane world can be used to suggest another in the magickal world. This is important in magick! Magicians may surround themselves with as many appropriate correspondences as they can to vividly affect the senses, making their magickal connection with the Spiritual realms easier and more vivid.

Magickal Properties of Herbs and Spices

Herbs/Spices	Magickal Properties
Allspice	Wealth, prosperity, enthusiasm
Anise	Protection of loved ones
Basil	Money, success, prosperity, love
Bay leaves	Psychic awareness, honor, courage
Caraway	Wisdom, intellectual success
Celery seed	Wisdom, financial gain
Chives	Warding off of diseases, protection
Cinnamon	Courage, psychic awareness, safety, love
Cloves	Material gain, success
Coriander	Alleviation of pain
Cumin	Protection from negative energy
Curry	Protection, passion, clarification of psychic power
Dill	Wealth, protection
Fennel	Good luck, protection
Ginger	Wealth, ingenuity, mental alertness
Lemon balm	Romance, happiness
Marjorum	Love, happiness
Mint	Passion, romance
Mustard	Psychic growth, wisdom
Nutmeg	Prosperity, business success
Oregano	Honor, peace
Parsley	Rebirth, new beginnings
Pepper	Elimination of negative energy, protection
Rosemary	Fidelity, good luck, protection, wisdom
Saffron	Psychic awareness
Sage	Memory, wealth, long life
Salt	Cleansing and clarifying
Summer savory	Wisdom
Tarragon	Money, success, protection
Thyme	Honor, courage, attraction of love
Vanilla beans	Enhanced memory, honor to ancestors

Magickal Properties of Salt*

Salt	Magickal Properties
Gray salt	Psychic endeavors and protection
Hawaiian red salt	Attraction of Earth Element and stability
Fleur de Sel	Ensured prosperity
Jurassic salt	Connection and honor to ancestors
Black salt	Increased psychic abilities
Kosher salt	Healing and blessings
Sea salt	Cleansing and dispelling negativity

All salts can be used for protection or purification.

Magickal Properties of Fruits and Vegetables

Fruits/Vegetables	Magickal Properties
Apples	Love, enhances magick
Artichokes	Prevents unwanted attention
Asparagus	Enhances sexuality
Avocado	Beauty spells
Bananas	Humor, sense of well-being
Beans	Reconciliation, protection, exorcism, resurrection
Beets	Love, passion
Berries	Protection from disease, passion
Cabbage	Fertility, profit, good luck
Carrots	Lust, fertility
Celery	Psychic power, mental work
Corn	Protection from negative forces
Cucumbers	Healing, lunar magick
Endive	Love, fertility
Fennel	Victory, clear vision, purification
Grapes	Fertility, money, mental power
Lemons	Cleansing, protection
Lettuce	Contentment, divination, sleep

continues

Magickal Properties of Fruits and Vegetables (continued)

Fruits/Vegetables	Magickal Properties
Melons	Intuition, creativity
Mushrooms	Peace, healing, prophetic dreams
Oranges	Prosperity, love
Peas	Fortune and profits in business
Pears	Love, enhances magick
Pineapple	Draws good luck, hinders lust
Potatoes	Wards away illness
Tomatoes	Repels evil, inspires love

Magickal Properties of Grain

Grain	Magickal Properties
Amaranth	Healing, protection
Barley	Love, offering
Corn	Nurturing, divination
Dahl	Stability, balance
Oats	Wealth
Quinoa	Health, psychic ability
Rice	Fertility, longevity, blessings
Rye	Loyalty, fidelity
Wheat	Fertility, abundance

Magickal Properties of Nuts and Seeds

Nuts/Seeds	Magickal Properties
Almonds*	Wisdom, prosperity, enduring love
Acorns	Fertility, wisdom
Cashews	Money
Grapeseed*	Banishment of negative energies or influences
Hazelnuts*	Fertility

Nuts/Seeds	Magickal Properties
Macadamias*	Wealth and empowerment for women
Peanuts*	Male sexuality, grounding
Pecans	Wealth, work
Sesame seeds*	Love, strength, abundance
Walnuts*	Wisdom

*Indicates this nut or seed is commonly pressed for use in oil form.

Magickal Properties of Meats and Seafood

Meats/Seafood	Magickal Properties
Chicken	Vitality, light-heartedness
Beef	Kindness, motherhood, nurturing
Duck	Loyalty
Oysters	Love, romance, passion
Pork	Intelligence
Salmon	Strength and wisdom
Shrimp	Triumph over adversity and sexual vitality
Tuna	Abundance
Turkey	Integrity, leadership, protection

Magickal Properties of Flowers

Flowers	Magickal Properties
Asters	Variety, patience
Black-eyed Susans	Justice
Borage	Courage
Chrysanthemums	Protection, happy home
Clover	Good luck, clairvoyance
Coneflowers	Good health, strengthened spells
Daisies	Innocence, love
Heather	Luck

continues

Magickal Properties of Flowers   (continued)

Flowers	Magickal Properties
Honeysuckle	Fidelity, attraction
Jasmine	Attraction
Lavender	Relaxation
Lilac	Luck, love
Lilies of the valley	Counter spells, attract fairies
Morning glories	Love, peace, mental health
Poppies	Charm for someone bewitched by love
Roses	Love, passion, friendship
Sunflowers	Truth, fame, recognition, granting of wishes
Violets	Love, honesty, virtue

Magickal Properties of Trees

Trees	Magickal Properties
Alder	Protection, divination, persistence, endurance, overcoming of obstacles
Apple	Choice, love, healing magick, wisdom, psychic journeying
Ash	Used in spells requiring focus, strength of purpose; links inner and outer worlds
Aspen	Competence, humility
Beech	Guidance from the past to gain insight, protection
Birch	Fertility, healing spells, cleansing and purification, patience, renewal
Blackthorn	Fate; outside influences that must be obeyed
Elder	Purifying; connection with Mother Earth, insight, psychic work, faery magick
Elm	Added stability and grounding to a spell
Fir	Clear vision, divination, psychic powers
Hawthorn	Protection, love, marriage spells, strength through adversity, connection with faeries
Hazel	Knowledge, wisdom, and poetic inspiration

Trees	Magickal Properties
Holly	Spells for sleep and rest; easing of the passage of death, connection with the Lord, home, protection
Larch	Warding off evil, protection, induced visions
Maple	Success and abundance
Oak	Protection, strength, success, stability, optimism, clarity of thought
Pear	Love, temptation
Pine	Released guilt
Poplar	Resistance, communication, endurance, conquest
Rowan	Protection; control over enchantment, connection with the wild world, challenging of old ideas
Willow	Cycles, rhythms, healing pain or illness, physical and psychic journeying, flexibility
Yew	Enhanced magickal and psychic abilities, induced prophetic visions, death and rebirth, wisdom, love

Magickal Properties of Gems

Gems	Magickal Properties
Amber	Success and joy in all things
Amethyst	Peace and serenity, positive self-image
Aquamarine	Calm nerves, good relationships
Bloodstone	Healing both physical and psychic wounds
Garnet	Forcefulness, yang energies
Hematite	Emotional stability
Jade	Money
Lapis lazuli	Psychic awareness, grounding
Moonstone	Intuition and personal growth, yin energies
Onyx (Black)	Powerful protection, banishing negative energies
Quartz (Clear)	Visions, clarity of thought, intensifies magick
Rose quartz	Self-esteem, love

Magickal Properties of Colors

Color	Magickal Properties
Red or pink	Love, affection
White	Truth, purity
Yellow	Happiness, friendship
Orange	Energy, bounty
Bronze	Happy home
Purple	Power, protection
Blue	Peace, mental health

Sun Cycles and Magickal Correspondences

Sun Cycle	Crystals and Gems	Herbs and Flowers
Samhain: The Dark Lord enters the underworld.	Obsidian, black onyx, bloodstone, amethyst, opal	Bay leaf, lavender, nutmeg, sage
Yule: The Sun God is born.	Quartz, blue sunstone, emerald, ruby, sapphire	Chamomile, rosemary, ginger, sage, cinnamon, mistletoe
Candlemas: The Sun God is a nursing infant.	Quartz, opal, moonstone, aventurine, sunstone	Angelica, basil, bay leaves, myrrh
Ostara: The Sun God is a small child.	Moss agate, green moonstone, orange calcite, rose quartz	Jasmine, rose, violet
Beltane: The Sun God is a young groom marrying the Goddess.	Quartz, sunstone, orange calcite, malachite	Frankincense, lemon balm, lemon thyme, saffron
Midsummer: The Sun God reigns supreme.	Amethyst, malachite, golden topaz, opal, quartz, azurite-malachite, lapis lazuli, diamonds	St. John's Wort, chamomile, lavender, trefoil, vervain

Sun Cycle	Crystals and Gems	Herbs and Flowers
Lammas: The Sun God becomes the Dark Lord and becomes an old man.	Tiger-eye, golden topaz, opal, citrine, ametrine	All herbs and grains
Mabon: The Dark Lord lays dying.	Amber, quartz, tiger-eye, citrine	Myrrh, hibiscus, marigold, sunflowers, rose petals

Full Moons and Their Spells

Full Moons	Spells and Rituals
January—Wolf Moon	Spells involving organization, ambition, career, politics; healing for the knees, bones, teeth, skin
February—Ice Moon	Spells involving science, freedom, friendship, breaking of bad habits or addictions; healing for the calves, ankles, blood
March—Crow Moon	Spells involving music, art, telepathy, dreams; healing for the feet and lymph glands
April—Planter's Moon	Spells involving authority, rebirth, leadership; healing for the face and head
May—Flower Moon	Spells involving love, money, acquisition; healing for the throat and neck
June—Strawberry Moon	Spells involving communication, writing, travel; healing for the arms, hands, and lungs
July—Blood Moon	Spells involving the home and for honoring lunar gods and goddesses; healing for the chest and stomach

continues

Full Moons and Their Spells (continued)

Full Moons	Spells and Rituals
August—Corn Moon	Spells involving authority, courage, fertility; healing for the upper back, spine, heart
September—Harvest Moon	Spells involving employment, health, diet; healing for the intestines and nervous system
October—Hunter's Moon	Spells involving justice, unions, balance (spiritual and otherwise), artistry; healing for the lower back and kidneys
November—Snow Moon	Spells involving power, psychic growth, sex; healing for the reproductive organs.
December—Cold Moon	Spells involving travel, sports, truth, animals; healing for the liver and thighs

Appendix D

Know Yourself, Know Your Natural Magick

When doing any kind of magick, especially Natural Magick, it is very useful to explore both inwardly and outwardly to see the effects of the magick you're working. In this appendix, we'll give you some ideas to help you begin this journey within and without, and hope you experience the same profound joy and reverence we have found in honoring Nature and living in resonant harmony with the natural world and all of the beings and entities that inhabit it.

Record Your Natural Magick

It's handy to keep records of your magickal workings so that over time you can easily see what works best for you. Making notes before and after creating magick will help you learn and grow as a Natural Magician.

Pre-Spellcrafting Notes

Begin by noting the time, place, and intent of your magickal purpose.

Date: _____

Phase of the Moon: _____

Moon in astrological sign: _____

Time of day: _____

Phase of my cycle (for women): _____

Magickal purpose: _____

My mood: _____

Magickal tools I will need: _____

_____

Magickal jewelry I will wear: _____

_____

Type and color of clothing I will wear: _____

_____

Entities or "other realm" beings I will call upon to help:

_____

_____

_____

_____

Ritual words I will use:

_____

_____

_____

_____

Names of other participants (if any):

_____

_____

_____

_____

Result: How will I gauge the effects of my magick?

_____

_____

_____

_____

Post-Spellcrafting Notes

In this section, note the results of your Natural Magick.

Unexpected occurrences:

_____

_____

_____

_____

_____

How I felt during the ritual:

_____

_____

_____

_____

Elements I would change or eliminate the next time:

_____

_____

_____

_____

_____

Tracking Your Spiritual Self

If you understand your own natural rhythms and learn your body's subtle signals, you will have a better feel for when magickal workings should occur or when you are most open to magick or "other realm" communication. Consider keeping a log similar to the following.

Waxing Moon:

Physically, I feel _____.

My emotional tone is _____.

My energy level is _____.

I feel especially active.   Yes/No

I feel especially wise.   Yes/No

I feel especially imaginative.   Yes/No

Waning Moon:

Physically, I feel _____.

My emotional tone is _____.

My energy level is _____.

I feel especially active.   Yes/No

I feel especially wise.   Yes/No

I feel especially imaginative.   Yes/No

Full Moon:

Physically, I feel _____.

My emotional tone is _____.

My energy level is _____.

I feel especially active.   Yes/No

I feel especially wise.   Yes/No

I feel especially imaginative.   Yes/No

New Moon:

Physically, I feel _____.

My emotional tone is _____.

My energy level is _____.

I feel especially active.   Yes/No

I feel especially wise.   Yes/No

I feel especially imaginative.   Yes/No

It will take many months to have enough data to draw conclusions. You can use this information to find out the best time to do a particular type of magick or to determine when you feel most powerful.

Daily Power Record

Use this self check-in at various times during the day to track the ebb and flow of your body's own natural rhythms. You are better able to act magickally when your energy level is high. Low-energy times are best for meditation and just being open to the inspiration of the world around you.

I wake up energized.   Yes/No

Before/after breakfast I feel _____

_____.

By mid to late morning I feel _____

_____.

Before/after lunch I feel _____

_____.

By mid to late afternoon I feel _____

_____.

Before/after dinner I feel _____

_____.

After dinner I feel _____

_____.

I am ready to go to bed by _____.

I fall asleep easily.   Yes/No

I sleep soundly.   Yes/No

Seasonal Spiritual Tracking

This will obviously take you at least a year to complete and it will take you several years to see a pattern developing. Some people feel more energized when the temperatures are cooler. Others find warm weather more conducive to magickal workings.

Summer

In general, during hot summer months, I feel (list as many adjectives as you can that apply):

_____

_____

_____

_____

Fall

In general, during cool fall months, I feel (list as many adjectives as you can that apply):

_____

_____

_____

_____

Winter

In general, during cold winter months, I feel (list as many adjectives as you can that apply):

_____

_____

_____

_____

Spring

In general, during balmy spring months, I feel (list as many adjectives as you can that apply):

_____

_____

_____

_____

Index

offerings, 234
oils, 35-37
pantries, 32
seasoning foods, 32-33
  garlic, 35
  onions, 35
  salts, 34
sharing after rituals
  Bannocks, 259-260
  Bûche de Noël, 252-254
  Hot Cross Buns,
    255-256
  Mulled Wine/Spiced
    Cider, 254-255
  Sangria or Berry Iced
    Green Tea, 259
  Spring Mint Julep, 257
  Strawberry Muffins, 258
  traditions, 252
snacks, 44
spring
  Almond Butter Cream,
    216
  Almond Paste, 215
  Crystallized Flowers,
    216-217
  Fiddlehead Frittata with
    Ham and Hollandaise
    Sauce, 211-212
  Hollandaise Sauce, 213
  May Basket Cake,
    213-215
  Spring Salad, 210-211
storing, 44-45
summer
  Cucumber-Yogurt
    Sauce, 221-222
  Juicy Fruit Crumble,
    224-225
  Midsummer Night's
    Cream, 225-226

Peasant Stew, 222-224
Spring Chicken Pasta
  Salad with Cucumber-
  Yogurt Sauce, 220-221
Sun, 143-144
teas, 43
traditions, 235
trees, 187-188
vinegars, 37
Water, 77-78
Winds, 132-133
winter
  Beef Roast in Old Ale,
    203-204
  Parsnip Purée with
    Garlic Cream, 205
  Spice Cake with Dried
    Fruit, 205-207
  Steaming Spiced
    Chocolate, 207
  Winter Stew, 202-203
Force, 4
Four Winds, 126
  East, 127
  foods, 132-133
  Native American tradi-
    tions, 133-134
  North, 126
  South, 127-128
  West, 128-129
Frost-on-the-Pumpkin Pie,
  196-198
fruits, 40-41
Full Moon rituals, 148-150

G

Ganzfeld experiments, 93
gardening, 118-119
  herbs, 120-121
  indoors, 121-122
  willow tea, 120

garlic, 35
garnets, 278
gems, 271, 274-275
ghee, 36
Ghobe, 83
ginger, 157
gnomes, 82-83, 166
goblets, 46
Goddesses
  Boreana, 126
  Eurana, 127
  Nona, 128
  Zephrina, 128
Gods
  Boreus, 126
  Euros, 127
  Notus, 128
  Zephyrus, 128
gold panning, 86-87
Golden Rule, 28
Grael, 108
grains, 38
grapes, 41
grapeseeds, 39
gratitude, 17-18
gray salts, 34
Greek mythology
  Apollo, 136
  Neptune, 70
  Poseidon, 70
  Prometheus, 60
green jasper, 278
Greeting the Dawn, 140-142
Groundhog Day, 137
Guardians, 102
  Guardians of the
    Watchtowers, 102
  inviting
    cakes and ale, 105-106
    meditation, 102-103
    ritual, 104-105
    sacred spaces, 103-104

Check Out These
Best-Sellers

Grammar and Style
SECOND EDITION

Laurie E. Rozakis, Ph.D.

1-59257-115-8 • $16.95

Buying and Selling a Home
FOURTH EDITION

Shelley O'Hara and Nancy D. Lewis

1-59257-120-4 • $18.95

Being a Groom
SECOND EDITION

Jennifer Lata Rung and Mark Rung

0-02-864456-5 • $9.95

Learning Spanish
THIRD EDITION

Gail Stein

0-02-864451-4 • $18.95

Personal Finance in Your 20s & 30s
SECOND EDITION

Sarah Young Fisher and Susan Shelly

0-02-864374-7 • $19.95

Organizing Your Life
FOURTH EDITION

Georgene Lockwood

1-59257-413-0 • $16.95

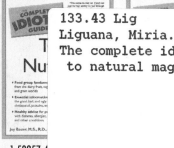

1-59257-

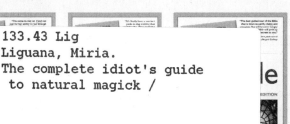

8.95

Calculus

W. Michael Kelley

0-02-864365-8 • $18.95

Music Theory
SECOND EDITION

Michael Miller

1-59257-437-8 • $19.95

The Perfect Resume
THIRD EDITION

Susan Ireland

0-02-864440-9 • $14.95

Playing the Guitar
SECOND EDITION

Frederick Noad

0-02-864244-9 • $21.95

1-59257-335-5 • $19.95

Knitting and Crocheting
SECOND EDITION
Illustrated

Barbara Breiter and Gail Diven

1-59257-089-5 • $16.95

More than *450 titles* available at
booksellers and online retailers everywhere

www.idiotsguides.com

ALPHA